# Christians and Jews in the Ottoman Arab World

## The Roots of Sectarianism

Bruce Masters' book explores the history of Christians and Jews in the Arab provinces of the Ottoman empire and how their identities as non-Muslims evolved over four hundred years. At the start of this period, in the sixteenth century, social community was circumscribed by religious identity and non-Muslims lived within the hierarchy established by Muslim law. In the nineteenth century, however, in response to Western influences, a radical change took place. Conflict erupted between Muslims and Christians in different parts of the empire in a challenge to that hierarchy. In the Balkans and Anatolia, sectarian animosities gave way to nationalist ones as religious identities were transformed by the political vocabulary imported from the West, while in the Arab provinces, the language of nationalism helped heal the rift between sectarian communities as their elites tentatively embraced a new political identity as Arabs. By contrast Arabic-speaking Jews experienced neither the outrage of their Muslim neighbors nor the internal struggle over identity experienced by the Christian communities. By maintaining their traditional religio-political boundaries, they were much slower to recast themselves as Arabs. As the author illustrates in this thought-provoking and lucid history, it is these religious and ethnic ambiguities which have to a large extent informed the rhetoric of religious fundamentalism in the empire's successor states throughout the twentieth century. In this way, the book negotiates the present through the past, thereby contributing to an understanding of the political and religious tensions of the modern Middle East.

BRUCE MASTERS is Professor of History at Wesleyan University. His publications include *The Origins of Western Economic Dominance in the Middle East* (1988) and (with Edhem Eldem and Daniel Goffman) *The Ottoman City between East and West: Aleppo, Izmir, and Istanbul* (1999).

# Cambridge Studies in Islamic Civilization

*Published titles in the series are listed at the back of the book*

# Christians and Jews in the Ottoman Arab World

## The Roots of Sectarianism

BRUCE MASTERS

*Wesleyan University*

CAMBRIDGE
UNIVERSITY PRESS

PUBLISHED BY THE PRESS SYNDICATE OF THE UNIVERSITY OF CAMBRIDGE
The Pitt Building, Trumpington Street, Cambridge, United Kingdom

CAMBRIDGE UNIVERSITY PRESS
The Edinburgh Building, Cambridge CB2 2RU, UK
40 West 20th Street, New York NY 10011–4211, USA
10 Stamford Road, Oakleigh, VIC 3166, Australia
Ruiz de Alarcón 13, 28014 Madrid, Spain
Dock House, The Waterfront, Cape Town 8001, South Africa

http://www.cambridge.org

First published 2001

Printed in the United Kingdom at the University Press, Cambridge

*Typeface* Times 10/12 pt    *System* 3b2   [CE]

*A catalogue record for this book is available from the British Library*

*Library of Congress Cataloguing in Publication data*

Masters, Bruce Alan, 1950–
Christians and Jews in the Ottoman Arab world: the roots of sectarianism / Bruce Masters.
      p.    cm. – (Cambridge studies in Islamic civilization)
Includes bibliographical references and index.
ISBN 0 521 80333 0
1. Christians – Arab countries – History.   2. Jews – Arab countries – History.
3. Turkey – History – Ottoman Empire, 1288–1918.   4. Islam – Relations – Christianity.
5. Christianity and other religions – Islam.   6. Islam – Relations – Judaism.
7. Judaism – Relations – Islam.   I. Title.   II. Series.

DS59.C48 M37 2001
305.6′09569–dc21    00–067486


ISBN 0 521 80333 0 hardback

For Russ and Sheila Murphy

*Sláinte agus saol agaibh*
*Talamh gan chíos agaibh . . .*
*Ó Bhealtaine amach*

# Contents

# Acknowledgments

This work was a long time in the making. Its origins lie in several different research projects on unrelated aspects of the history of Aleppo and Syria. When I set out on the journey, it was not my intention to write about non-Muslims as the main actors. Rather I wanted to assess how the peoples of the Middle East adapted to the changes they experienced in the Ottoman Empire's last century. In seeking to understand the West's impact on the peoples of the Ottoman Empire, however, each research avenue I embarked upon led me back to the non-Muslims. I simply could not ignore the communities where that impact was felt first.

The research for this project was conducted primarily at the National Archives in Damascus, where Mme. Daᶜd al-Hakim was gracious and helpful as always, the Prime Minister's Archive in Istanbul, and the Public Records Office in London. I want to thank the staff of all three institutions for their help and the governments of the Republic of Turkey and the Syrian Arab Republic for granting me permission to conduct research in their state archives. I would also like to thank the funding bodies that made research in the region possible. These include the Fulbright Commission, the American Research Institute in Turkey, and Wesleyan University.

As a result of its rather lengthy gestation period, this study has gone through several different incarnations, has been presented in part at various academic venues, and has been commented upon by various people at different times and in a variety of places. Parts of it have appeared as papers delivered at Middle Eastern Studies Association conferences over the past decade and a lecture series at the National University of Ireland-Maynooth, Republic of Ireland. I have also discussed my conclusions at talks given at Rice, Princeton and, what was for me the most personally satisfying, before my social science colleagues at the Davenport Public Affairs Center, Wesleyan University. Of those who have critiqued versions of the work, either in part or *in toto* or otherwise given encouragement, I would like to thank Leila Fawaz, Dina Rizk Khoury, Daniel Goffman, Abdul-Karim Rafeq, Molly Greene, Ruairí Ó hUiginn, and Ussama Makdisi. I also would like to thank Marigold Acland at Cambridge University Press for being the editor most of us in the scholarly profession can only dream of finding. Lastly, I would like to thank my Wesleyan colleague, Russ Murphy, who over literally hundreds of cups of coffee during the past five years has patiently heard the genesis of every argument I make in this book with good humor and more than a bit of skepticism. I dedicate this book to him and to Sheila, his lifelong soul mate, for their hospitality and friendship over the years.

# Note on transliteration and terms

I have chosen to transcribe Arabic names and technical terms following the modified system used by the *International Journal of Middle Eastern Studies* without the diacritical marks beyond the use of an apostrophe for the *hamza* in the middle of a word and a raised case "c" for the "ᶜayn." Ottoman Turkish names and terms are transcribed according to the rules of Modern Turkish except that I have retained voiced final consonants, Mehmed rather than Mehmet.

The choice of terms for places and peoples is more difficult. What should we call the lands that constituted the Ottoman Arab provinces? Egypt presents no difficulty as all agreed both then and now that the valley and delta of the Nile constituted one geographical unit although there was some dispute over where to demarcate the southern boundary. But elsewhere the names we now call the various parts of the Fertile Crescent and their inhabitants in English had no currency for most of the Ottoman centuries. For the Europeans, there was a clear distinction between Palestine as the "Holy Land" of the Christians or *Eretz Israel* of the Jews and Syria which otherwise incorporated all the habitable lands south of the Taurus Mountains and between the Mediterranean and the Syrian Desert. The name Lebanon was used by both locals and Europeans but referred only to the mountains in the northern part of the present-day republic of the same name. The Ottoman authorities if pressed for a single name would have called the lands south of Anatolia simply Arabistan. Some modern scholars prefer the term *Bilad al-Sham* (the country of Damascus) as that was the term sometimes employed by Ottoman Arabs living in Damascus. Those authors who lived in Damascus' northern rival Aleppo never used that designation, however, and would have most probably bristled had they been told that was the name of their country. In an attempt to minimize confusion, I have used the current political designation for the most part even if in the case of some, i.e. Iraq, they are completely anachronistic. I have chosen to use Syria as cultural designation to mean all the Western arch of the Fertile Crescent unless Lebanon or Palestine is specifically mentioned. I do so without any underlying political agenda.

Similarly vexing is the question of what we should call those Arabic-speakers of the region. I have used Arab as simple expedient but only Bedouin would have been called by that name for most of the Ottoman centuries. Reflecting identities that were current in the Ottoman period I have chosen *Rum* as a collective noun for Arabic-speaking Greek Orthodox Christians and "Franks" for Western Europeans generally, and those who were Roman Catholics specifically. Those were the terms preferred by the inhabitants of the Ottoman Arab world. They also convey to the reader the ambiguities inherent in any potential ethnic identities in the period.

# Introduction

The question of the conditions under which Jews and Christians lived in premodern Islamic societies remains contested. It is unfortunately not solely an issue of arcane academic interest. History, or more often only a half-remembered myth, informs nationalist ideologies prevalent in the successor states to now-vanished Muslim empires across Eurasia from Sarajevo to New Delhi. The dispute over the writing of the past is perhaps the most strident in the territories of the former Ottoman Empire where competing, endogenously selective memories of former defeats and atrocities serve to validate violence directed at those deemed to be outside the boundaries of the "nation." Political activists who seek a return to an Islamic golden age add further urgency to the debate with their call for the establishment of authentically Muslim governments in nation-states that are also home to non-Muslim minorities. The Islamists promise to their non-Muslim fellow citizens the same levels of security and justice they assert were present in the political community (*umma*) founded by the Prophet Muhammad.[1] That such a call for the return to an idealized past can provoke fears in one religious community and fervent optimism in another is testimony to the stark difference with which a common history can be remembered by Muslims, Christians, and Jews.

Recent Western scholarship on the Ottoman past has not been helpful in clearing up the ambiguities surrounding the historical experience of the empire's ethnic and religious minorities. Historical revisionists – and who does not seek to be a revisionist when it comes to the writing of history – have generally avoided topics that serve to segregate the peoples of the Ottoman Empire into monolithic, vertically constructed, sectarian communities. The impulse comes in partial response to the political manipulation of religious identities by the Western powers in the Ottoman *ancien régime*,

---

[1] See, for example, the reputed "Manifesto of the Islamic Revolution in Syria" contained in the appendix of Umar Abd-Allah, *The Islamic Struggle in Syria* (Berkeley, CA, 1983), p. 218; Gudrun Krämer, "Dhimmi or citizen? Muslim–Christian relations in Egypt" in *The Christian–Muslim Frontier: Chaos, Clash or Dialogue*. Edited by Jørgen Nielsen (London, 1998), pp. 33–49.

the "Eastern Question," during the nineteenth century. Marxian models that give primacy to class over alternate social identities have inspired further revisionism. More recently still the discourse of "post-colonialism" and the stinging critique leveled by Edward Said against the assumptions and agenda of established Western scholarship on the Middle East ("Orientalism") have deprecated the writing of Ottoman history with what is perceived as an unwarranted emphasis on religious differences. This critique decries the metaphor of a religious mosaic for the Ottoman Empire so often employed by Western scholars as serving to highlight an artificial distinction between the West, as "modern" and secular, and an unchanging "Orient" constructed as being mired in religious bigotry.[2]

The criticism of the abuses of "Orientalism" as an academic discipline by Said, and those influenced by him, has been both thoughtful and substantive. Even if Westerners were not entirely responsible for the rise of sectarian animosities in the Middle East in the nineteenth century, Western observers penned much of the early literature on sectarian relations in the Ottoman Empire. They were typically biased against Muslims and their descriptions and analyses often distorted the reality of the complexity of the relationships that linked Muslims, Christians, and Jews in the twilight of the empire. As such, the received Western historical record on the conditions under which the religious minorities in the Ottoman Empire lived is tainted and requires care when consulted. Furthermore some of those who have written on the subject more recently have done so to advance the political claims of one ethnic community over another. In response to the political manipulation of research agenda surrounding the Ottoman Empire's religious minorities, many of those who would deconstruct the "Orient" avoid religion as a category of identity in their historical analyses altogether. To write or not to write about the history of non-Muslims living in Muslim states has become, and perhaps always was, all too often a political act.[3]

This is easily illustrated by a brief comparison of contemporary scholarship on the Arabic-speaking Christian and Jewish communities. The Arab nationalist historiographical tradition, established by Muhammad Kurd-ʿAli's monumental *Khitat al-Sham* in the 1920s, presented an integrated and comprehensive imagining of the history of the Arab people of Syria which recognized sectarian differences but chose not to highlight them in the grand narrative.[4] Rather, Kurd-ʿAli's historical vision emphasized the commonality of a Syrian Arab past. Religious differences were rendered

[2] Edward Said, *Orientalism* (New York, 1978); and his *Covering Islam: How the Media and the Experts Determine How We See the Rest of the World* (New York, 1978).
[3] This is not to say that there has not been some excellent scholarship on non-Muslims in the Ottoman Empire. *Christians and Jews in the Ottoman Empire*. Edited by Benjamin Braude and Bernard Lewis. 2 vols. (New York, 1982); *The Jews of the Ottoman Empire*. Edited by Avigdor Levy (Princeton, NJ, 1994).
[4] Muhammad Kurd-ʿAli, *Khitat al-Sham* [A Map of Syria]. 6 vols. (first published Damascus, 1925–28, 2nd edn. Beirut, 1969–72).

largely irrelevant in his recasting of Syria's history with Christianity and Judaism having been given a properly Semitic – read Arab in Kurd-ᶜAli's historical imagination – pedigree. All the monotheistic faiths were thus equally valid expressions of what Kurd-ᶜAli conceived to be the Syrian people's special place in world history as the receivers and transmitters of divine truths.

Arab nationalist historians after Kurd-ᶜAli shared his desire to create a unitary vision of a linguistically based nation with a common history. In the nationalist-tinged construction of the past by some contemporary Arabs, Ottoman rule was every bit as imperialistic and oppressive as is the empire that lingers in the collective folk memory of Greeks or Serbs. There are significant differences, however. The Balkan Christians could conflate "Turks" and "Muslims" into one monolithic, and inherently evil, people. Muslim Slavs in Bosnia were thus configured as "Turks" in the political imagination of many of their Serb neighbors as was the case for Greek-speaking Muslims on Crete with tragic results for both peoples. Such a stark sectarian dichotomy was impossible in the Arab nationalist historical imagination, as Islam remained, even for the most secular among them, an integral part of the Arab people's heritage (*turath*). Instead, the Ottomans have often been characterized as imperialists who prefigured the later Europeans, with their tyranny compounded by their lax adherence to Islamic values and mores. Historians with Islamist, rather than nationalist, sympathies have moderated this view recently. While still critical of some sultans, they credit those in the early centuries, as well as Abdül-Hamid (1876–1909), as having served as the defenders of Islam.[5]

Most twentieth-century European and North American scholars of Ottoman Syria have chosen not to single out the Christians for special attention whether consciously following the Arab nationalist paradigm or not. The same can be said for those researching the histories of Egypt and Iraq. There are some notable exceptions, but these serve to remind us how much research remains to be done on the individual Christian communities in the Ottoman Arab provinces.[6] With the influence of Arab nationalist

[5] Karl Barbir, "Memory, Heritage, and History: The Ottoman Legacy in the Arab World" in *Imperial Legacy: The Ottoman Imprint on the Balkans and the Middle East*. Edited by L. Carl Brown (New York, 1996), pp. 100–14; Rifat Ali Abou-el-Haj, "The Social Use of the Past: Recent Arab Historiography of Ottoman Rule" *International Journal of Middle Eastern Studies* 14 (1982): 185–201; Abdul-Karim Rafeq, "Ottoman Historical Research in Syria since 1946" *Asian Research Trends* (Tokyo) 2 (1992): 45–78. James Reilly, "Past and Present in Local Histories of the Ottoman Period from Syria and Lebanon" *Middle Eastern Studies* 35 (1999): 45–65. Maurus Reinkowski, "Late Ottoman Rule over Palestine: Its Evaluation in Arab, Turkish and Israeli Histories, 1970–90" *Middle Eastern Studies* 35 (1999): 66–97.
[6] John Joseph, *Muslim–Christian Relations and Inter-Christian Rivalries in the Middle East: The Case of the Jacobites in an Age of Transition* (Albany, NY, 1983); Matti Moosa, *The Maronites in History* (Syracuse, NY, 1986). The missionary enterprise has received more attention: Charles Frazee, *Catholics and Sultans: The Church and the Ottoman Empire, 1453–1923* (London, 1983); Bernard Heyberger, *Les chrétiens du proche-orient au temps de la*

historiography infusing much of the writing of the Ottoman Arab past in the West, it has often seemed patently disloyal to politically concerned scholars to focus one's research on the religious differences among Arabic-speakers. To place Christians at the center of any research agenda might aid and abet those who would promote the politics of sectarianism in the region by providing unintended fodder for their polemic. As such, even the acknowledgment of the existence of separate religious communities in the Ottoman Arab past has been sometimes deftly sidestepped in the historical literature.

In sharp contrast, the Israeli–Palestinian struggle has generated numerous contemporary studies on the conditions of Jewish life in various Islamic societies. The history of the Jewish experience in Islam, written in the nineteenth century, was largely the product of European Jewish intellectuals. In contrast to the "Orientalist" literature on the Christians in the Muslim lands, it typically painted an optimistic picture of a Muslim–Jewish symbiosis in the medieval period that contrasted favorably with the dismal historical record of the treatment of Jews in Christian Europe. That tradition was carried forward into this century by S. D. Goitein and by those who would depict the Ottoman Empire as a haven for Jews expelled from Spain in the aftermath of the *reconquista*.[7]

The history of the Jews in Muslim Arab societies was rewritten with an emphasis on the darker side of their experience in the wake of their virtual disappearance from the Arab lands after the establishment of the State of Israel in 1948. Prompting a call for historical revisionism, the Tunisian-born Albert Memmi suggested that more Jews had been killed in pogroms in the Muslim world than in all of Christian Europe's long history of anti-Semitism before the advent of the combined twentieth-century horrors of Nazism and Stalinism.[8] This claim subverts the image cultivated in the nineteenth century of a Jewish–Muslim golden age in order to justify Israel as a haven for Jews fleeing from what the author posits as the inherent religious intolerance of Muslim societies.[9] Most of the subsequent scholarship on Jewish communities in the Arab lands has not been as strident as Memmi's, but it has typically presented the Jews as having a history distinct from that of their Muslim and Christian neighbors.

*réforme catholique* (Rome, 1994); Derek Hopwood. *The Russian Presence in Syria and Palestine, 1843–1914: Church and Politics in the Near East* (Oxford, 1969); Uygur Kocabaşıoğlu, *Kendi belgeleriyle Anadolu'daki Amerika: 19. yüzyılda Osmanlı İmparatorluğu'ndaki Amerikan misyoner okulları* [America in Anatolia: American Missionary Schools in the Nineteenth-Century Ottoman Empire from their own Documents] (Istanbul, 1989); A. L. Tibawi, *American Interests in Syria, 1800–1901* (Oxford, 1966).

[7] S. D. Goitein, *Jews and Arabs: Their Contacts through the Ages* (New York, 1955); Stanford Shaw, *The Jews of the Ottoman Empire and the Turkish Republic* (New York, 1991). For further discussion, see Mark Cohen, *Under Crescent and Cross: The Jews in the Middle Ages* (Princeton, NJ, 1994), pp. 3–13.

[8] Albert Memmi, *Jews and Arabs* (Chicago, IL, 1975). Translated by Eleanor Levieux. p. 27.

[9] See also: Bat Ye'or, *The Dhimmi: Jews and Christians under Islam*. Translated by David Maisel, Paul Fenton, and David Littman (Rutherford, NJ, 1985).

The reasons for not writing Ottoman history with religious identities at its core are obvious. Beyond the fear of the potential for contributing to ongoing polemics, there is the nagging doubt that an emphasis on religion as a social category in the historical discourse might distort our understanding of the Ottoman past. Christopher Bayly has raised the question of whether ordinary people in premodern India had a well-defined sense of sectarian consciousness that would conform to our contemporary construction of social identity.[10] It is a valid question for the sultan's subjects as well. In trying to assess to what degree religion shaped their everyday behavior, we must remember that Islam as a system of belief had been established in the Arab Middle East for almost a thousand years when the Ottomans arrived. Christians and Jews had been a minority for most of those centuries and most Muslims in the region could boast of a lineage that had been Muslim for generations. That reality stands in stark contrast to Mughal India where non-Muslims remained numerically, if not politically, dominant and many Muslims had only recently converted. The situation in India in the sixteenth and seventeenth centuries more closely resembled the religious flux characteristic of the Ottoman Balkans in roughly the same period where the boundaries between different faiths were more porous than that found in the major cities of the Ottoman Arab world. There the historical record left by the Muslim and non-Muslim elites alike suggests that urban Christians and Jews had adapted to being governed by Muslim legal norms and categories. In the process, they assimilated the social distinctions and boundaries imposed by an Islamic world-view, as well as its language, as their own.

Given the pervading influence of Islamic law, religion served as the primary test which established who was included within any individual's larger political community and who stood outside it for most of the history of the Ottoman period. A religiously ordained cosmology lay at the heart of the psychological world-view of each of those who inhabited the Ottoman Arab provinces. Religious faith served as an internalized anchor to each individual's sense of broader community and as the primary signifier of his or her identity to those outside it. Custom, law, and the state mandated that this was so for each of the sultan's subjects, whether he or she was an actual believer or not. Moreover, religion possessed an inherently political dimension in Ottoman society. The Ottoman sultans proclaimed their public adherence to Islam's traditions and norms, even if some might have been lax in their interpretation of that faith's injunctions once safely behind the palace walls and out of the public gaze.

An individual's legal status for most of the Ottoman period was vested in one's religious identity as much as it was in one's gender. Being female

---

[10] C. A. Bayly, "The Pre-history of 'Communalism'? Religious Conflict in India, 1700–1860" *Modern Asian Studies* 19 (1985): 177–203.

and/or non-Muslim carried differing degrees of subordination when dealing with a Muslim male under the legal hierarchy imposed by Islamic law (shariᶜa). Judith Tucker has recently explored the role of Islamic law in defining women's place in Ottoman Syria;[11] this volume seeks to explicate the legal position of the non-Muslims. As was the case in the definition of gender roles, the law's interpretation of the rights and obligations of Jews and Christians could change over time and from place to place. Clearly wealthy women and non-Muslims enjoyed access to power and privilege that were unimaginable to either the Muslim urban poor or peasants. But in cases dealing with women or non-Muslims, the Islamic courts when pressed upheld the social hierarchy that privileged Muslim males. The outward sign of women's dependency in the Ottoman period was the veil (*hijab*); for non-Muslims it might mean the requirement that they wear clothes dyed blue or black, or red shoes as was the case in eighteenth-century Aleppo. As a strict adherence to the law was only rarely enforced, it was more often the case what Christians and Jews could not wear: anything green (as the Prophet's own color) or white turbans. Such injunctions gave rise to a sartorial code whereby one would often know what faith the person approaching on the street professed. Simply put, you were what you wore.

In the public space of the bathhouses where clothing was shed, custom required non-Muslim men in Aleppo to wear towels identifying their religious faith. In Ottoman Cairo, it required Jews and Christians to wear colored string or religious amulets in the bathhouse;[12] similar regulations existed in Jerusalem.[13] In the case of women bathers for whom customary practice and sensibilities did not require a towel to cover them at all times, a judge in Aleppo decreed that Muslim and non-Muslim women should visit the bathhouses on separate days, lest the social division between the religious communities be blurred.[14] In fourteenth-century Cairo, the judge ibn al-Hajj had reached a similar conclusion.[15] Clothing served as a semiotic device to let members of one's own community know one belonged and as a marker to those outside it of difference. Law and customary practice decreed that Jews or Christians be immediately identifiable to each other and to the people of Islam, even if an individual's phenotype or dialect could not easily establish his or her religious community.

The question of who constituted the majority and the minority was thus transparent within the Ottoman Empire in the early modern period. Islamic

---

[11] Judith Tucker, *In the House of the Law: Gender and Islamic Law in Ottoman Syria and Palestine* (Berkeley, CA, 1998).

[12] Galal el-Nahal, *The Judicial Administration of Ottoman Egypt in the Seventeenth Century* (Minneapolis, MN, 1979), p. 56.

[13] Amnon Cohen, *Jewish Life under Islam: Jerusalem in the Sixteenth Century* (Cambridge, MA, 1984), p. 73.

[14] Damascus, Aleppo Court records, vol. LXXXIV, p. 56.

[15] Leila Ahmed, *Women and Gender in Islam: Historical Roots of a Modern Debate* (New Haven, CT, 1992), pp. 120–21.

law, as interpreted by the state's religious scholars (the *ᶜulama*), established the political subordination of non-Muslims to Muslims. Even in regions where Muslims were the numerical minority, they were, in effect, the legal majority as long as their territory fell under the sway of the *dar al-Islam* (House of Islam). The importance of European merchants in local economies and the rise of West European military power increasingly undermined that hierarchical ordering of intercommunal relationships after the sixteenth century. That the Europeans were also Christians inevitably altered Muslim attitudes toward the native Christians who shared their landscape. Local Christians would serve for some Muslims in the nineteenth century as convenient surrogates for the anger that could only rarely be expressed directly against the Europeans. But Muslim disquiet also emerged as a result of changes in the social and economic hierarchy governing Christian–Muslim relations. The degree of change was, in turn, brought about by each community's reaction, or inaction, to the penetration of Western political and economic hegemony with the gradual emergence of what Immanuel Wallerstein has labeled the "capitalist world system."[16]

The imbalance in the rate of acceptance of the "new" by individuals in the different religious communities sowed the seeds of social disruption. Ottoman political rhetoric in the centuries before the Tanzimat reforms of the nineteenth century enshrined "tradition" as a virtue and one did not comfortably question the ways of the ancestors. Anything labeled by Muslim religious scholars as innovation (*bidᶜa*) was tantamount to being forbidden and the embrace of the new carried the potential for religious censure.[17] Christian and Jewish religious leaders were equally wary of change. Yet things were always changing in the Middle East as institutions evolved or new ones were invented, secure behind the façade of the myth of an unchanging tradition. But when change was injected into the region in the form of Western education and political ideology by Christian Europeans themselves, rather than indirectly through neutral middlemen, Muslims were slower to embrace the new than were the region's Christians. The rate of acceptance among the Christians was in itself uneven and involved selective adaptation of Western ideas. Not all embraced the future proffered by the Europeans with equal enthusiasm. Nonetheless, the *status quo* in Ottoman society was forever transformed as individual Christians chose to assimilate certain aspects of "modernity" as defined and advanced by the Europeans. In the process, those who embraced, and profited from, the new began to distance themselves socially, economically, and perhaps even psychologically from their Muslim neighbors.

The Jews of the Ottoman Arab provinces were generally slower to

[16] Immanuel Wallerstein, *The Modern World System*. 3 vols. (New York, and San Diego, CA, 1974, 1980, 1989).
[17] Halil İnalcık, *The Ottoman Empire: The Classical Age 1300–1600* (London, 1973), pp. 179–85.

appropriate European innovations than was the case for some of the region's Christians. They, as individuals, had even more reason than the Muslims to view the arrival of the Christian Europeans with ambivalence and perhaps even alarm, given Europe's history of anti-Semitism and the avowed intent to convert them voiced by the Christian missionaries of various denominations who followed the merchants. The Jews from Iberia, the *Sephardim,*[18] arriving in the major commercial centers of the Arab provinces in the sixteenth century were an exception. Many of the Sephardic Jews had sojourned in the Italian city-states before finding their way eastward and brought with them new technologies and business practices from Europe as well as a knowledge of Italian, the lingua franca of Mediterranean trade. Indeed, they were often considered to be Europeans by the Ottoman officials and European consuls alike and were afforded European diplomatic protection. Although there was intellectual exchange and intermarriage between the Sephardim and the Arab Jews, an introduction to a European imagined "modernity" for the latter would have to await the establishment of the Alliance Israélite Universelle in 1860 when it would be packaged by European Jews for them specifically.

The blend of European ideas and economic change that accompanied the incorporation of the Ottoman Empire into the "capitalist world system" was not always fortuitous for the region's religious minorities. Fatma Müge Göçek has suggested the new Ottoman middle classes that emerged in the nineteenth century were bifurcated, with two, largely disconnected social groups – the bureaucratic and the commercial bourgeoisie. The bureaucrats were Muslim while the merchants were predominantly non-Muslim. She proposes that this voluntary segregation contributed to ever growing cultural and political chasms, which rendered asunder the various religious communities.[19] The principal ideological outcome was the emergence of ethnically based nationalisms among the empire's diverse peoples with calamitous results – the fate of the Armenians and Greeks of Anatolia or the various Muslim populations in the Balkans.

Although sectarian unrest occurred in Egypt and the Fertile Crescent, Arabic-speaking Christian intellectuals and community leaders eventually were able to articulate several options with which to configure their political community as the empire collapsed under the weight of myriad ethnic antagonisms. Their choices were usually very different from those explored by their coreligionists elsewhere in the empire. This was due, in part, to the very crucial fact that Christian Arabs shared a common language and

[18] There is a tendency to refer to all Jews from Muslim lands as *Sephardim,* rather than distinguishing *Sephardim* from *Mizrachim* (literally, "Easterners"). I will use the term more narrowly to mean only those Jews from Iberia, and their descendants, who in the Ottoman period continued to speak Judeo-Spanish (*Ladino* or *Judezmo*).
[19] Fatma Müge Göçek, *Rise of the Bourgeoisie, Demise of Empire: Ottoman Westernization and Social Change* (New York, 1996).

culture with their Muslim neighbors. Configured solely as religious communities, they were also clearly in the numerical minority almost everywhere, unlike the Christians in the Balkans or even in the ethnically contested regions of Anatolia where the various communities could at least pretend they were in the majority by manipulating suspect census data. The political realities recognized by Christian Arabs were remarkably similar to those facing the Jews throughout Ottoman Europe who found the rising tide of Balkan Christian nationalism to be often accompanied by the old demon of anti-Semitism. The choices for Christian Arabs and Ottoman Jews alike were to retain a distinct communal identity as in the past or to identify themselves within the parameters of a political community that would include their Muslim neighbors. Only among a very few did the possibility of religiously based nationalisms – "Greater Lebanon" and Zionism – intrude before the First World War.

In a movement away from defining community solely by religious faith, the non-Muslim elites in the Arab provinces increasingly chose the option of a secular political identity, whether Ottomanism or Arabism, as the empire stumbled into the twentieth century. The choice of those who would embrace a collective identity that would create a space for them within the wider Muslim majority became all the more appealing as some Muslim intellectuals also began to articulate tentative definitions of political community, devoid of sectarian dissonance. Sectarian violence had erupted earlier in the Ottoman Arab provinces than it did in Anatolia. That the Arab elites, Muslim and non-Muslim alike, were able to avoid any further open ruptures along religious lines, when the empire collapsed and neighboring Anatolia exploded into a paroxysm of ethnic violence, says much about the sea change which had occurred in their articulation of their political identity.

Benedict Anderson suggests that identification with the concept of "nation" can only arise among a people when there is a sense of political community, i.e. a shared identity more widely defined than by lineage alone. Anderson acknowledges, however, not every community conceives itself within the framework of a nation, which he defines as an "imagined political community – and imagined as both inherently limited and sovereign."[20] The prerequisite for his nationhood is the acknowledgment by individuals that a political compact links them to others with whom they share a recognized affinity beyond family, clan, or tribe. The parameters for inclusion can vary, depending on how the collective identity is constructed or "imagined." A shared language is perhaps the most elementary basis for recognition of mutual affinity, but geography, historical memory, or religion can also help shape the boundaries of community. More often that not, it is a

[20] Benedict Anderson, *Imagined Communities: Reflections on the Origin and Spread of Nationalism* (London, 1991).

combination of more than one of these "necessary conditions." But whatever the basis for the political affinity, Anderson contends that it must first be "imagined" by the elites who then have to inculcate the masses with that articulation before it can take hold of the collective consciousness of those who would constitute the nation. His definition is thus at odds with those who consider ethnic/national identities to be primordial, the inevitable by-products of a shared language and culture.[21]

Nation, as Anderson defines it, is a West European concept and a relatively recent one at that. Although a seemingly parallel political ideology linking culture, history, polity, and geography emerged independently in East Asia with the Middle Kingdom of the Han Chinese, Europeans introduced the idea of nation to most of the remaining world. This occurred under less than optimal circumstances. The spatial delineation of a nation was often left to those who drew the maps and the mapmakers outside of West Europe's core were rarely indigenous. Even where the collective identity of a colonized people coalesced into a "proto-nation" (to borrow Eric Hobsbawm's term[22]), it arose in opposition to conquest and often appropriated the political categories imposed by the invaders on the indigenous inhabitants of a place. Thus, the Gaels who inhabited Britain's island neighbor had never conceived themselves as being collectively "Irish" until they were labeled as such by those who sought to conquer them. While they had several synonyms for their island home, they did not associate any of those with what they chose to call themselves. Rather, they saw the world, much like the early Greeks, in stark cultural terms *Gael* versus *Gall*, or "us" and "everyone else."[23] It was arguably a simplistic distinction, but one that was shared by many peoples around the globe. By the end of the nineteenth century, however, most of the world's inhabitants had learnt similarly to define their own sense of an imagined community within the parameters of the European concept of the nation-state or in conscious opposition to it – the path chosen by Marxists and late twentieth-century Islamists. Given the political and economic hegemony established by the West, they could not ignore it.

Anderson's nation is at odds with the political traditions of tribal or dynastic regimes that had served the peoples of the Middle East for centuries.[24] It also runs contrary to the Muslim concept of *umma* (the community of believers) which holds out its own dream of an "imagined political community," rooted in the authenticity of the Prophet's tradition

---

[21] Clifford Geertz, "The Integrative Revolution: Primordial Sentiments and Civil Politics in the New States" in *Old Societies and New States*. Edited by Clifford Geertz (New York, 1963), pp. 105–57.

[22] Eric Hobsbawm, *Nations and Nationalisms since 1780* (Cambridge, 1990).

[23] Joep Leerssen, *Mere Irish and Fíor-Ghael: Studies in the Idea of Irish Nationality, its Development and Literary Expression prior to the Nineteenth Century* (Cork, 1996).

[24] See the contributions to *Tribes and State Formation in the Middle East*. Edited by Philip Khoury and Joseph Kostiner (Berkeley, CA, 1990).

(*Sunna*). But the political *umma* has proven far too tenuous to support a unitary state for long as its very inclusiveness makes it unstable, even as it remains a political ideal to which many ordinary Muslims aspire.

Ethnic pride (*ʿasabiyya*) had, of course, existed in Islamic societies before the introduction of European political models.[25] But nationalism was only comprehensible as the basis of a political ideology for most Middle Easterners in the nineteenth century after Western political categories were assimilated into local realities. An illustration of this appropriation of a national identity as constructed by Westerners is found in the articulation of "Turkishness" (*Türkçülük*). Throughout most of the Ottoman period, European visitors to the sultans' realms used the label "Turk" indiscriminately to mean any Muslim, regardless of his or her mother tongue. To become Muslim was to "turn Turk." Yet for any proper Ottoman gentleman at the sultan's court that term would have sounded vulgar if applied to him until the end of the nineteenth century when Muslim Ottoman intellectuals began to privilege language as the basis of a constructed national identity. Only then could the *Turchia*, which had haunted the imagination of West Europeans in the centuries after the fall of Constantinople, become the *Türkiye* of the Young Turks.

In contrast to the Muslim ideal of an indivisible *umma*, the evolution of the non-Muslim religious communities of the Ottoman Empire into officially recognized religio-political bodies (*millets*) with powers of taxation and collective representation in the eighteenth century provided opportunities for the empire's non-Muslims to create Anderson's "imagined communities." The possibility of "nation" replacing religious community took root most easily among those peoples for whom religious identity and language were conflated. Greeks and Armenians could make the intellectual leap from a community based solely on sectarian identity to one that was reconfigured by adding mother tongue as a criterion for inclusion without too much confusion. The religious identity of both peoples already possessed a strong potential for an imagining of a national identity along the lines suggested by Anderson as their languages of liturgy, and hence literary expression, resembled their spoken vernaculars. Each community also preserved a collective memory of its own historic kingship to aid in the imagining of the possibility of, and therefore the pressing necessity for, national sovereignty. But even among Greek-speakers, it was not apparent to all that a resuscitated Byzantine Empire, rooted in Orthodoxy and with Constantinople as its redeemed capital, would be solely the preserve of Hellenes.[26]

The framers of other potential proto-nationalities in the Ottoman

---

[25] Metin Kunt, "Ethnic-Regional (*Cins*) Solidarity in the Seventeenth-Century Ottoman Establishment" *International Journal of Middle East Studies* 5 (1974): 233–39.

[26] Paschalis Kitromilides, "'Imagined Communities' and the Origins of the National Question in the Balkans" *European Historical Quarterly* 19 (1989): 149–94.

Balkans could restrict the boundaries of inclusion by employing the criterion of language to create autonomous exarchates with complementary and newly reconfigured national histories. Rumanians, Serbs, and Bulgarians employed this model of the "invention of tradition" in the nineteenth century.[27] Religion, as defined by loyalty to autonomous exarchates, combined with language, helped to articulate compelling, and therefore historically self-evident, parameters of the imagined community for emerging Balkan nationalist identities. The creation of an ideology wedded to the concept of nation was obviously more difficult for peoples who shared a common tongue but held a variety of previously mutually exclusive religious identities: Albanians, the Bosnian Slavs, and Arabs.

The Orthodox Christian Arabs (or simply the *Rum* in both contemporary Arabic and Ottoman Turkish texts), who comprised the largest single Christian community in the Arab provinces, were subsumed in the eighteenth century in a *millet* dominated by Greeks, who occasionally exercised linguistic imperialism over their non-Hellenic coreligionists. A subordination of the linguistic identity of the non-Greek communities within the Orthodox *millet* to a newly realized national identity, articulated in the language of the patriarchate, was possible in the Balkans where some Vlachs and Slavs apparently were willing to abandon their mother tongue for the Greek of the Mother Church. Such an option, however, does not seem to have been possible for Syria's Orthodox Christians. Even if contemporary European and Ottoman sources referred to them as "Greeks," their ties of language and culture to their Muslim Arab neighbors prevented easy assimilation into *Hellas*. A strong sense of localism and a reaction to Greek ecclesiastical hegemony, however, did eventually lead some of the Rum to lobby for their own separate *millet* to be articulated in Arabic (the so-called Greek Catholics, *Melkit Katolikler* in Ottoman Turkish, *Rum kathulik* in Arabic).

Language created barriers for the integration of Christian Arabs into a Hellenic *ethnos*, but Arabic did not necessarily serve as bedrock for an Arab national consciousness. The majority of the *millet* of the Rum in the Fertile Crescent did not choose to join the Melkite Catholic *millet* when that option became available and continued to be served by a predominantly Greek hierarchy until the start of the twentieth century.[28] Furthermore, the overwhelming majority of those who shared Arabic as a mother tongue were not Christians. Arabic-speaking peoples inhabited contiguous regions with a myriad of traditions and political histories. Even for those who lived within a common cultural zone such as the *Bilad al-Sham* (geographical

---

[27] Dimitrije Djordjevic and Stephen Fischer-Galati, *The Balkan Revolutionary Tradition* (New York, 1981). *The Invention of Tradition*. Edited by Eric Hobsbawm and Terence Ranger (Cambridge, 1983).

[28] Hopwood, *Russian Presence*, pp. 159–200. The Arab laity of the patriarchate of Jerusalem were still protesting Greek control of the higher offices in the year 2000.

Syria) or Egypt, their confessional allegiances might pit at times community against community – Orthodox versus Catholic, Sunni versus Shi<sup>c</sup>a. Nonetheless, the creation of the Melkite Catholic *millet* had unintentionally provided a locally based politics of identity expressed in Arabic. The implications of that for the further articulation of an ethnic identity based in language for all Arabic-speaking Christians reached far beyond the Melkites alone.

We can plot the history of the religious minorities in the Ottoman Arab world as a narrative of change and adaptation from their initial contacts with European merchants and missionaries to the articulation of national identities at the end of the empire. This transformation affected only a small minority of urban dwellers. But they would emerge as their communities' intellectual and economic elites. Change came slowly and incrementally over several centuries for the vast majority of Muslims, Christians, and Jews of the empire alike, only to arrive with a disruptive fury in the nineteenth century when Ottoman bureaucrats in Istanbul imposed it by imperial decree. Although the number of people who personally experienced any direct impact of European economic or intellectual penetration was small, they were the historical actors who determined the collective, political trajectory of their coreligionists. The Christian elites of the empire, and to a lesser extent their Jewish counterparts, were the first of the sultan's subjects to encounter and assimilate Western ideas in any systematic way. They were also among the first to imagine, if ever so tentatively, a political identity drawn along ethnic/linguistic lines.

This characterization of the transformation of the status of the non-Muslims is, of course, not original with me. Robert Haddad advanced a similar argument for the Syrian Christians, as did Charles Issawi for all of the non-Muslims of the empire.[29] I am indebted in particular to the pioneering essay by Haddad that piqued my interest to pursue this study and to reexamine his assumptions. I do not substantially alter his characterization of the role of the Catholic–Orthodox religious confrontation in giving rise to a Syrian identity. But I differ from these earlier works by identifying the transformation as starting before the eighteenth century and by placing these developments squarely within the context of Ottoman history. Previous studies of the non-Muslims have relied heavily on European accounts and documentation, often ignoring the indigene "voice." I have sought to correct that imbalance by using sources written by Arabic-speaking non-Muslims, as well as records of the Ottoman authorities. The bureaucrats in the capital were not unaware of the transitions that were occurring in the realm they administered. Their actions often

---

[29] Robert Haddad, *Syrian Christians in Muslim Society: An Interpretation* (Westport, CT, 1970); Charles Issawi, "The Transformation of the Economic Position of the *Millets* in the Nineteenth Century" in *Christians and Jews in the Ottoman Empire*. Edited by B. Braude and B. Lewis. (Princeton, NJ, 1982), vol. I, pp. 261–85.

played a decisive role in determining the fate of the empire's religious minorities and in formulating their political identities. The construction of social community was very much a product of an ongoing interaction between the Ottoman bureaucrats, representing the sultan, and his subjects, Muslim and non-Muslim alike.

This study examines the evolution of sectarian relations and political identities in the Ottoman Arab provinces over four centuries from the arrival of the Sultan Selim's army in Syria in 1516 to the start of the First World War. Given the breadth of its geographical and historical parameters, not all communities will be dealt with equally. I will not be discussing Christians and Jews outside the core provinces of the Fertile Crescent and Egypt, except tangentially. Their exclusion is seemingly justified as the Ottoman regime only sporadically exercised political control over the Arab territories on the empire's periphery and the question of whether North Africa or Yemen were ever properly "Ottoman" remains. Within the Fertile Crescent, this study privileges the history of the non-Muslims of the Syrian provinces. It was there that the European influence was the most profound and the social transformation of the minorities concomitantly the most dramatic. Moreover, Syrian Christians and Jews often served as the principal transmitters of new knowledge and ideas outside their native cities to other regions of the Arabic-speaking Ottoman world.

Geographical Syria has also received the most attention from contemporary scholars of the Ottoman Arab past. These have researched many of the primary sources on non-Muslims, both in the archives of its provincial centers and in Istanbul, to an extent not yet reproduced for the other provinces. Their findings provide comparative materials for my own archival research largely focused on Aleppo. Within greater Syria, this study draws heavily on examples from that city and highlights the emergence of Catholic communities there. I justify that emphasis on two counts. Firstly, until the rapid growth of Beirut and Alexandria in the nineteenth century, Aleppo was the major locus of intercultural contact in the Arab east (*Mashriq*). Secondly, the city was home to the largest urban concentration of non-Muslims in the Ottoman Arab lands and the social evolution at the heart of this study was an urban phenomenon. As such, its religious communities were often in the vanguard of historical developments that would occur elsewhere later. I am also treating in greater detail the story of the city's Melkite Catholics as they were the first people in the region to define their communal identity through language. Hopefully, others will be tempted to test the characterizations I outline here with case studies outside Syria. The Jewish community of Baghdad, for example, seems one that clearly is in need of its own monograph.

This study focuses on change. In part, the approach is a reaction to scholarship that posits that institutions in the Ottoman Empire were relatively static until the nineteenth century. But I also want to suggest to the reader that the peoples of the Arab provinces of the Ottoman Empire were not simply passive recipients of a changing world order imposed from without by the Europeans. Rather they took an active lead in devising strategies to cope with change and benefit from it, thereby determining their own futures. The question of the demographic fate of non-Muslims in the Arab world in the twenty-first century is still unresolved as their presence in the region continues to decline due to emigration.[30] Whatever their future, however, I would like the reader to come away with an appreciation of the remarkable social, cultural, and political transformations they experienced in the Ottoman past.

[30] Youssef Courbage and Philippe Fargues, *Christians and Jews under Islam*. Translated by Judy Marbro (London, 1997), pp. 174–95.

CHAPTER 1

# The limits of tolerance: the social status of non-Muslims in the Ottoman Arab lands

| | |
|---|---|
| The cold lasts as long as the Christian fasts. | (Syrian proverb) |
| A Jew when bankrupt searches his old account books. | (Baghdadi proverb) |
| A Copt without cunning is like a tree without fruit. | (Egyptian proverb) |

Proverbs inform us that the Arabic-speaking peoples in the Ottoman centuries reduced sectarian differences to simplistic, if usually benign, clichés. Urban folk wisdom more commonly imposed stereotypes on the tribal peoples who loomed as the ultimate "other" in the imaginations of town dwellers or on residents of neighboring towns and regions in a reflection of fiercely held local identities and loyalties. It is significant, however, that the Muslim majority in the region's cities and towns perceived their non-Muslim neighbors as existing outside the boundaries of their social community. Differences in public behavior were noted and passed down in proverb to become received tradition. Such stereotypes highlight the social distance separating the religious communities in the cities of the Ottoman Arab world. Jews and Christians might share residential quarters and work place with Muslims, but they were seldom, if ever, included in the collective "we" in the consciousness of their Muslim neighbors.

This impression finds confirmation in the written record left to us by Muslim chroniclers of the Ottoman centuries where non-Muslims' lives went largely unremarked. There were, of course, exceptions. In times of natural disasters or during attacks by outsiders, all the inhabitants of a city might come together in common cause, forgetting sectarian differences in a spirit of civic cooperation. An example of such collaboration was the Christian participation in the defense of Mosul in 1743 when an apparition of the Virgin Mary sanctified the defenders and was duly noted by a Muslim chronicler.[1] But the exceptions draw attention to the silence prevalent elsewhere in the

---

[1] Dina Rizk Khoury, *State and Provincial Society in the Ottoman Empire: Mosul, 1540–1834* (Cambridge, 1997), p. 67.

narratives. That sense of psychological separation was reciprocated by Christian chroniclers who frequently employed the undifferentiated collective "Islam" when referring to their Muslim neighbors and rarely commented on events in the larger Muslim world unless they had direct bearing on the fate of their own religious community. Almost every chronicler in the early Ottoman centuries, whatever his faith, seemed to have been bound by an unspoken rule that the affairs of religious communities outside his own would be of no concern to the posterity for whom he wrote.

We know that the religious communities were psychologically separated from each other, if not segregated by law, but it is difficult to reconstruct the parameters of social distance or, alternatively, the opportunities for cross-communal interaction on a personal level that might have existed. Complicating our discussion, much of what the historical record says about sectarian relations was written by European observers, whether Jews or Christians, whose impartiality is often questionable. Furthermore, social boundaries and taboos shifted across the empire. Conditions observed in one town might not be found in another; circumstances might also change over time even in the same location. It is precisely the arena of everyday behavior and attitudes where historians have the fewest clues as to the nature of the interactions among the various communities in the Ottoman Empire: what did people actually think of one another? What was the extent of social contact among individuals from different religious communities? Was tolerance or intolerance the rule?[2]

Most historians agree that the Islamic court records from various cities in the Ottoman period establish that any economic discrimination urban non-Muslims faced was relatively light. The head-tax (*jizya*), for which all adult male non-Muslims were liable but which was often assessed collectively on their religious community, was undoubtedly irksome. But it was rarely financially debilitating as the rate was based on one's ability to pay. Many avoided paying it altogether, much to the ire of their community leaders who found themselves having to make up the difference. In times of political turmoil when the long arm of the state became too attenuated to enforce its writ, Christians and Jews might find themselves the special victims of financial extortion from local Ottoman officialdom. But wealthy Muslims felt the squeeze as well. Legally, non-Muslims could not engage in the lucrative business of tax farming. But individual Christians and Jews did hold tax farms in the eighteenth century, an indication that restrictions limiting the participation of non-Muslims were not always enforced. Otherwise, Christians and Jews were free to seek their livelihood unimpeded by

[2] Dominique Chevallier raises some of these same questions in his short but insightful "Non-Muslim Communities in Arab Cities" in *Christian and Jews in the Ottoman Empire*. Edited by B. Braude and B. Lewis (New York, 1982), vol. II, pp. 159–65. Unfortunately, he does not give any answers.

state interference. Some flourished economically under these conditions and by the end of the Ottoman period, many of the wealthiest individuals in the Ottoman Arab cities were non-Muslims.

There is also little question that Jews and Christians had any established political rights. But that was true for the Muslim subjects of the sultans as well. However, many among the Muslim elite in the Arab cities of the empire had come to believe by the eighteenth century that they did have a stake in the regime. It was self-avowedly Muslim and so it was by definition theirs. Typical of this identification with the House of Osman, the early eighteenth-century Damascene chronicler Muhammad bin Kannan took an avid interest in the Ottoman sultans' campaigns as the champions of Islam. His loyalty was not absolute as the author's allegiance seemed to falter when he noted that the Ottoman armies had engaged in battle the equally Sunni Afghan army of Nadir Shah. Concluding the entry, he simply asked God to end the fighting without his usual invocation, "May God grant the sultan victory."[3] Non-Muslims had no such illusions. They might feel personally loyal to an individual sultan or governor who had dealt with their community fairly, but they knew the state was not theirs. It was only at the end of the empire, when its political elite sought to introduce the idea of Ottoman citizenship, that the definition was broad enough to welcome the inclusion of Jews and Christians.[4] Cognizant that there was a psychological distance between the Muslims and non-Muslims in the Ottoman era, we need to explore the origins of that attitude and examine how it might have influenced intercommunal relations in the Ottoman period.

## The roots of difference: *ahl al-dhimma*

Muslims in the Ottoman Arab lands provided complex, and often varied, responses to their Jewish and Christian neighbors. This was in no small part due to the ambivalence toward the two faiths found at the very core of Islamic traditions. Western scholars and observers of Muslim societies have alternatively ascribed to Islam, as a normative social construct, religious toleration and fanaticism. Both characterizations are possible, as Muslim states historically have manifested these apposite tendencies at different times and in different places. The primary inspiration for Islamic attitudes, the Qur'an, itself shows considerable vacillation when dealing with its sibling monotheistic faiths. The Qur'an recognizes the validity of the

[3] Muhammad bin Kannan al-Salihi. *Yawmiyyat shamiyya* [Damascus Diary], *min 1111 h. hatta 1153 h.–1699 m. hatta 1740 m.* Edited by Akram Hasan al-ᶜUlabi (Damascus, 1994), p. 382. See also, Bruce Masters, "The View from the Province: Syrian Chroniclers of the Eighteenth Century" *Journal of the American Oriental Society* 114 (1994): 353–62; Khoury, *State and Provincial Society*, pp. 156–87.
[4] Selim Deringil, *The Well-Protected Domains: Ideology and the Legitimation of Power in the Ottoman Empire 1876–1909* (London, 1998).

prophets of both Judaism and Christianity. Indeed, it claims them as its own. Needless to say, neither Christian nor Jewish traditions reciprocated that generosity toward their younger sibling. The Qur'an, however, warns those Jews and Christians who were the Prophet Muhammad's contemporaries of God's eternal damnation should they reject his mission. Furthermore, it directly negates doctrines they held to be the essential truths of their faith.

Western scholars have interpreted the Qur'an's apparent ambiguity towards the earlier monotheisms as arising from the historical context in which the sacred text was revealed.[5] They note the Qur'an was delivered over twenty years, during which Muhammad transformed himself from a prophet without political power to the head of a state at war with those who doubted his role as messenger of God. As such, they suggest that the Qur'anic verses reflect the historical progression of the Prophet's ministry. In the earlier revelations delivered in Mecca, God, through His Prophet, appealed to the believers of the other "heaven-sent" religions to acknowledge Muhammad as legitimately delivering His message. Revelation made the links to the two earlier faiths manifest by incorporating biblical tales into the Qur'an, thereby establishing them as sacred text for Muslims. This invocation of the two earlier traditions sought to widen the appeal of the message of the Prophet Muhammad to Arabian Christians and Jews by demonstrating the continuity of the revelations given to him with those of their own prophets. This secular interpretation maintains the Prophet found that, once in power, his fellow monotheists refused to accept that his message was from their shared God and even mocked his apparent ignorance of their holy books. In response, the tone of revelation toward non-Muslims turned more critical.

But Muhammad was also the political head of the fledgling Muslim state. Acting as such, he established a binding precedent for his successors when dealing with non-Muslims through his agreement with the Jewish tribes of Medina, which Western scholars have dubbed the "Constitution of Medina." Thereafter, Muslim authorities would recognize the rights of believers in the monotheistic faiths to remain at peace within the *umma*, as long as they recognized Islam's political authority over them.[6] This clientage was embodied in the concept of the *ahl al-dhimma* (literally "the people of the contract," in the singular *dhimmi*) which guaranteed the rights of the non-Muslims to property, livelihood, and freedom of worship in return for extra taxes (the *jizya*) and the promise not to help Islam's enemies. Most Muslim commentators do not share this contextual view of an evolution of attitudes toward non-Muslims expressed through divine revelation,

---

[5] Montgomery Watt, *Muhammad at Mecca* (Oxford, 1953) and *Muhammad at Medina* (Oxford, 1956); Maxime Rodinson, *Mahomet* (Paris, 1968).
[6] R. B. Serjeant, "The 'Constitution of Medina' " *Islamic Quarterly* 8 (1964): 3–16.

however. Rather, they hold that any apparent inconsistencies Western scholars find within the Qur'an arise out of human inability to grasp the innate coherence of the divine text.[7]

With Muhammad's death in 632, revelation ceased. Both the Qur'an and the historical actions taken by the Prophet in his lifetime had left the Muslims with a mixed legacy in the representation of the relative merits and failings of the "Peoples of the Book." While Christianity and Judaism were valid, at least in the abstract, some of their doctrines as understood by contemporary Jews and Christians were wrong. It was, however, left to God alone to punish the non-Muslims for their obstinacy on the final Day of Judgment. Until then, Muslims should leave them in their theological error unharmed. Jews and Christians must show, in return, their political subordination to the people of Islam by paying the *jizya*. This rather rudimentary formula for coexistence was based on the realities of an Arabia where the vast majority of the inhabitants had already accepted, at least nominally, the Prophet's message. It was soon in need of radical revision following the success of the Muslim armies in the decades following his death.

The Muslims had reached the borders of both China and the kingdom of the Franks by 750 with a string of military successes, equalling those of Alexander the Great or Chingiz Khan. Victories on the battlefield brought millions of non-Muslims into the *umma* and necessitated a reevaluation of the status of non-Muslims in the Muslim state. Despite the Western stereotype of Muslim conquerors with sword in one hand and the Qur'an in the other, Muslims did not expect their new subjects to embrace Islam. Rather theirs was a war for political control and booty, not for the hearts and minds of the non-believers who possessed a "Book." The options for the few surviving polytheists in the Middle East were less generous. Muslim expectations for the maintenance of the *status quo ante* were short lived, however, as numerous former Christians, Jews, and Zoroastrians accepted the Prophet's message.

Initially, the Arab Muslims made little distinction between those non-Arabs who accepted Islam and those who did not. All non-Arab adult males, Muslim converts or not, had to pay the *jizya* and all conquered lands were subject to a tax assessed on their productivity (*kharaj*). The new converts to Islam were considered to be without proper, i.e. Arab, lineage and became legally the clients (singular *mawla*, plural *mawali*) of Arab tribesmen so as to conform to the preIslamic social hierarchy that still prevailed as normative. By contrast, Arab tribesmen who remained Christians but fought for the *umma* were accorded a status close to that of Muslim Arabs. Christian Arab poets received the caliph's largess and theologians such as St. John of Damascus were welcomed at the court of the

[7] R. Stephen Humphreys, *Islamic History: A Framework for Inquiry* (Princeton, NJ, 1991), pp. 258–59.

Umayyad dynasty (661–750).[8] Such behavior must have loomed as a stark injustice in the minds of the newly converted and added to the potential for anti-Christian prejudice among them. Partially in response to their grievances, a new legalistic tradition emerged in the urban centers of Iraq and the Hejaz through which scholars sought to define God's law and to limit the abuses of an Islamic kingship. In the process, this legal tradition delineated the rights and obligations of both Muslims, regardless of ethnic origin, and non-Muslims within the Muslim state.

A revolution shook the *umma* in 750. It had gained strength among the believers, in part, out of the their sense of grievance generated by the regime's treatment of non-Arab Muslims. The new rulers, the Banu ᶜAbbas (Abbasids, 750–1258) in Baghdad, tried to steer the ship of state on a decidedly more Muslim course with the help of an emerging intellectual class of legal scholars, the ᶜulama. Social unrest, as well as religiously couched arguments, eventually led to a reformulation of Muslim identity. It was to be a broader and more inclusive one than had existed before. Although the believers still assigned merit to those of the Prophet's lineage (*ashraf*, singular *sharif*), the newly emergent legal tradition eliminated the distinction between Arab and non-Arab origins in determining the social standing of any individual Muslim within the community of believers.

Islam, as a political ideology, became more legalistic over time, enshrining what might have been temporary historical expediencies as holy law (*shariᶜa*). This was particularly true in its formulation of the conditions under which non-Muslims might enjoy Islam's protection. It is almost impossible to state with any certainty what percentage of the people in Islam's core lands of North Africa, the Fertile Crescent, and Iran had embraced Islam by 750, but as Muslims gained ground numerically, non-Muslims became increasingly marginalized within the Muslim state. As a political expression of that marginality, their social and political subordination to the people of Islam was given concrete legal form in a document known as the "Pact of ᶜUmar." Although its historic origins are debated, the "Pact of ᶜUmar" became an integral part of the Muslim legal tradition by the ninth century. It would govern how subsequent Muslim states treated their non-Muslim subjects from the time of the Abbasids until the Ottoman reforms of the nineteenth century.

Muslim tradition states that the Caliph ᶜUmar ibn al-Khattab (634–44) issued the "Pact" to the Christians of Jerusalem, or alternatively Syria as a whole, following its fall to the Muslim armies. Although Western scholars have ascribed the formulation to the Umayyad caliph, ᶜUmar II (717–20), it may be that its final formulation is a composite of many different agreements between Muslims and non-Muslims. Although the core of these may originally date from the time of the Prophet, they were modified with

---

[8]  Philip Hitti, *History of the Arabs* (New York, 1970), pp. 195–96.

increasing severity over time.[9] A written version of the agreement entered into Muslim legal texts by the ninth century in a standard formula invariably ascribed to the Caliph ᶜUmar ibn al-Khattab. Later versions elaborated on the conditions and added new restrictions, all the while claiming to be the original "Pact." In its earliest renditions, the "Pact" stipulated that in return for the Muslims' pledge of safe-conduct for their persons and property (*aman*), the non-Muslims agreed to the following:

> They would be subject to the political authority of Islam.
>
> They would not speak of the Prophet Muhammad, his Book, or his faith.
>
> They would refrain from committing fornication with Muslim women. This was extended to include marriage between non-Muslim men and Muslim women. Marriage between Muslim men and *dhimmi* women was allowed, following the Prophet's example, as long as the children were brought up as Muslims. But non-Muslim wives of Muslim men were free to worship according to their own faith.
>
> Non-Muslims were forbidden to sell or give a Muslim anything that was in violation of Islamic law, i.e. carrion, pork, or alcohol.
>
> The display of crosses or the ringing of bells in public was not permitted, nor any public proclamation of "polytheistic" belief to a Muslim.
>
> No new churches or synagogues could be built.
>
> Non-Muslims must wear the girdle over their cloaks and were to differentiate themselves from Muslims by their headgear, mounts, and saddles. This was expanded later to prohibit non-Muslims from riding either horses or camels, limiting them to mules and donkeys.
>
> Non-Muslims should not teach their children the Qur'an, nor use Arabic in their personal seals.
>
> No non-Muslim could hold a Muslim as a slave.
>
> No public religious processions, such as those traditionally held at Easter, were to be allowed.

The formula guarantees in return that Muslims would not interfere in any internal decisions made by the leadership of the non-Muslim religious communities in regards to personal status law or contracts unless all parties agreed to Muslim adjudication.[10]

---

[9]  C.E. Bosworth, "The Concept of *Dhimma* in Early Islam" in *Christians and Jews in the Ottoman Empire*. Edited by B. Braude and B. Lewis (New York, 1982), vol. I, pp. 37–51.

[10]  For English translations of versions of the "Pact of ᶜUmar" as they have survived in the Islamic legal literature, see *Islam from the Prophet Muhammad to the Capture of Constantinople*, vol. II *Religion and Society*. Edited and translated by Bernard Lewis (New York, 1974), pp. 216–23.

If we compare these conditions to other premodern codes regulating relationships between conquerors and the conquered, the "Pact of ᶜUmar" seems almost benign. The "Statutes of Kilkenny" promulgated in Ireland in 1366 by the Anglo-Normans sought to stop the assimilation of the ruling French-speaking elite into the culture of the ruled by prohibiting the use of Gaelic language, music, dress, and sport among the Normans.[11] The "Pact of ᶜUmar" displays no such fears. If anything, the injunctions seem designed to insure that non-Muslims remained distinct from Muslims by their dress and by limiting their assimilation into the culture of the Muslims. While the "Pact" allows non-Muslims to retain their own customary practices in regards to personal status law, it established a public disdain for those practices in the eyes of the Muslim legal scholars and, by extension, the state. More importantly, it codified that Muslims had precedence over non-Muslims in any public space the communities might share. The call to prayer might disturb a non-Muslim's slumber, but the ringing of church bells or the chants of the non-believers should not inconvenience a Muslim.

These annoying, rather than life-threatening, prohibitions established the social inferiority of non-Muslims in a Muslim society. Non-Muslims had to pay the *jizya*, but the amount assessed in the Ottoman period was usually more symbolic than onerous. A non-Muslim's testimony was accepted in the Muslim courts, except in those cases where a ruling of guilt would result in the imposition of criminal sanctions against a Muslim. As such, a non-Muslim had nothing to fear when entering into commercial contracts with Muslims. There were no prohibitions on where non-Muslims might live or work, even if the dead were to be buried separately. Nor was any separation of trades by confession mandated. Yet it is clear from the injunctions that the social status of a Muslim was higher than that of a non-Muslim in much the same way that the codification of tradition as law established the social and legal superiority of men over women.

This translated into an institutionalized indifference among the Muslim elites to the non-Muslims as expressed in the literature extant from Islam's classical age. While Muslim historians showed interest in the Christian states predating the rise of Islam and geographers might discuss European Christian societies, little notice was paid to the indigenous Christians who were their neighbors. This omission is all the more telling as Muslim historians often relied on accounts written by their Arabic-speaking Christian contemporaries for information on early Christianity and the Byzantine Empire.[12] Indifference in the public record gave way to open Muslim hostility toward Christians in response to the reports of atrocities committed by the Franks against Muslim civilians in Christendom's first

---

[11] J. A. Watt, "The Anglo-Irish Colony under Strain, 1327–99" in *A New History of Ireland*, vol. II *Medieval Ireland, 1169–1534*. Edited by Art Cosgrove (Oxford, 1993), pp. 352–96.

[12] Nadia Maria El-Sheikh, "Arab Christian Contributions to Muslim Historiography on Byzantium" *Bulletin of the Royal Institute for Inter-Faith Studies*, 1/2 (1999): 45–60.

crusade to capture the Holy Land in 1098. The potential for inter-confessional antagonism was further fueled by the heated counter-rhetoric of crusade and jihad that continued for the next two centuries. Although with the exception of the Armenian kingdom of Edessa (present day Urfa), Middle Eastern Christians did not welcome the arrival of their coreligionists from Europe, Muslim attitudes toward local Christians deteriorated as their loyalty became suspect. Surviving Muslim legal documents from the period take on a harsher tone, illustrating the shift in attitudes. In the aftermath of the trauma of the Crusades, the "Pact of ʿUmar" was often rewritten with further refinements on the preexisting restrictions. For example, the requirement that non-Muslims wear clothing of a specified color became much more widespread in this period.[13]

The percentage of Christians in the population of the Muslim lands declined sharply after the crusading period. They disappeared entirely from Muslim-ruled areas of Spain and North Africa. The process of conversion and assimilation into Arabic-Muslim society seems to have accelerated in the core lands of the Arab Middle East as well, as Coptic and Syriac ceased to be widely used as vernaculars and survived primarily as languages of liturgy. Whereas the Christians had once been the majority in the Fertile Crescent, they were a numerical minority almost everywhere by the Mamluk period (1250–1516), if not before.[14] Jews survived in these regions as much more coherent communities than did the Christians and, generally, with less open hostility from their Muslim neighbors. But there can be no question that official Muslim tolerance for Jews had ebbed as well. In regions where there were no Christians, and especially in territories where the Shiʿa tradition predominated such as Yemen and Iran, the Jewish communities might be subjected to oppressive measures similar to those Christians sometimes suffered elsewhere.[15]

Muslims did not universally share this hardening of sectarian attitudes expressed by Islam's legal establishment. During the turbulent centuries of the Crusades, Islam's mystics, the Sufis, were redefining what it meant to be Muslim. The literalism of the *Qurʾan* was seen in their cosmology to be only an exterior truth which paled when compared to the inner knowledge (*maʿarifa*) of God that could be gained from the Sufi quest. A key figure in the Sufis' legends and lore was Jesus who was believed by some to embody the inner truth of religion as Muhammad had the outer. The external forms

---

[13] Donald Little, "Coptic Converts to Islam during the Bahri Mamluk Period" in *Conversion and Continuity: Indigenous Christian Communities in Islamic Lands, Eighth to Eighteenth Centuries.* Edited by Michael Gervers and Ramzi Jibran Bikhazi (Toronto, 1990), pp. 263–88.

[14] Nehemia Levitzon, "Conversion to Islam in Syria and Palestine and the Survival of Christian Communities" in *Conversion and Continuity: Indigenous Christian Communities in Islamic Lands, Eighth to Eighteenth Centuries.* Edited by M. Gervers and R. Bikhazi (Toronto, 1990), pp. 263–68.

[15] Hayyim Cohen, *The Jews of the Middle East, 1860–1972* (New York, 1973), p. 3.

of Christian and Muslim worship were equally irrelevant for the Sufis in their quest for eternal realities. As such, whether one started on the road to God from church, mosque, or synagogue was not as important as that one started on the quest for truth at all. This relativism could lead to greater cultural tolerance of non-Muslims in an expression of religious brotherhood. This is not to suggest all Sufis embraced a more tolerant view of non-Muslims. Rather Sufism offered an emotional and intellectual counterweight to the Islamic legal scholars' efforts to codify a rigid separation between the religious communities. In doing so, it added yet another layer of ambivalence to that which already pervaded Muslim attitudes toward non-Muslims.

Sufism also provided an Islamic façade for the ongoing syncretism between Christian belief and practice and those of Muslims on a popular level. Christians had been visiting holy shrines throughout the region before the arrival of the Muslim armies and many of these continued to exercise a spiritual pull over converts to Islam and their descendants. Some of the shrines were accepted into popular Islam with the continued remembrance of their original namesake, as was the case of the Virgin's reputed tombs in Jerusalem and Lebanon or her well in Ephesus/Selçuk. Others were transformed into shrines for more authentic Sufi saints, allowing for the joint observance of feast days by Muslims and Christians, even if they evoked a different name in their remembrances. This was particularly true for the most popular of Near Eastern saints, St. George. In his incarnation as Khidr-Ilyas (a conflation of the Prophet Elijah, the mythical sprite Khidr, and the Christian saint), he became the Sufi saint *par excellence*, transforming the saint's numerous reputed burial places throughout Syria and Palestine into sites of pilgrimage for both Muslims and Christians.[16]

Elsewhere, in the Syrian town of Homs, a popular Sufi festival coincided with the Christians' celebrations of Holy Week.[17] In Egypt, the *Shamm al-nasim* (Breath of Spring) holiday – of properly Christian origins being the Monday after Easter – was, and is still, celebrated by Muslims and Copts alike.[18] There was less syncretism between Jews and Muslims in their sacred geography, although members of both communities visited certain holy places that held shared religious significance. These included Abel's tomb in the environs of Damascus, the Tomb of the Patriarchs in Hebron, and the

[16] Heyberger, *Les chrétiens du proche-orient*, pp. 57–61. William Dalrymple, *From the Holy Mountain: A Journey among the Christians of the Middle East* (New York, 1988), pp. 339–44; Hanna Batatu, *Syria's Peasantry, the Descendants of its Lesser Rural Notables, and their Politics* (Princeton, NJ, 1999), pp. 105–06; Eugene Rogan, *Frontiers of the State in the Late Ottoman Empire: Transjordan, 1850–1921* (Cambridge, 1999), pp. 37–38.
[17] James Reilly, "Inter-Confessional Relations in Nineteenth-Century Syria: Damascus, Homs and Hama Compared" *Islam & Muslim Christian Relations* 7 (1996): 218.
[18] Huda Lutfy, "Coptic Festivals of the Nile: Aberrations of the Past?" in *The Mamluks in Egyptian Politics and Society*. Edited by Thomas Philipp and Ulrich Haarman (Cambridge, 1998), pp. 254–82.

tomb of Joshua outside of Baghdad. The tomb of the Prophet Nahum in
the village of Qara Qosh in Mosul province, today's northern Iraq, was
ecumenically maintained by local Christians and visited by Muslims and
Jews alike.[19]

## Ambiguities of inter-confessional relations in Ottoman society

QUESTION:    The Christians of a certain village hold public celebrations three days
out of the year in accordance to their ancient traditions during which time they
sing and dance. Although they have caused no harm to any Muslims, the Jews
have complained and have sought to prevent the celebrations. Can they?

ANSWER:    The people of Islam must stop this. Whoever says, "They cause no
harm" is lying and has no religion. If the infidels (*kâfirler*) hold their festival on a
Friday, they are infringing on Muslims' rights and causing harm. It is not
appropriate here to say whether they or the Jews are the more accursed
community. The religious communities should be separate.

Ruling of Ebusuûd Efendi[20]

The Ottoman elite shared the negative and positive impulses toward non-
Muslims, contained within the competing Islamic traditions. The empire
owed its initial existence to its role as a border outpost of a crusading Islam
in the early fourteenth century. That the territory controlled by the House
of Osman grew from a mini-statelet, consisting of only a few dozen square
miles of rugged mountainous terrain, to a world empire was due in part to
the legitimacy and the momentum the Ottomans gained by their dogged
pursuit of holy war (*gaza*) against the infidels. There was hardly a decade in
the entire six hundred years of the dynasty's history when it was not at war
with one Christian rival or another. But much of the imagery of holy war
associated with the Ottomans' early centuries was an invention of tradition
by later generations.[21] The realities of the dynasty's origins were more
ambivalent. The House of Osman relied on the services of Christian allies
from its earliest victories over other Christians. Its sons bedded Christian
women, as did their sons so that most Ottoman sultans had both formerly,
and in some cases still, Christian mothers and consorts.

Despite the fact that Anatolia had been a solidly Christian territory
before the battle of Manzikert/Malazgırt in 1071, its Islamization proceeded
quickly as Greek and Armenian Christians accepted the faith of those who
held military and political power. There is no evidence of wide-scale forced

[19] David d'Beth Hillel, *Unknown Jews in Unknown Lands: The Travels of Rabbi David d'Beth
Hillel.* Edited by Walter Fischel (New York, 1973), p. 78.
[20] Ebussud Efendi's *fatwa*s cited in this work are taken from M. Ertuğrul Düzdağ, *Şeyhülislam
Ebussuud Efendi fetvaları ışığında 16. asır Türk hayatı* [Turkish Life in the Sixteenth Century
in Light of the Fatwas of Şeyhülislam Ebussuud Efendi] (Istanbul, 1983), p. 96.
[21] Cemal Kafadar, *Between Two Worlds: The Construction of the Ottoman State* (Berkeley, CA,
1994).

conversions either in Anatolia or later following the Ottoman conquests in the Balkans, with the possible exception of the Albanians. We must, therefore, assume the pull to the new faith was a combination of economic and political incentives, coupled with the undeniable appeal of Islam as a dynamic faith. The reasons given by those who converted on Cyprus (conquered in 1571) and Crete (after 1669) were mixed. Christian men on Crete embraced Islam as way of getting into the military; Christian women everywhere typically converted either to get rid of their husbands or to claim a portion of their fathers' and/or husbands' estates. But still other men and women simply stated that their former faith was "false and corrupt" (*bâtil ve fâsid*) and they embraced the "true faith" that was Islam.[22]

Islam's emotional and spiritual appeal to the sultans' Christian subjects was increased by the syncretistic interpretations which were being preached by the wandering Sufi mendicants who visited the villages of Anatolia and later the Balkans. Prominent among these were the adherents of the Bektaşi order who blended elements of Christianity with Islam, retaining a special place for Jesus and Mary and a fondness for wine while adding reverence for Ali. The retention of Christian customs by the order must have seemed comforting and familiar to the region's Christian peasants, often physically remote from their own clergy. Confirming this assumption, the strongholds of Bektaşi belief in the Ottoman lands were found among the Albanians, Pomaks, and Bosnians – the only Balkan peoples to apostatize in any great numbers – and in the ranks of the Janissary corps, which was conscripted from the Christian subjects of the sultans.[23]

It was, perhaps, only in the Ottoman cities that Islam was practiced in its more recognizable, contemporary form. There the Ottoman sultans sought to promote a state-sponsored version of Islam, preached by men who were graduates of state-supervised seminaries and paid salaries from the sultans' coffers as urban Islam became institutionalized to a degree unknown before.[24] That cooptation created a weapon which could be wielded against the sultans should they veer too far from what the men of religion had constructed as orthodoxy. These men of religion formed the core of what might be considered the empire's Muslim intelligentsia. They were its scientists, historians, and poets, as well as its legal scholars. Their ethnic and social origins were as diverse as the population of the empire itself. As such, we might expect them to represent a diversity of outlooks. But as a social

---

[22] Ronald Jennings, *Christians and Muslims in Ottoman Cyprus and the Mediterranean World, 1571–1640* (New York, 1993) pp. 137–42; Molly Greene, *A Shared World: Christians and Muslims in the Early Modern Mediterranean* (Princeton, NJ, 2000), pp. 36–44, 93–95.

[23] Alexander Lopasić, "Islamization of the Balkans with Special Research to Bosnia" *Journal of Islamic Studies* 5 (1994): 163–86.

[24] Halil İnalcık, *The Ottoman Empire: The Classical Age 1300–1600* (London, 1973), pp. 165–72.

and intellectual class, they held remarkably similar world-views, undoubt-edly molded, as hoped for by the state's bureaucrats, by their shared educational experience. The differences that did occur among them followed the demarcation in intellectual world-views already established – legalism versus mysticism. Although it must be noted that a single individual scholar might display both tendencies in his literary interests, producing legal commentary and mystical poetry without any apparent internal psycho-logical confusion.[25]

This Ottoman Muslim intelligentsia has left as its legacy volumes of religious commentary, history, and poetry. But that literature, as was the case in Islam's classical age, is largely silent about the non-Muslims amongst whom the authors lived. There was an occasional comparative discussion of the pulchritudinous merits of women from various non-Muslim ethnic groups or poems in praise of Christian taverns and beauties, but more serious literature seems in retrospect strangely taciturn. Evliya Çelebi, the inveterate traveler of the seventeenth century who usually took great interest in describing the various ethnic groups he encountered, could visit Damascus and Aleppo without mentioning that there were any non-Muslims in either city. He did, however, express surprise that the *Rum* of the Lebanese port cities spoke not *Rumca* (Greek) but Arabic.[26] There were, of course, exceptions but these formed an interesting parallel with the rare woman who found her way into Ottoman historical narratives.[27] Muslim male chroniclers usually mentioned Muslim women or non-Muslims only as negative examples, symbols of the corruption on the body politic and even then only after the individual in question had fallen from power.

In the absence of literary sources, the judicial rulings (*fatwa*, plural *fatawi*) of leading Ottoman jurists provide some insights into everyday relations between individuals of differing religious traditions. The most important of these collections are those delivered by the men who served as chief justice of the empire, the *Şeyhülislâm*. Rulings were issued in response to specific, yet supposedly hypothetical, legal queries submitted to the Justice by anyone in the empire. Once a ruling had been delivered, it could be entered as evidence into any court case where it had relevance. The judge at the local court did not have to accept the Justice's *fatwa* as definitive, but in the regions that were within the effective control of the state most would probably defer to his judgment.[28] Further afield, in southern Syria and Palestine, the *fatwa*s of the *Şeyhülislam* in Istanbul were not as normative,

[25] Cornell Fleischer, *Bureaucrat and Intellectual in the Ottoman Empire: The Historian Mustafa Âli (1541–1600)* (Princeton, NJ, 1986).

[26] Evliya Çelebi, *Evliya Çelebi Seyahatnamesi* [Travelogue] vol. IX. Edited by Mehmed Zillîoğlu. Istanbul, 1984, pp. 151–55; 201–11.

[27] Leslie Pierce, *The Imperial Harem: Women and Sovereignty in the Ottoman Empire* (New York, 1993), pp. 267–85.

[28] Haim Gerber, *State, Society, and Law in Islam: Ottoman Law in Comparative Perspective* (Albany, NY, 1994), pp. 79–112.

although local *muftis* were equally important in shaping the character of the law as practiced in the provincial courts.[29]

Among the various esteemed gentlemen who held the post of Şeyhülislâm, the most respected was undoubtedly Ebussuûd Efendi (d. 1574) who served the sultans Kanunî Süleyman and Sarhoş Selim between 1545 and 1574. Ebussuûd's fame rested on the quality of his responses, his longevity in office, and the fact that Süleyman's reign was viewed with historical hindsight by later generations as a halcyon age of Islamic justice. It would follow if Ebussuûd were the chief justice during the period, he must have been the most judicious of men. His rulings continued to have a normative effect on Ottoman jurisprudence long after his death and can be taken, as much as any one collection can, to be an exemplar of the opinions of the Ottoman legal establishment.[30] His *fatwas* illustrate the complex web of social relationships connecting Muslims, Christians, and Jews in the Ottoman Empire. Sometimes they suggest a casual intermingling of peoples we might construe as tolerance. These include references to the giving of red dyed eggs by Christians to their Muslim neighbors at Easter and the reciprocal sharing of meat sacrificed at the Muslim Feast of the Sacrifice (*Kurban Bayramı*). But they also offer evidence that intercommunal tensions could flare up into violence, not only between Muslims and non-Muslims but between Christians and Jews as well.[31]

The rulings by Ebussuûd help us to understand why. He is careful to maintain the conditions established by the "Pact of ⁽Umar" for non-Muslims' behavior. These included the right to maintain their own legal traditions, the right to property, and safety of person, even if that meant passing as a Muslim by donning a white turban in a place where it might prove dangerous to be identified as a *dhimmi*.[32] But at the same time, non-Muslims had to accede to the social superiority of Muslims by doing nothing to disturb their peace and sense of well-being. The language employed in his responses further helps us to deconstruct Ebussuûd's public attitude toward non-Muslims. Eschewing the legalistic, and value-neutral, term *dhimmi*, he often preferred instead *kâfir* (infidel), semantically close to the colloquial Turkish slur for non-Muslims, *gâvur*. Interestingly, he like many of his contemporaries reserved the term exclusively for Orthodox Christians with Jews and Armenians identified by their communal affiliation. That was, no doubt, conditioned by his derisory view of their Trinitarian beliefs. The Justice wanted the social line to be clearly drawn between Muslims and non-Muslims, even asserting that Muslims should not speak a language used by non-Muslims lest the division between the two

---

[29] Tucker, *In the House of the Law*, pp. 1–36.
[30] Richard Repp, "Qanun and Shari⁽a in the Ottoman Context" in *Islamic Law: Social and Historical Contexts*. Edited by Aziz al-Azmeh (London, 1988), pp. 124–45.
[31] Düzdağ, *Ebussuud Efendi fetvaları*, pp. 91–94.
[32] *Ibid.*, no. 358, p. 89.

communities be blurred.[33] In the end, his public opinion of non-Muslims is probably best summarized by his own pronouncement, "The communities should be separate."

A similar public disdain cannot be attributed to ʿAbd al-Ghani al-Nabulusi (d. 1731) who was, for a time, mufti of Damascus – the provincial equivalent of the *şeyhülislâm* – and who might serve as an exemplar of the Ottoman intellectual tradition rooted in mysticism. ʿAbd al-Ghani al-Nabulusi was a prolific writer whose works ranged from amatory poetry to a treatise on the proper care and propagation of olive trees. But it is in one of his travel narratives, *al-Haqiqa wa al-majaz fi rihlat bilad al-Sham wa Misr wa al-Hijaz* (The Truth and the Marvel of a Journey in Syria, Egypt, and the Hejaz) that we find indications of his attitudes toward non-Muslims. His was not an ordinary travelogue for it chronicled a voyage of interior discovery across the spiritual geography of the Middle East. Al-Nabulusi gave little space to physical features of the lands he traversed, but rather dwelt on the mystical links between the places he visited and various Sufi saints, past and present, with whom they were associated. Included in his extended pilgrimage were visits to Christian holy places: the Monastery of Mar Taqla at Maʿalula, the reputed grave of the Virgin Mary in Lebanon, and the largely Christian villages of Nazareth and Bethlehem. His descriptions of these places were reverential and highly informed about contemporary Christian practices and beliefs. In his description of Nazareth, for example, he discussed details of Jesus' life that he attributed to the apocryphal Gnostic gospel of St. Peter. His description of Bethlehem included a poem extolling the quiet charm of the village and the generosity of its monks whose singing sent him into mystical rapture.[34]

His travel narrative was not the only example of al-Nabulusi's written respect for Islam's sibling faiths. His dream book gives many examples of the blessings a dreamer will encounter should he or she perchance dream of Jesus.[35] In addition, al-Nabulusi wrote at least two essays in defense of Sufi masters under attack by orthodox Muslim critics for being lenient in their treatment of non-Muslims. The first was a defense of the thirteenth-century Andalusian poet, al-Shushtari, whom had been accused of using Christian imagery by one of al-Nabulusi's contemporaries. Al-Nabulusi explained in his commentary what the terms used by al-Shushtari meant for Christians and how they corresponded appropriately to Sufi concepts and beliefs, thereby collapsing the differences between Christianity and Sufism in regard to the authenticity of their respective spirituality. In 1692, he wrote a

---

[33] *Ibid.*, nos. 527 and 528, p. 118.
[34] ʿAbd al-Ghani al-Nabulusi, *al-Haqiqa wa al-majaz fi rihlat bilad al-Sham wa Misr wa al-Hijaz* [The Truth and the Crossing of a Journey to Syria, Egypt, and the Hejaz], (Damascus, 1989), pp. 299, 365–66.
[35] Annemarie Schimmel, "Dreams of Jesus in the Islamic Tradition" *Bulletin of the Royal Institute for Inter-Faith Studies* 1/1 (1999): 207–12.

polemic against an unnamed Turkish scholar who had derided Muhyi al-Din ibn al-ᶜArabi (d. 1240) for allowing that Jews and Christians might enter paradise.[36] In fact, al-Nabulusi's positive views towards non-Muslims seem conditioned by the mystical outlook of ibn al-ᶜArabi, his spiritual mentor. This interpretation is supported by a lengthy *fatwa* issued by al-Nabulusi in 1712 on the nature of God. It presents a discussion of God's being that is clearly informed by the works of ibn al-ᶜArabi. What is, perhaps, unanticipated about the *fatwa* is that it was issued in response to three questions posed to the shaykh by the Patriarch of Antioch, Athanasios Dabbas. That these two men could engage in a philosophical discussion of the nature of God from a mysticism rooted in their respective faiths as intellectual equals suggests that not all Muslim intellectuals shared Ebussuûd Efendi's disdain for non-Muslims.[37]

## Christians and Jews in a Muslim world: the record of the qadi courts and the central state archives

Studies based on the registers of the qadi courts of various Ottoman Arab cities have provided rare insights into the social interactions of ordinary people in the early modern Middle East.[38] Useful as these records are, however, they can be problematic for our investigation.[39] The registry of the cases was usually brief and often formulaic. What might have been an emotional confrontation at court was recorded in a condensed entry, with a straightforward and even detached style. Only rarely was testimony recorded verbatim and we are left to ponder the silences. There are other omissions as well. Murders, or other public outrages against non-Muslims, were only rarely brought to court, due in no small part to the invalidation of non-Muslim testimony against Muslims in cases where a penalty might result. We must, therefore, turn to Christian and Jewish sources, or to the registry of petitions from those communities for redress from the sultan, for the elaboration of incidents of overt hostility by Muslims against non-Muslims. An example of these alternative voices is found in the account by the eighteenth-century chronicler of Aleppo, Yusuf Dimitri ᶜAbbud of the death of Hanna ibn ᶜAziza, a Christian, murdered by Taha al-Fattal, a Muslim. Taha had asked Hanna for work but when the latter replied he did

[36] Omaima Abou-Bakr, "The Religious Other: Christian Images in Sufi poetry" in *Images of the Other: Europe and the Muslim World before 1700.* Edited by David Blanks (Cairo, 1997), pp. 96–108; Michael Winter, "A Polemical Treatise by ᶜAbd al-Gani al-Nabulusi against a Turkish Scholar on the Religious Status of the *Dhimmi*s" *Arabica* 35 (1988): 92–103.
[37] Bakri Aladdin, "Deux *fatwa*-s du Šayh ᶜAbd al-Gani al-Nabulusi" *Bulletin d'Études Orientales* 39–40 (1987–88): 9–37; Heyberger, *Les chrétiens du proche-orient*, pp. 40–42.
[38] See studies by Abdul-Karim Rafeq, André Raymond, Amnon Cohen, Galal el-Nahal, Abraham Marcus, James Reilly, and Margaret Meriwether listed in the bibliography.
[39] Dror Ze'evi, "The Use of Ottoman Shari'a Court Records as a Source for Middle Eastern Social History: A Reappraisal" *Islamic Law and Society* 5 (1998): 35–36.

not have anything for Taha to do, Taha pulled his dagger and killed him. There being only Christian witnesses no charges against Taha were ever brought to court.[40]

While Christians and Jews appeared frequently in the Muslim courts in the Arabic-speaking provinces and apparently showed no hesitancy to press cases involving breach of contract against Muslims, the recorders of their testimonies have left semiotic evidence it was not on the basis of complete equality. Individual Christians and Jews were always identified by their religion when entered into the records, an indication that the court scribes considered "Muslim" to be the norm and unnecessary for notation. Non-Muslim men were further set apart from their Muslim contemporaries by the scribes in both Aleppo and Damascus who recorded their patronymic as "*walad*," for example, Jirjis walad Tuma (George, son of Thomas), as opposed to the "*ibn*" reserved for Muslims, for example, Muhammad ibn Hasan. In an interesting contrast, Arabic-speaking legal clerks indiscriminately recorded Muslim, Jewish, and Christian women as "*bint*" (daughter). Dead Muslims were referred to as the "deceased" (*mutawaffa*) while dead non-Muslims had simply "perished" (*halik*). As if such devices were not enough to make the distinction clear, Jewish and Christian masculine names shared with Muslims were spelled incorrectly in the Syrian courts. Thus "Yusuf" (Joseph) would indicate a Muslim, while "Yasif" would let us know the individual was either a Christian or a Jew. The name "Musa" (Moses) shared by men from all three religious communities would be written correctly with the letter "*sin*" in the case of a Muslim, and incorrectly with the letter "*sad*" if the bearer were not.[41] Muslim chroniclers in Egypt often employed similar misspelling of names of non-Muslims when recording them in their histories.[42]

The testimony of a non-Muslim was accepted in court with the swearing of the appropriate oath, on either the Torah or the Gospels (*Injil*). Despite the Qur'anic injunction that the testimony of two non-Muslim males, or two Muslim women for that matter, was required to equal that of one Muslim male, non-Muslims and women testified against Muslim males on an equal basis. There was a difference, however, between the two classes of witnesses. Women of whatever faith were generally required to present two male witnesses as to their identity, while non-Muslim males were accepted

---

[40] Yusuf Dimitri ʿAbbud al-Halabi. *al-murtadd fi taʾrikh Halab wa Baghdad* [A Revisiting of the History of Aleppo and Baghdad]. Edited by Fawwaz Mahmud al-Fawwaz, M.A. Thesis, University of Damascus, 1978, p. 118.

[41] Najwa al-Qattan. "The Damascene Jewish Community in the Latter Decades of the Eighteenth Century" in *The Syrian Land in the 18th and 19th Century*. Edited by Thomas Philipp (Stuttgart, 1992), p. 204; Abdul-Karim Rafeq "Craft Organizations and Religious Communities in Ottoman Syria (XVI–XIX Centuries)" in *La Shiʿa nell'Impero ottomano* (Rome, 1993), pp. 33–34.

[42] Michael Winter, *Egyptian Society under Ottoman Rule 1517–1798* (London, 1992), pp. 204–05.

on their own recognizance. The physical descriptions of non-Muslim males were sometimes recorded as an apparent identity check, however, as was often the case for slaves. Such physical descriptions were rarely, if ever, added in the case of free Muslim males. Despite such hints of possible discrimination, at least in the eyes of the recording secretary, non-Muslim men and women were frequent visitors to the Muslim courts. But, as non-Muslims often relied on Muslim witnesses to win their civil cases against Muslims, we can assume that they understood the efficacy of having Muslim testimony to sway a Muslim judge to their side.[43]

The court records taken together from the various Arab cities give us a relatively positive picture of intercommunal relations in the seventeenth and eighteenth centuries, although we must remember the caution that non-Muslims may have been reluctant to bring charges in cases involving physical attacks against them. Non-Muslims and Muslims often lived in the same quarters. But almost every Arab city also had quarters which were becoming almost exclusively non-Muslim over the course of the Ottoman centuries. Such residential clustering was necessitated for Jews by the Talmudic injunction that they live within a limited walking distance from their synagogues and in many cities only one existed. The emergence of predominantly Christian quarters, however, supports the hypothesis of a psychological distancing between the different religious communities that led them to cluster together residentially with their coreligionists even when the law did not require it.[44] But even those neighborhoods that were overwhelmingly populated by either Jews or Christians often housed a few Muslim families, as was the case of the predominantly Christian quarter of Bab Tuma in Damascus or the Jewish quarter of Bahsita in Aleppo.[45]

Muslims and non-Muslims worked together in many of the trade guilds and went as a collective unit to voice guild concerns before the court, although the names of Muslims were always listed first in such depositions. But if there were any Muslims in a guild, the head (*shaykh*) was invariably a Muslim, even if the membership were overwhelmingly non-Muslim as in the case of the guilds of silk weavers in Aleppo and Damascus. In many such guilds, however, the *shaykh*'s second in command (*yiğit başı*) was a non-Muslim. Not all the trades were integrated, but religiously segregated guilds consisting only of Muslims usually involved low prestige jobs such as tanners or porters, the membership of which was typically of tribal origin. There were also some trades that were exclusively Jewish and/or Christian

---

[43] Najwa al-Qattan, "*Dhimmis* in the Muslim Court: Legal Autonomy and Religious Discrimination" *International Journal of Middle East Studies* 31 (1999): 429–44.

[44] Jean-Claude David, "L'espace des chrétiens à Alep: ségrégation et mixité, stratégies communautaires (1750–1850)" *Revue du Monde Musulman et de la Méditerranée* 55–56 (1990): 152–70.

[45] Colette Establet and Jean-Paul Pascual, *Familles et fortunes à Damas: 450 foyers damascains en 1700* (Damascus, 1994), pp. 165–66.

(for example, the *kashrut* butchers, physicians and goldsmiths in most cities, the Sasuni Armenian bakers in Aleppo). By and large, however, the court records demonstrate that the work places and markets of the Ottoman Arab cities were well integrated with a casual mixing of persons following different religious traditions.

The court records also suggest there was a large degree of assimilation into Islamic legal practices by Arabic-speaking non-Muslims in the Ottoman period. Non-Muslims could only resort to the Muslim courts if all concerned parties agreed to Muslim adjudication. Otherwise, Muslim judges were to return the cases to the appropriate religious authorities in the minority community in accordance with the Pact of ᶜUmar. Apparently, records from non-Muslim judicial bodies have not survived in any Ottoman Arab city, other than the *responsa* literature of some of the more eminent rabbis.[46] There is, however, anecdotal evidence that the Jews maintained religious courts in several cities, as did the Greek Orthodox Patriarchate in Damascus. We know of the latter from an imperial order in 1805, instructing the city's governor to execute an Orthodox priest who had been found guilty by the patriarch's court on charges of embezzlement.[47]

Nevertheless, Christians and Jews did not hesitate to rely on the Muslim courts on many different occasions when they were not required to do so by law. Christian males most commonly invoked the shariᶜa to divorce their wives. Divorce was permitted to Eastern-rite Christians, but as many in Aleppo and the Lebanese coastal cities became Uniate Catholics in the eighteenth century, it was no longer an option under their canon law. Despite the Catholic injunction against divorce, Aleppo's new Catholics continued to appeal to the Muslim courts for divorce settlements. Even resident Venetian merchants in the city invoked the shariᶜa on occasion to divorce their wives, something they could not have contemplated doing at home.[48] Non-Muslim women in Aleppo, on the other hand, usually converted to Islam in order to divorce their husbands in a Muslim court. Once Muslim, the only grounds for women in largely Hanafi Syria to initiate divorce proceedings, without their husbands' compliance, lay in the Shafaᶜi school of law which permitted a wife to divorce her husband on grounds of desertion. As such, there is the occasional entry in the records of the Shafaᶜi judges in Aleppo of a Christian woman appearing before them to announce her conversion to Islam and then immediately divorcing her

[46] Joseph Hacker, "Jewish Autonomy in the Ottoman Empire: Its Scope and Limits. Jewish Courts from the Sixteenth to the Eighteenth Centuries" in *The Jews of the Ottoman Empire.* Edited by A. Levy (Princeton, NJ, 1994), pp. 153–202; Marc Angel, "The Responsa Literature in the Ottoman Empire for the Study of Ottoman Jewry" in *The Jews of the Ottoman Empire.* Edited by A. Levy (Princeton, NJ, 1994), pp. 669–85.
[47] Istanbul, BOA, Ahkâm-ı Şam-ı Şerif, vol. VI, p. 18.
[48] Damascus, Aleppo Court records, vol. XIX, p. 112; Heyberger, *Les chrétiens du proche-orient,* pp. 76–77.

absent husband.[49] In both Damascus and Jerusalem, however, there were cases of non-Muslim women initiating divorce proceedings against their husbands on grounds supplied by Islamic law, without their previous conversion to Islam.[50]

Christians in Syria frequently brought charges against fellow Christians in the Muslim courts, especially as confrontations developed between Catholic and Orthodox factions. The Jews in the Ottoman Arab cities were more conservative of their traditions and less eager than the Christians to bring internal community disputes before the qadi and into the Muslim public gaze. English factors, resident in Aleppo in the late seventeenth century, claimed the local rabbis had issued injunctions forbidding any of their community from bearing testimony against another Jew in the Muslim courts.[51] Whether or not this was true, there are very few cases registered in the Islamic court registers in that city reflecting intra-communal strife among the city's Jewish population. That was not the case in sixteenth-century Jerusalem or eighteenth-century Damascus, however, as Jews in those two cities frequently brought intracommunal conflicts to the Muslim courts for adjudication.[52] Unfortunately, no one has yet researched the qadi records of Baghdad to discover to what degree the numerically larger Jewish community there relied on the Muslim courts.

While the court records show evidence of cooperation between individual members of the disparate religious communities, they also document moments of sectarian dissonance in cases typically initiated by Muslims. On August 16, 1658, a delegation of Muslims from the quarter of Kharab-khan in Aleppo charged Christians in the quarter with selling alcohol (*khamr*) and drunken behavior. The Christians replied they had an imperial order that allowed them to sell alcohol. The judge ruled that their license did not permit them to get drunk and he ordered them to desist from selling alcoholic beverages in future.[53] Christians were free to engage in what was considered to be offensive behavior in Muslim eyes, as long as it was behind the walls of their homes. But they were not at liberty to offend Muslim senses or sensibilities in any public space.

Sectarian dissonance could at times also become violent. In the seventeenth century, a group of Jews in Cairo brought charges against some Muslims whom they claimed had harassed them with stones as they proceeded through a Muslim cemetery with their own dead for burial in an adjacent Jewish cemetery.[54] The judge ruled in the Jews' favor and ordered the Muslims to desist from any such interference. The problem did not go

---

[49] Damascus, Aleppo Court records, vol. II, p. 381; vol. XIX, p. 95.
[50] Al-Qattan, "*Dhimmis*," pp. 434–35; A. Cohen, *Jewish Life*, pp. 131–32.
[51] London, PRO, SP 105/113, p. 263, dated June 23, 1671.
[52] A. Cohen, *Jewish Life*, pp. 115–19; al-Qattan, "*Dhimmis*," pp. 432–37.
[53] Damascus, Aleppo Court records, vol. III, p. 668.
[54] el-Nahhal, *Judicial Administration*, p. 57.

away, however. It emerged again in the eighteenth century when a judge ruled in a very similar case against the Jewish plaintiffs.[55]

That is not to say Christians and Jews invariably accepted injustice with resignation. Individual subjects of the sultan of whatever faith held the right of direct appeal to him for justice. This was a long-established, and well-trodden tradition in Islamic political theory and practice and one that the Ottoman sultans embraced as their patrimony. The Islamic tradition is replete with stories of the first four caliphs (the "Rightly-guided" exemplars of Sunni tradition) extending justice to non-Muslim petitioners, even at the expense of their trusted lieutenants. The Ottoman sultans could do no less than follow the example of their illustrious predecessors

Gaining the sultan's ear, however, did not necessarily result in swift justice. The Porte's response in 1757 to a petition from a group of "poor Jews" (reaya-ı Yehud fukarâsı) in Jerusalem provides evidence of that. The Jews had complained that, even though they had received a court order forbidding the practice, government officials continued to tax the burial of indigent Jews who came to Jerusalem from "other places" to die and so be buried in Eretz Israel. The sultan's order reminded the city's governor that a fatwa had outlawed this practice previously and that Sultan Ahmed had banned the requests for unlawful taxes from the Jewish community of Jerusalem in 1724.[56] But the imperial order of 1757 seems to have gone the way of the one issued in 1724. In response to yet another such complaint arising from the city's Jewish community in 1758, the governor was ordered immediately to bury the Jewish dead, whose coffins were apparently piling up, unburied in the streets, even if they had not paid the jizya while alive.[57] In a related complaint to the one lodged by Jerusalem's Jews, the Jews of Aleppo complained in 1795 that they were being taxed on funerals. The Porte responded that time by stating that the shari$^c$a forbade the taxing of dead men, or living women and children. Furthermore, the order went on to say such acts were in violation of previously issued sultanic writ (kanun) and fatwas. But the document noted that similar complaints had arrived in Istanbul from non-Muslims in Belgrade, Ankara, and Kayseri, a suggestion that the practice was widespread.[58]

The bureaucrats in the capital were generally consistent in interpreting the rights and obligations of the non-Muslims as long as they fell within the parameters of the Pact of $^c$Umar. They were less consistent in the application of sultanic law (kanun). But the state bureaucrats in Istanbul could only rarely compel distant provincial officials to honor the sultan's wishes. Governors were routinely rotated from one provincial center to another.

[55] Michael Winter, Egyptian Society under Ottoman Rule 1517–1798 (London, 1992), pp. 217–18.
[56] Istanbul, BOA, Ahkâm-ı Şam-ı Şerif, vol. II, p. 66.
[57] Istanbul, BOA, Ahkâm-ı Şam-ı Şerif, vol. II, p. 95.
[58] Istanbul, BOA, Ahkâm-ı Halep vol. V, p. 181.

This encouraged their noncompliance and facilitated the spread of innovative, if illegal, practices for the creation of wealth throughout the empire, for example, the tax on Jewish funerals. The Holy Land in particular with its Jewish and Christian pilgrims and large population of resident clergy and rabbis seems to have been viewed as a potential trough of illegal gain to the Ottoman officials stationed there. Complaints of officials charging illegal taxes on pilgrims and religious institutions arrived from Jews and Christians throughout the eighteenth century, with seemingly little relief ever effected.[59]

The Porte's chronic inability to enforce its own rules must have seemed to the non-Muslims an indication of its disinterest in insuring the law was applied fairly when it came to them. In fact, other complaints arising from Muslims in Palestine in the eighteenth century show it was a general failure to compel local officials to enforce most orders emanating from Istanbul and not just those in which non-Muslims were involved. But the apparent impotence of the sultans to enforce their own decrees helps to explain why the collective folk memories of so many non-Muslims in the former Ottoman Empire are filled with examples of oppression and abuse. There was an obvious disjuncture between the theory and practice of Ottoman law in the eighteenth and early nineteenth centuries. That experience might lead non-Muslim victims of injustice to blame the sultan himself for their misery. In similar cases, Muslim chroniclers tended to blame the local authorities as their world-view clung to the proposition that the sultan must always be a paragon of justice. Non-Muslims were not so sanguine about where true culpability lay.

## Conclusion

Having examined intercommunal interactions as depicted in the law court records and the *fatwa*s, the question remains, "What did people really think?" Was there anything approaching genuine tolerance? The answer rests in what we mean by tolerance. Visitors to Aleppo, for example, whether Simeon of Lviv in the seventeenth century, Alexander Russell in the eighteenth century, or Rabbi Hillel in the early nineteenth century, all reported Aleppo's Muslim population as being tolerant toward the believers of other faiths, intermingling with them without any overt hostility. Russell wrote that while the Christians often complained of being singled out by the authorities for oppression, they were in fact no more the target of venial behavior on the part of the city's officials than were the Muslims. And what attention they did draw was usually the result of their internal squabbling.

[59] Amnon Cohen, "The Ottoman Approach to Christians and Christianity in Sixteenth-Century Jerusalem" *Islam & Christian Muslim Relations* 7 (1996): 205–12; Jacob Barnai, *The Jews in Palestine in the Eighteenth Century: Under the Patronage of the Istanbul Committee of Officials for Palestine.* Translated by Naomi Goldblum (Tuscaloosa, AL, 1992), pp. 21–22; Istanbul, BOA, Ahkâm-ı Şam-ı Şerif, vol. II, pp. 28–29; vol. VI, p. 6.

But he did add that they were "liable to suffer from the insolent petulancy of their Turkish neighbours."[60]

If we mean mutual respect between members of the different communities, then again we have a mixed answer. Russell's characterization of "insolent petulancy" would hardly seem to qualify. The historical record shows that some Muslim intellectuals such as al-Nabulusi had genuine regards for their Christian contemporaries. For the ordinary Muslim men and women who filled the streets of the empire's cities, mixing with non-Muslims on a daily basis, the *fatwa*s show that their social acceptance of non-Muslims could vary almost as dramatically as could be found among the Muslim elites. In many cases, there were networks of social exchange and reciprocity across sectarian lines, for example, the exchange of special foods on religious holidays and the joint celebration of certain saints' feast days. There were also instances of violence. But indifference, perhaps tinged with contempt as manifested by Ebusuûd Efendi, rather than overt hostility seems to have been the emotional norm governing intercommunal relations in the period before the sectarian outbursts of the nineteenth century.

While there were few rigid barriers separating individuals of different faiths from each other, there was concomitantly little to draw them together, beyond commerce or natural disasters. Without the routinization of interpersonal relations across religious lines, individuals in each community could remain secure at night, behind their locked quarter gates, with the confidence borne of deep conviction that theirs alone was the true faith. Violence might occasionally erupt over a slight that members of the majority community felt had been rendered them by the minority, but more typically the violence was an insult rather than a blow. Friendships were also possible across sectarian divides. More frequently still were political alliances between individuals, or even extended families, of different faiths, established and nurtured by mutual interests and needs. But the traditions of all the communities agreed with Ebusuûd Efendi that it was indeed better for everyone concerned if the religious communities remained separate. In this regard, Ottoman Arab cities did not differ greatly from other premodern cities where different religious communities shared a common space. Sudhir Kakar has described the relationship between Hindus and Muslims in Hyderabad as "They were more than strangers, not often enemies but less than friends."[61] That characterization would seem appropriate for the cities of the Ottoman Arab world as well.

The question remains whether the confessional loyalties and religious identities in Ottoman Syria were "primordial," i.e. normative and primary, or "circumstantial" arising out of conditions which were perhaps peculiar

---

[60] Alexander Russell, *A Natural History of Aleppo* (London, 1794), vol. II, pp. 41–42.
[61] Sudhir Kakar, *Colors of Violence: Cultural Identities, Religion, and Conflict* (Chicago, IL, 1996), p. 10.

to time and place and not always present in the consciousness of Ottoman Syrians. It most probably can never be satisfactorily answered. Reacting against those historians who posit Muslim fanaticism against non-Muslims as having been a constant reality in Middle Eastern societies, James Reilly stresses that the relationships between the religious communities were multi-faceted and not always confrontational. Membership in a particular religious community did not necessarily give rise to a sense of "ethnic" solidarity.[62]

However valid that cautionary advice, interpretations of Islamic law did play a normative role in ordering the everyday experience of Muslims and non-Muslims alike, at least in the cities where that law was enforced. As long as confessional identity determined one's legal and political status, if it were not primordial, then it was very close to being essential in structuring the relationships across sectarian frontiers. There was also a psychological separation that arose from communal endogamy. The passing of individual lives was marked by events that occurred solely within their own religious community, in terms of their life span – baptism or circumcision, marriage, and burial – and in the passing of a single year, i.e. the calendar of religious festivals. The names and the demarcation of the months and the very numbering of the years varied, with each community marking the passage of a shared time differently.[63]

Religious identities in the Ottoman period did not exclude the "imagining" of community along something other than sectarian lines. But religion was at least the primary basis of identity, beyond family, clan, or gender, for members of the Muslim and non-Muslim communities alike for most of the Ottoman period. If for no other reason that was their core identity mandated by the state, law, and tradition. This was especially true in the cities where the $^c$ulama acted as the enforcers of the shari$^c$a's writ and they more typically shared the world-view of Ebussuûd Efendi than that of al-Nabulusi. It was undoubtedly less the case in the region's thousands of villages where more heterodox religious traditions prevailed and the casual intermingling of people of different faiths was common before the hardening of sectarian boundaries in the nineteenth century.[64] Tensions between members of the different religious communities did, on occasion, flare to violence in the Ottoman Empire before the nineteenth century. That is not to say that an atmosphere of latent confrontation was endemic to all inter-confessional contacts, or that religious fanaticism was the rule. The various

---

[62] Reilly, "Inter-Confessional Relations," pp. 213–24.
[63] Edhem Eldem, "Istanbul: From Imperial to Periphalized Capital" in *The Ottoman City between East and West: Aleppo, Izmir, Istanbul*. Edhem Eldem, Daniel Goffman, and Bruce Masters (Cambridge, 1999), pp. 153–56. Jason Goodwin, *Lords of the Horizons: A History of the Ottoman Empire* (New York, 1998), pp. 306–08.
[64] Ussama Makdisi, *Culture of Sectarianism: Community, History, and Violence in Nineteenth-Century Lebanon* (Berkeley, CA, 2000); Rogan, *Frontiers of the State*, pp. 37–38.

religious communities in the Arab Ottoman world shared much in common with their neighbors beyond that most basic glue of social cohesion, language. Their music, cuisine, and material culture were also generally indistinguishable.[65] But as long as religion lay at the heart of each individual's world-view, the potential for society to fracture along sectarian lines remained.

[65] Kay Kaufman Shelemay, *Let Jasmine Rain Down: Song and Remembrance among Syrian Jews* (Chicago, IL, 1998).

CHAPTER 2

# The Ottoman Arab world: a diversity of sects and peoples

Historians differ as to why Sultan Yavuz Selim (1512–20) moved south in 1516 in a campaign that would topple the Mamluk regime. It may have been a preemptive strike against a potential ally of his archenemy Shah Ismail Safavi in Iran, a strategic move to secure the lucrative spice trade of the Levant, or to block European expansion into the soft underbelly of Islam.[1] Whatever his reasons, Selim's decisive intervention brought the historic Muslim capitals of Damascus and Cairo into a rapidly expanding empire. Selim's son, Kanûnî Süleyman (1520–66), would add Baghdad to the patrimony of the House of Osman, as well as much of the North African littoral. By 1600, most of the Arab lands were nominally subject to the Ottoman sultan, with indigenous elites able to maintain their independence only in Morocco and the more remote regions of the Arabian Peninsula and the North African interior. But the further afield from the Ottoman heartland one traveled, the less effective was Ottoman control or influence and it was only in the core Arab provinces of the Fertile Crescent and Egypt that Ottoman policies had any long-lasting effect on the relationships between Muslims and non-Muslims. And even in Egypt, the ability of the sultans to effect policy was questionable by the mid-eighteenth century.

Muslim–Christian relations were at low ebb when the Ottomans arrived in the Arab lands. The Mamluk sultans had embarked on an ideological, as well as a military, campaign against the Christians in the aftermath of the Crusades. Their armies leveled churches and monasteries while the bureaucratic arm of the state imposed severe restrictions on their Christian subjects. Tamerlane (Timur-i lenk), while not adverse to massacring Muslims in their thousands, showed a particular penchant for wreaking devastation on the Christian communities which lay in his path at the beginning of the fifteenth century. Egypt, which survived largely outside the zone of direct military conflict, witnessed an outpouring of Islamic legal

[1] P. M. Holt, *Egypt and the Fertile Crescent, 1516–1922: A Political History* (London, 1966); Palmira Brummett, *Ottoman Seapower and Levantine Diplomacy in the Age of Discovery* (Albany, NY, 1994).

polemic against the Christians that led, on occasion, to mob attacks on the remaining Coptic churches and monasteries. An increasing rate of conversion further reduced the Copts to an isolated minority.[2] This prolonged time of troubles could only intensify the Christians' self-view as being isolated communities of believers, punished by God for some unidentified sins.[3] In the aftermath of these disasters, Christianity in the Arab east was in psychological and numerical decline. Jewish communities in the region did not attract the same level of Muslim hostility and fared better than their Christian neighbors. But with the possible exception of the community in Cairo with its connections to the Mamluk court, the Jews of the Arab lands could hardly be characterized as flourishing on the eve of the Ottoman conquest.

The Jews and Christians in the region were undoubtedly ambivalent, if not completely indifferent, to the change in the dynastic succession of the sultans who exercised sovereignty over their lives, but they were to receive a respite under the new regime. The Ottoman bureaucrats were, unlike the Mamluk beys, usually indifferent as to the existence of non-Muslims under their control. The Ottoman sultans were still winning victories against European armies on the battlefield and the presence of Christians so distant from the war zone in central Europe must have seemed unimportant to most Ottoman officials posted in the Arab lands, beyond the collection of their taxes. In the case of the Sephardic Jews, the sultans welcomed them into their realm as potentially revenue-producing subjects. More importantly, the political tradition honored by the Ottoman sultans was to grant autonomy to the various social groupings that made up the population of their empire. This afforded the Christians and Jews in the Ottoman world fairly wide-ranging freedom to order their communal affairs as they saw fit. Ottoman official nonchalance further allowed them to recover some of the losses they had endured under the Mamluks, including the discrete repair of damaged churches and synagogues and, in a few rare cases, permission to build new ones, in an apparent disregard of the injunctions of the Pact of ᶜUmar.

## The sectarian landscape of the Ottoman Arab lands

Alexander Russell noted that the Jews of eighteenth-century Aleppo spoke a dialect of Arabic distinct from that shared by the city's Christians and Muslims; this was also true for the much larger Jewish community in Baghdad.[4] Almost everywhere else, urban Jews, Christians, and Muslims were indistinguishable from each other by their accent or their material

---

[2] Aziz Atiya, *A History of Eastern Christianity* (Notre Dame, IN, 1968), pp. 96–98.
[3] Joseph, *Muslim–Christian Relations*, pp. 16–17; Atiya, *ibid.*, pp. 274–76.
[4] Russell, *A Natural History*, vol. II, pp. 59–60; H. Cohen, *Jews of the Middle East*, pp. 37–38.

culture. It was true that the dress of the non-Muslims might identify their
confessional community in some areas as was required by the Pact of
ʿUmar or in others by their own customary preference. But the fact that the
dress code was frequently invoked by governors eager to extract bribes from
wealthy non-Muslims suggests even in their daily costume Muslims and
non-Muslims were not always easily identifiable to the outside observer.
European visitors to the region, whether Christians or Jews, frequently
noted with a degree of disgust and alarm that their erstwhile coreligionists
were "Turks" in all but name. That same degree of assimilation did not
characterize the Christians who lived in the upland periphery of the Arab
Fertile Crescent where their isolation prevented complete assimilation into
the culture of the Muslim majority of the lowlands. It was the opposition
between orthodoxy and heterodoxy in religious belief, but also between
assimilation and cultural resistance.

The most notable example of this "freedom of the mountain" could be
found among the Maronites of Mount Lebanon who enjoyed an autonomy
verging on independence throughout most of the Ottoman period, due in no
small part to their symbiotic political relationship with the Druzes.
Although that relationship would break down in the nineteenth century, the
two communities lived in relative harmony in the earlier Ottoman centuries,
even occasionally going to war together against a common outside enemy as
was the case in 1772 when the Emir Yusuf al-Shihab occupied Damascus,
supported by his Druze and Maronite retainers.[5] The Maronites were the
spiritual descendants of Christians who had accepted the articulation of
Christ's nature (monotheletism) put forward in the attempted compromise
between orthodoxy and monophysitism by the Byzantine Emperor
Heraclius (610–41). Unfortunately for their subsequent future, they were
the only Christians to do so. They thereby cut themselves off theologically
from either of the dominant intellectual traditions of the Christian East.
Although the community originally was located in northern Syria, over time
most of the Maronites migrated to the safety of the Lebanese mountains
where they formed the absolute majority in some districts. By the Ottoman
period, the Maronites had abandoned Syriac in favor of Arabic as their
vernacular and had assimilated much of the Arabo-Muslim culture as their
own. But the Maronite secular and religious leadership appealed to Sunni
Muslim authority only rarely.

The elites of the community could flaunt in their mountain redoubts their
disregard for many of the legal restrictions imposed on non-Muslims
elsewhere – building new churches and monasteries, openly carrying arms,
and riding horses. What was unthinkable in the rest of the sultan's domains
could occur almost seamlessly in Mount Lebanon, with the open conversion

[5] Mikha'il Burayk al-Dimashqi. *Ta'rikh al-Sham* [History of Damascus] *1720–1782*. Edited by Qustantin al-Basha (Harrisa, Lebanon, 1930), p. 96.

to Christianity by individuals from two politically dominant clans of the Mountain, the Sunni Shihab and the Druze Abu-Lamma[c], in the early nineteenth century without apparent repercussion.[6] The conversion of the Abu Lamma[c]s was even sanctified by a *fatwa* issued in 1847 by Muhammad al-Halawani, mufti of Beirut, who wrote that as the Druzes already were unbelievers, their conversion to Christianity was acceptable as the Prophet had said, "Unbelief constitutes one nation."[7] Other Maronites, outside the community's heartland in Kisrawan, lived among Muslim majorities more circumspectly, in Damascus and Aleppo or in religiously mixed villages such as those in the Shuf and the Jabal [c]Amil in Lebanon or the Jabal al-[c]Alawiyyin in Syria. The community in Aleppo, in particular, gave the Maronites an urban face as well as a rural one and Aleppine Maronites would play a crucial role in the community's transition to a European defined "modernity" in the Ottoman period.

The existence of their patriarch and church hierarchy outside the zone of direct Ottoman control gave the Maronites everywhere an opportunity for freedom of political action not shared by most other Christians in the Ottoman period. Sunni Muslims might have added that it also gave them an arrogance unknown among, or undreamed by, Christians elsewhere in the Arab world. Exploiting that autonomy, the hierarchy of the Maronite Church entered into dialogue with Rome long before any of the other Eastern-rite churches and thus secured a special relationship with the Latin West. This was reflected in the early European travel narratives whose authors almost invariably singled the Maronites out for special attention and favorable comment; William Biddulph, an Englishman who visited Syria in 1600, referred to them as the "free" Christians of Syria.[8] Basking in that special relationship with the West, Maronites could be found in Europe, taking advantage of both trade and educational opportunities long before other Christians in the region. Individual Maronites were also among the first to collaborate with European merchants and missionaries in their quest for profits and souls, respectively. Indeed, no other Christian community in the Arabic-speaking Levant would tie its fortunes so closely to those of the West, first to Catholic Europe generally, and later to France specifically.

The Jacobites, the followers of Ya[c]qub Barda'i, were another highland community who enjoyed a large degree of anonymity, and therefore autonomy, in the Ottoman period. Sometimes called the Syrian Orthodox,

6  Joseph Abou Nohra, "L'evolution du système politique libanais dans le contexte des conflits régionaux et locaux (1840–1864)" in *Lebanon: A History of Conflict and Consensus*. Edited by N. Shehadi and D. Haffar Mills (London, 1988), p. 35.
7  Reported in a letter sent by Eli Smith, an American missionary in Lebanon to Revd. R. Anderson, Boston, dated March 10, 1846. Papers of American Board of Commissioners for Foreign Missions (ABCFM), held by Harvard University, microfilm series, reel 544, letter 163.
8  Samuel Purchas (ed.). *Purchas his Pilgrimes* vol. VIII (Glasgow, 1905), p. 273.

or more simply the *Suryani* in Arabic and Ottoman Turkish, the Jacobites were Monophysite Christians and the ideological heirs to the bitter theological battles waged within Christendom in the fifth century AD to define the nature of Christ. The Monophysites, who chose to emphasize Christ's divine nature at the expense of his human one, lost the theological battle at the Council of Chalcedon in 451. Thereafter, they were relegated to the ranks of heresy and obscurity, in the eyes of the dominant Nicene Christian tradition represented both in Constantinople and Rome.

The Jacobites had probably been the numerical majority in the hill country of the Jazirah (northern Iraq and southeastern Turkey) before the advent of the Crusaders. But they suffered a severe contraction in their numbers due to war and conversion to Islam in the aftermath of the bloody struggles between Islam and Christendom. By the start of the Ottoman period, the Jacobites were largely confined to an arc of territory stretching from Mosul north to Diyarbakır. Beyond the boundaries of that zone, they constituted significant minorities in cities such as Aleppo and Urfa. They could even be found in Damascus. But the see of their Patriarch was in the remote monastery of Dayr Zaʿafaran, outside of Mardin. It was an appropriate location as the true heartland of the Jacobites lay not in the cities but in the dozens of villages that dotted the mountains between Mardin and Midyat, known to the Jacobites as Tur Abdin. Throughout their homeland, the Jacobites lived as a minority among either Muslim or Yazidi Kurds with whom relations could vary over time, but whose tribal aghas rarely enforced the shariʿa regulations on their Christian subjects.[9]

Despite centuries of a cultural Arabization of the Jacobites in the cities, most of the rural Jacobite population retained Aramaic as a spoken vernacular well into the Ottoman period. The Jacobite peasantry spoke a dialect of Aramaic known as *Turoyo* in the Tur Abdin, or a mixture of Aramaic and Arabic called simply *fallahi* (peasant) in the plains to the north of Mosul.[10] However, the language had virtually ceased to be written by the community's intellectual elite by the time of the arrival of the Ottoman armies. Rather, literate Jacobites, like their contemporaries among the Maronites in Lebanon, often chose to write Arabic in Syriac script (*karshuni*). Curiously, given their late assimilation as Arabic-speakers, Jacobites stuck to their preference for Arabic as their mother tongue more assiduously than did their Muslim neighbors in cities such as Diyarbakır, Mardin, and Urfa where the Muslim population was increasingly Turcophone. At the start of the Republican period, it was generally only the Jacobite Christians who retained Arabic as their spoken

[9] Joseph, *Muslim–Christian Relations*, pp. 22–24; Martin van Bruinessen, *Agha, Shaikh, and State: The Social and Political Structures of Kurdistan* (London, 1992), pp. 24–25.
[10] Joseph, *ibid.*, pp. 18–29; D. Khouri, *State and Provincial Society*, p. 190.

vernacular in the cities of southeastern Turkey. If their mountain isolation provided the Maronites with a sense of freedom that would fan the ambitions of some for a Christian Lebanon in the twentieth century, the mountains did not nurture the Jacobites. Indeed, they only seemed to have heightened their sense of isolation from the larger world. The Jacobites had enjoyed a flowering of their literary culture in Syriac in the centuries preceding the disaster of the Crusades, but they produced few intellectuals in the Ottoman period. Served by an often venial and unresponsive clergy, the Jacobites were prime candidates for apostasy, whether to Islam or later to Catholicism.

There were also communities of Nestorian Christians (*Kildani* or alternatively *Nasturi* in Arabic and Ottoman Turkish, later to be known as Assyrians in the West) living beside the Jacobite villagers in the plains to the north of Mosul, most notably in the large village of Telkayf. The Nestorians were followers of a theological tradition anathematized by the Orthodox Christian mainstream in 431 at the Council of Ephesus for their emphasis on the human nature of Christ. The proponents of what would become the doctrine of their church insisted that Jesus' human nature and his divine one could not be conflated. They therefore refused to recognize Mary as the "Mother of God," calling her simply the "Mother of Jesus." That apparent denigration of Mary's status led to riots in Constantinople in the fifth century, but established the Nestorians as doctrinally much closer to Islam's understanding of Jesus' nature than was the case for other Christians.[11]

Higher still in the mountains, above the zone shared with the Jacobites, other Nestorian Christians and Jews were scattered throughout the more remote regions of Kurdistan. In the mountains, the Nestorians were largely a tribal people in their communal and economic organization. Although they retained Aramaic as their mother tongue, they were otherwise largely indistinguishable from their Kurdish-speaking tribal Muslim neighbors in their social organization or customs. As was the case with the Maronite mountaineers, the mountain Nestorians were well armed and willing to defend their rights with militancy unknown among their coreligionists of the lowlands.[12] The Nestorian community had enjoyed special favor during the Mongol period as many of the Mongol khans had either converted to Nestorian Christianity or married Nestorian women. In the wake of the Mongol collapse, the Nestorians' Muslim neighbors viewed them as having collaborated with the Mongol terror. They suffered greatly in the post-crusading period from retaliatory raids, launched by various Muslim armies; Ismail Safavi, the Iranian shah, was reported to have massacred all

[11] Robert Haddad, "Conversion of Eastern Orthodox Christians to the Unia in the Seventeenth and Eighteenth Centuries" in *Conversion and Continuity*. Edited by Gervers and Bikhazi (Toronto, 1990), pp. 451–52.
[12] Robert Betts, *Christians in the Arab East* (Atlanta, GA, 1975), pp. 51–52.

the Christians of Baghdad during his occupation of the city in 1508.[13] As the result of such outrages, the community virtually disappeared from the urban centers of Iraq.

The Nestorians were a scattered community when the Ottomans arrived, even more remote from the metropolitan centers of Christianity in both east and west than were the Jacobites. Unlike other Christian communities who received a respite after 1516, the Nestorians' troubles did not end with the arrival of the Ottomans. The Nestorians' homeland lay astride the frontier between the Ottoman and Iranian empires and their villages were frequently reduced to battlefields with the soldiers on both sides enslaving the unfortunate inhabitants. Although the enslavement of non-combatant *dhimmi*s had been specifically outlawed by Ebussuûd Efendi in the sixteenth century, a large number of Jewish and Christians slaves seized in Iranian Azerbaijan went on sale in Aleppo in 1726, following the Ottoman campaign against Tabriz. Local Jews and Armenians promptly redeemed slaves taken from their own religious communities in Iran. The hapless Nestorians had no such saviors and were purchased as slaves by local Muslims and Christians, including the wife of the British consul in the city.[14]

In the fifteenth century, the office of the supreme prelate of the Nestorians, the catholicos, passed into the hands of one extended family, with spiritual authority transferring from uncle to nephew. Initially, those holding the see resided in Iranian territory at Urumia while the majority of their flock remained on the Ottoman side of the border. In the seventeenth century, the Nestorians around Mosul, angry at a mere child's elevation as catholicos, broke from the church and acknowledged the Latin Pope as their spiritual head.[15] In the aftermath of the schism, the patriarchal see of the "traditionalist" faction moved to the village of Qudshanis (Kochanes in British and American missionary correspondence) in the heartland of the Nestorian tribal confederations, amidst the almost impenetrable mountains of what is today the Turkish province of Hakkâri.[16] The pro-Catholic faction retained the name Chaldean while the traditionalists in the mountains simply called themselves *Suryani*, helping to confuse outsiders as to the theological distinctions between Nestorians and Jacobites. In truth, the laity and even many of the clergy of both communities had largely forgotten the theological differences that divided them and outsiders were not completely wrong to conflate the two traditions. In the nineteenth century

[13] Yusuf Rizq-Allah Ghanima, *Nuzhat al-mushtaq fi ta'rikh Yahud al-ʿIraq* [A Nostalgic Ramble through the History of the Jews of Iraq] (Baghdad, 1924), p. 154.

[14] Düzdağ, *Ebussuud Efendi fetvaları*, n. 439; Damascus, Aleppo Court records, vol. XVIII, pp. 833, 835, 839; vol. LI, pp. 66, 75, 158.

[15] Frazee, *Catholics and Sultans*, pp. 55–58.

[16] J. F. Coakley, *The Church of the East and the Church of England: A History of the Archbishop of Canterbury's Assyrian Mission* (Oxford, 1992), pp. 14–17; Atiya, *Eastern Christianity*, pp. 273–78.

after contact with American and British archaeologists excavating ancient Ninevah, the traditionalists chose to call themselves Assyrians, thereby creating a link to a glorious, if somewhat questionable, past.

The Jews of this upland region did not adopt the tribal political organization of their Kurdish Muslim or Nestorian neighbors. They were nonetheless integrated culturally into the larger Kurdish society in which they lived and generally spoke Kurdish although some, like the Nestorians, retained Aramaic as their vernacular. Jews were to be found either as peasant farmers in scattered, predominantly Muslim villages or as craftsmen in the major Kurdish towns – Zakho, Sulaimaniyyah, and Amadiyyah – where they established an economic niche as goldsmiths and jewelers.[17] Despite their isolation, the Jews of Kurdistan retained a strong Jewish communal identity, preserving their religious tradition in accordance with the precepts of the Talmud.[18] Due to that important religious link to the people of Israel, they were not as isolated culturally or spiritually as were their Nestorian or Jacobite neighbors, who until the arrival of the European missionaries had no metropolitan connections with any coreligionists outside their mountains. Even so, the Kurdish Jews were largely a peripheral people in the consciousness of the lowland Jewish communities in the Arab provinces.

The religious geography became simpler once one came down from the mountains. Non-Muslims lived in villages and cities throughout the Fertile Crescent. But there was a significant disparity between the Iraqi and the Syrian provinces in the pattern of their settlement. The two lowland Iraqi provinces, Baghdad and Basra, had at the start of the Ottoman period only tiny remnants of their once numerically strong Christian communities. These were augmented over time as Iranian Armenians and Arab Christian migrants from northern Iraq and Syria established themselves in the two cities. In contrast to central and southern Iraq, Christians were to be found in significant numbers in the province of Mosul, both in the provincial capital and its hinterlands. Iraq's Jews had weathered the aftermath of the Crusades and the Mongols more successfully than had the Christians, and there were thriving Jewish communities in all the Iraqi cities. That of Baghdad may have been numerically the largest Jewish community in the Arab east. With a community which was both large and wealthy, Baghdad served as one of the leading intellectual centers for Arab Jews throughout the Ottoman period, producing rabbis of wide renown throughout the Jewish communities of the East.

Geographical Syria (*bilad al-Sham*) contained the largest concentration of Christians in the Ottoman Arab lands but the Jewish population outside of

---

[17] Hillel, *Unknown Jews*, pp. 71–82; Erich Brauer, *The Jews of Kurdistan.* Edited and completed by Raphael Patai (Detroit, MI, 1993).

[18] Hillel, *ibid.*, pp. 73–82.

Palestine was comparatively less significant than was that of Iraq. Scholarly estimates of the ratio of Christians in the region that is today demarcated into Syria, Lebanon, Jordan, Israel, and Palestine range from a fifth to a third of the total population, which probably was between a million and a million and a half souls in 1516. Christians were scattered throughout all four Syrian provinces: Aleppo, Damascus, Tripoli, and Tyre. Some regions such as Mount Lebanon, the villages on the eastern slopes of the Anti-Lebanon range, the Hawran, or the villages surrounding Jerusalem and Nazareth in Palestine, had very high concentrations of Christians. There were even Christian Bedouin in the Trans-Jordan.[19] Significant Christian minorities were present in all of Syria's cities and towns, with the exception of Hebron, but the largest communities were those of Damascus and Aleppo.

Most of the Christians of the Arabic-speaking lowlands at the time of the Ottoman conquest were Greek Orthodox by tradition with the Patriarch of Antioch, resident in Damascus by the sixteenth century at the latest, serving as their primate and spiritual leader. During the Mamluk and early Ottoman centuries, the connection between Antioch and Constantinople was attenuated. Although the Patriarch of Constantinople claimed supreme authority, the Byzantines appointed by the Ecumenical Patriarch to the see only rarely took up their post. In their absence, a tradition developed whereby the clergy and laity of Damascus chose whom they wished as patriarch, invariably a local Arab cleric. The Orthodox Christians of Syria were not completely isolated from their brethren in the Byzantine world, as priests and monks continued to travel between Constantinople and Syria. But an Arabization of the church hierarchy occurred in the absence of control exercised by the Greek church as the community accommodated itself to being a minority church within a Muslim state. Unlike their coreligionists in Anatolia who wrote their Turkish vernacular using the Greek alphabet, Orthodox Arabs wrote their vernacular in the same script as did their Muslim neighbors. Nonetheless, the spiritual link of Syria's Orthodox Christians to Constantinople, as well as their continued use of Greek as their language of liturgy, created linguistic confusion as to their ethnic identity for Europeans and Ottoman officials alike. This was in no small part due to the name they chose to call themselves.

The Orthodox Christian Arabs of Syria were called Melkites (*malakiyyun*, "the king's men") in the early centuries of Arab rule. It was reputedly a term of derision imposed by the Muslims on those Christians who remained true to the faith of the Byzantine emperors. But over time, those same Christians took up the name as a badge of pride.[20] By the Ottoman

[19] Rogan, *Frontiers of the State*, pp. 30–31.
[20] Maksimus Mazlum, *Nabdhah ta'rikhiyya fi ma jara li-ta'ifat al-Rum al kathulik mundhu sanat 1837 fi ma baʿduha* [An Historical Tract on What Occurred to the Melkite Catholics from 1837 onwards] (no place of publication, 1907), p. iv.

conquest, however, the term seems to have dropped out of common usage by either the community or the Muslim authorities. Instead, these Arabic-speaking Orthodox Christians called themselves simply the *Rum*, a collective noun which could mean alternatively "Byzantines," "Anatolians," "Greeks," or "Orthodox Christians" in Ottoman Turkish, while in Syrian Arabic, *Rum* could also mean "Ottomans," in addition to the other possible meanings. These myriad lexical possibilities provided endless opportunities for ethnic misidentification by all those who were outside the community. The Catholic faction among the Rum in Syria in the eighteenth century revived the name Melkite, in an attempt to place distance between themselves and the Orthodox of the see of Constantinople. The term was slow to catch on in the popular imagination of the laity in Syria, however. Orthodox Arab chroniclers of the eighteenth century continued to label their own faction the Rum and the other "Catholics" (*ta'ifa kathulikiyya*) or more commonly "those who follow the religion of the Franks." Catholic authors appropriated the collective Rum for themselves and labeled their opponents simply "heretics" (*al-aratiqa*).

The Copts of Egypt comprised the other numerically large Christian community in the Ottoman Arab territories with perhaps between ten to fifteen percent of Egypt's total population, estimated variously at the time of the Ottoman conquest to be between two and three million people.[21] Their spiritual head, the Patriarch of Alexandria, had long before 1517 moved his actual see to Cairo. As was the case with the Jacobites and the Armenians, the Copts had embraced the Monophysite definition of Christ's nature and had been persecuted under the Byzantines. But they had also possessed before the arrival of the Muslim armies in the seventh century the potential for becoming a "national" church, not unlike that of Armenia where language, identification with territory, and faith would provide the foundation for a strong ethnic identity. The continued erosion of the community's numbers through conversion to Islam and the virtual disappearance of the Coptic language as a spoken vernacular had, however, erased any possibility of a Coptic "nation" centuries before the advent of Ottoman rule in Egypt.

After almost a millennium of assimilation into the dominant Arabic culture, the Copts were culturally or physically indistinguishable from their Muslim neighbors who were, after all, largely descended from Coptic converts. Egyptian Muslims and Copts shared a variety of folk practices that they deemed to be religiously ordained – abstinence from pork, the use of *zar* (magical healing), and the circumcision of both their sons and daughters (clitoridectomy). These undoubtedly blurred the cultural divide between the two communities. Adding to the potential for their cultural assimilation, the Copts were widely distributed geographically across Egypt.

---

[21] Otto Meinardus, *Christian Egypt: Faith and Life* (Cairo, 1970), p. 367.

Although they were proportionally a larger minority in Upper Egypt than in the Delta, outside a few villages such as Akhmim, they constituted a majority nowhere.

In addition to these indigenous Arabic-speaking Christians, Armenians were ubiquitous in the demographic mix of the cities of the Arab Middle East. It was, however, only in the trading cities of Aleppo and Basra that the Armenians came to constitute an important numerical component of the overall Christian population, before the tragic deportations of the Anatolian Armenians in the early twentieth century.[22] Even if their numbers were small, Armenians contributed to the commercial life of the cities of the region in which they dwelled with their connections to a wider trading diaspora that stretched already in the sixteenth century from Amsterdam to India. That cosmopolitanism aided them in adapting to the changes abroad in the world beyond the Middle East. As a people, they were instrumental in the introduction of new consumer technologies from the West, i.e. printing, photography, sewing machines, and eventually automobile mechanics, to the Arab lands in the last decades of the empire.

The Jews who lived in what would become the core of the Ottoman Arab provinces were almost entirely an urban people in 1516. There were exceptions: the Jews of Kurdistan already mentioned and the inhabitants of a few villages in Palestine.[23] But these were a tiny minority of the total. Jewish communities existed in all the major urban centers of the Arab world with those of Cairo, Aleppo, Damascus, and Baghdad being the largest. There were also smaller communities of Qaraite (non-Rabbinical Jews whose ancestors followed the traditions of the Jewish diaspora before the composition of the Talmud) in Egypt, Damascus, and Palestine. The Qaraites clung doggedly to the faith of their fathers, even while earning the derision of those who viewed that tradition as having been superseded by the Talmud. As in the case of the various Christian sects, differences in religious customs sometimes led to conflict between followers of the disparate traditions.[24] Whether Rabbinical or Qaraite, the Jews outside of the holy cities of *Eretz Israel* were almost entirely Arabic-speakers in the early sixteenth century and had assimilated as fully into the Arabo-Muslim culture surrounding them as had their Christian neighbors.

In contrast to that assimilation, the Jewish communities in Palestine had diverse ethnic origins and spoke in many tongues. Safed, a center for the study of the Jewish mystical tradition of the *Kabbalah*, had separate quarters for Jews from Portugal, Cordoba, Castile, Aragon, Hungary,

[22] Avedis Sanjian, *The Armenian Communities in Syria under Ottoman Dominion* (Cambridge, MA, 1966), pp. 46–53.
[23] Abraham David, *To Come to the Land: Immigration and Settlement in Sixteenth-Century Eretz-Israel*. Translated by Dena Ordan (Tuscaloosa, AL, 1999), pp. 24–35.
[24] el-Nahal, *Judicial Administration*, p. 42; Barnai, *Jews in Palestine*, p. 164.

Apulia, Seville, and Germany in the sixteenth century.[25] As the list suggests, Jews of Iberian origin (the *Sephardim*) increasingly found their way to Palestine in the sixteenth century and probably constituted the majority of the Jews in the Holy Land in the first century of Ottoman rule. Jewish immigrants to Palestine continued to come from diverse places in the eighteenth century with the migration of Eastern European *Hassidim* following the death of Baal Shem-Tov in 1760.[26] Millenarianism fueled much of the immigration to Palestine, nurtured by the immigrants' desire to be buried in Jerusalem to wait for the coming of the Messiah when many believed they would be physically resurrected. As such, the immigrants were often elderly and impoverished Jews from throughout Europe and the Middle East. But numerous Jewish scholars also came to find solace, freedom from persecution, and intellectual community in *Eretz Israel*. Throughout the Ottoman period, Jerusalem, Tiberias, and Safed served as shared physical spaces where Jewish intellectuals from throughout the diaspora could meet and exchange ideas in a cultural nexus parallel to that provided by Mecca and Medina for their Muslim contemporaries.

The Sephardic Jews were the most economically dynamic group to migrate to the Ottoman Arab cities in the sixteenth and seventeenth centuries. The migrants were a part of general population movement of Jews from the Christian Mediterranean to the Ottoman lands in the aftermath of their expulsion from Spain in 1492. Some had settled first in the port cities of Italy before moving on and retained valuable trade contacts with the Sephardic diaspora in the western Mediterranean and beyond, stretching to Amsterdam and the New World.[27] Many had been prosperous in their old homelands and brought whatever capital was movable with them. They also brought European technology and mercantile practices. Sephardic Jews established the empire's first printing presses and served as bankers in all the major cities. Although the majority of the Sephardic immigrants settled in Palestine, the Balkans, or in the cities of western Anatolia, others found their way to Aleppo, Damascus, and Cairo. It was only in Aleppo and Jerusalem among the Arab cities, however, that the community was sufficiently large to maintain its spoken tongue, Judeo-Spanish, until the end of the empire. Elsewhere, the Sephardic Jews were assimilated over time into the Arabic culture of their coreligionists. There is anecdotal evidence that the Sephardic and Arab Jews did not always share the same space peacefully.[28] This was most apparent in Aleppo where, by the end of the eighteenth century, the wealthy merchants among the

[25] Amnon Cohen and Bernard Lewis, *Population and Revenue in the Towns of Palestine in the Sixteenth Century* (Princeton, NJ, 1978), p. 158.
[26] Barnai, *Jews in Palestine*, pp. 37–39.
[27] Jonathan Israel, *European Jewry in the Age of Mercantilism 1550–1750* (Oxford, 1985).
[28] Hacker, "Jewish Autonomy in the Ottoman Empire," pp. 168–69.

Sephardim, the *Signores Francos*, had established a separate synagogue and benevolent societies for their own community.[29]

## How many?

The question of the number of non-Muslims in the Ottoman Arab provinces and the related issue of their percentage of the overall population remain contested by historians. Ömer Lutfi Barkan initiated the debate when he asserted that the extant Ottoman tax records revealed there were 113,358 Muslim households in the Syrian provinces in the period between 1520 and 1535, but only 914 Christian and no Jewish households.[30] That return of less than 1 percent of the total households as being Christian, not to mention the total absence of Jews, seemed to be historically counterfactual when compared to Ottoman census returns of the late nineteenth century where the number of non-Muslims was much more robust. His findings were immediately challenged by Charles Issawi but without any countervailing documentation.[31] Undaunted by the criticism, Barkan returned to the Ottoman registers for the latter decades of the sixteenth century, with the following results for four key Ottoman Arab provinces.

|          | Settled Muslims | Christians | Jews |
|----------|-----------------|------------|------|
| Aleppo   | 81,203          | 3386       | 233  |
| Baghdad  | 39,379          | 4035       | 603  |
| Damascus | 86,369          | 7867       | 2068 |
| Tripoli  | 34,316          | 11,768     | 307[32] |

The ratio of non-Muslims to Muslims improved with Barkan's second set of data, but there were still apparent anomalies. Both Christians and Jews seemed to have been significantly undercounted in Aleppo in comparison to Damascus, while Christians were apparently overrepresented in Baghdad at the expense of the city's Jewish population. Without questioning Barkan's results, a recent study has contrasted the low percentage of Christians in the population of the Syrian provinces in the first century of Ottoman rule with their greater representation in the Ottoman censuses at the end of empire to suggest that the Christian population increased at a

---

[29] Joseph Sutton, *Magic Carpet: Aleppo-in-Flatbush* (New York, 1971), pp. 173–75.

[30] Ömer Lutfi Barkan, "Essai sur les données statistiques des registres de recensement dans l'empire ottoman aux XVe et XVIe siècles" *Journal of the Economic and Social History of the Orient* 1 (1957): 20.

[31] Charles Issawi, "Comment on Professor Barkan's Estimate of the Population of the Ottoman Empire, 1520–1530" *Journal of the Economic and Social History of the Orient* 1 (1957): 329–31.

[32] Ömer Lutfi Barkan, "Research on the Ottoman Fiscal Surveys" in *Studies in the Economic History of the Middle East*. Edited by M. A. Cook (London, 1970), p. 171.

much faster rate than Muslims during the Ottoman period.[33] The hypothesis for this dramatic demographic phenomenon, if true, is the Christians had a higher birth rate than Muslims and a lower morbidity rate in times of pestilence.

The proposition that the Christians had a higher birth rate than Muslims in the sixteenth to the eighteenth century is unanswerable given our sources. The only extant data to confirm that claim are contained in the estate records of the deceased from various urban centers (Arabic, *dafatir al-mukhallafat*; Ottoman Turkish *tereke defterleri*). The survival of these records is spotty and most scholars agree that Christians are severely underrepresented in those records that are extant.[34] Even so, there is nothing in them to suggest that Christians had more children than did Muslims. A recent study of the elite Muslim families of Aleppo in the late eighteenth and early nineteenth century found that relatively few of their children reached adulthood but it did not examine the patterns present among the Christian elite of the city. As such, the question of whether there were sectarian differences in the average number of those who survived childhood in the city remains.[35] There is also little evidence to support the assumption that Muslims suffered a higher rate of morbidity from disease than did Christians, at least in the early centuries of Ottoman rule. Chronicles written by Christians in the eighteenth century suggest their community suffered from repeated visitations of plague and other diseases at rates that were comparable to those experienced by their Muslim contemporaries.[36] Accounts from the nineteenth century, however, indicate that by then Christians were using quarantines in times of plague.[37] But it is not at all certain that Christians enjoyed an advantage over their Muslim neighbors in terms of lower morbidity rates from disease before the concept of quarantine became more widely practiced by them, having been borrowed from the Europeans.

There were also two further negative constraints on Christian population growth that would have had an impact on the population counts of the late Ottoman period. The Christians continued to suffer a diminution of their numbers through conversion to Islam throughout the Ottoman centuries. Both the court records and Christian chronicles record a steady defection of Christians to Islam, albeit even if it were only a handful in any given year. Secondly, by the time the Ottoman censuses had become relatively reliable at the end of the nineteenth century, Christians were migrating out of the

[33] Courbage and Fargues, *Christians and Jews under Islam*, pp. 61–67.
[34] Establet and Pascual, *Familles et fortunes à Damas*, p. 32.
[35] Margaret Meriwether, *The Kin who Count: Family and Society in Ottoman Aleppo 1770–1840* (Austin, TX, 1999), pp. 217–32.
[36] ʿAbbud, *al-Murtadd*, pp. 102–07.
[37] Assaad Kayat, *A Voice from Lebanon* (London, 1847), pp. 11–12; Mikha'il Mishaqa *Murder, Mayhem, Pillage and Plunder: The History of Lebanon in the 18th and 19th Centuries.* Translated by Wheeler Thackston, Jr. (Albany, NY, 1988), p. 103.

empire at a rate disproportionate to that of their Muslim neighbors.[38] Both of these trends would have worked to reduce demographic advantages the Christians might have enjoyed due to either higher fertility or lower morbidity rates over their Muslim neighbors.

A plausible reason for the apparent disjuncture between the percentage of non-Muslims in the reported population of Syria in the sixteenth century and that of the nineteenth is, of course, that there was an undercount of Christians in the earlier period. The Christians of the Fertile Crescent were still largely a rural population in the sixteenth century, fairly remote and therefore less likely to be enumerated accurately.[39] Support for this hypothesis comes from scattered data points from across the region in the sixteenth and seventeenth centuries. *Jizya* records from the city of Aleppo suggest that an impressive growth in the Christian population occurred in the seventeenth and early eighteenth centuries. The tax register used by Barkan listed 309 Christian households and 15 Christian bachelors in the city in 1584–85; it also listed 7,881 Muslim and 233 Jewish urban households.[40] The much higher figure he supplies for Christian households in the province's villages and towns, compared to those in the provincial capital (3,386 to 309) is noteworthy as the Ottoman censuses of the late nineteenth century show that Christians had all but disappeared from the province's villages. It also provides an interesting counterpoint to the province's Jewish population, all of whom apparently lived in the provincial capital. We must be careful with this latter assumption as well, however, as *jizya* registers from the second half of the seventeenth century indicate the presence of Jews in two provincial towns, Kilis and Aintab (Gaziantep).

The number of Christian *jizya* payers in Aleppo rose to 2,500 in 1640 and to 5,391 in 1695.[41] Significantly, at the latter date only 2,254 Christian *jizya* payers were listed as living elsewhere in the province, a ratio of roughly two to one in favor of the city. That stands in stark contrast to Barkan's findings of a ratio of one urban Christian for every eleven peasants in the century before. In further support of a migration hypothesis, 1,234 Christian males, or 23 percent, were listed as newcomers to the city in the register compiled in 1695. The Jewish total of 875 males for the same year was not divided into separate categories, but the returns for the community represented almost a doubling of their number (450) registered in 1672. This increase suggests migrants were augmenting the Jewish community in the city as well.[42] That assumption is strengthened by the fact the Jews were listed in

[38] Kemal Karpat, "The Ottoman Emigration to America, 1860–1914" *International Journal of Middle Eastern Studies* 17 (1985): 175–209.
[39] Antoine Abdel-Nour, *Introduction à l'histoire urbaine de la Syrie ottomane (XVIe–XVIIIe siècle)*. Beirut, 1982, pp. 59–60.
[40] *Ibid.*, p. 66.
[41] Damascus, Aleppo Court records, vol. XXII, p. 21; Istanbul, BOA, MM 3498.
[42] Istanbul, BOA, MM 9489, p. 127.

two categories in the 1672 enumeration – 377 *Yehud-ı Araban* (Arab Jews) and 73 *Yehud-ı Efrenk* (Frankish Jews), suggesting the relative ratio of Arabic-speaking Jews to the more recently arrived Sephardim. We also have anecdotal evidence from the court registers that Jews were migrating to Aleppo from southeastern Anatolia in the latter part of the century and they, rather than Sephardic Jews, may have accounted for the increase.

Evidence from the Aleppo court records, including the registration of groups of newly arrived migrants, suggests Christians continued to come into the city in significant numbers in the first decades of the eighteenth century. In 1740, 8,120 Christian males registered as paying the *jizya*.[43] Thereafter in the eighteenth century, the returns were always below that figure, for example, 7,213 in 1756.[44] Even so, we cannot be certain that the returns for the later date represent a true demographic decline. The Armenian patriarch in Istanbul registered a complaint in 1757 on behalf of his clergy in Aleppo charging that the city's governor had illegally granted exemptions from paying the *jizya* to the city's Maronites in the previous year.[45] By the second half of the eighteenth century, irregularities in the ways in which the *jizya* was assessed and collected had become so ingrained in the bureaucratic culture of Aleppo that the registered returns are meaningless, a reality noted with alarm by the bureaucrats in Istanbul.[46]

Whatever their actual numbers, the growth in the population of Christians and Jews in Aleppo is all the more impressive as the total number of people living in the city apparently remained relatively constant after the middle of the seventeenth century, i.e. approximately 100,000 inhabitants.[47] The number of Christian *jizya* payers in 1740 represents a staggering increase of twenty-five-fold over the figures returned in 1585. There is little doubt Aleppo's Christian population grew substantially over the course of the first two Ottoman centuries, even if Barkan's figures are tainted by a severe undercount. Physical evidence is to be found in the expansion of the largely Christian suburbs known collectively as Judayda to the north of the city walls in the sixteenth to the eighteenth century. The city's court records also document a substantial migration of formerly rural Christians from northern and central Syria, as well as southeastern Anatolia, to the city, confirming the hypothesis created by the *jizya* returns.[48] Large-scale migration ended in the middle of the eighteenth century and thereafter Aleppo's

---

[43] Ferdinand Taoutel, "Watha'iq ta'rikhiyya ʿan Halab fi al-qarn al-thamin ʿashar" [Historical Documents on Aleppo in the Eighteenth Century] *al-Mashriq* vol. 41 (1947), pp. 252–53.

[44] Damascus, Aleppo Court records, vol. LXXXVII, pp. 13–31.

[45] Istanbul, BOA, Ahkâm-ı Halep, vol. II, p. 203.

[46] Hidemitsu Kuroki, "Dhimmis in Mid-Nineteenth Century Aleppo: An Analysis of Jizya Defters" (unpublished paper).

[47] André Raymond, "The Population of Aleppo in the Sixteenth and Seventeenth Centuries" *International Journal of Middle Eastern Studies* 16 (1984): 447–60.

[48] Bruce Masters, "Patterns of Migration to Ottoman Aleppo in the 17th and 18th Centuries" *Journal of Turkish Studies* 4 (1987): 75–89.

population decreased to approximately 80,000 souls in 1800, with the Christians constituting approximately 20 percent of the total and Jews, 5 percent. It did not start to rebound again until the second half of the nineteenth century.

Research on other Ottoman Arab cities, although still fragmentary, suggests similar demographic trends occurred elsewhere. The Ottoman *Tapu Tahrir* registers for Mosul in 1525–26 recorded 1,138 Muslim households and 138 bachelors, 553 non-Muslim households and 85 bachelors. In 1557, there were 1,846 Muslim adult males in the city, 692 Christians, and 105 Jews. In 1575–76, their numbers had grown to 2,204 Muslims, 812 Christians, and 145 Jews.[49] The number of adult non-Muslim males, including both Jews and Christians, in the city further increased from 1,538 in 1691 to 2,307 in 1729; by 1834, their number had reached 3,822. In 1845, it was estimated that there were 6,000 Christians in the city out of a total population of 43,000 inhabitants.[50] Corroborating the theory of rural flight, the number of Christians in the hinterlands of Mosul declined substantially over the course of the seventeenth century, even if the decline was not as precipitous as occurred in Aleppo province.[51] In 1845, French consular officials estimated that the Christian rural population of Mosul province still exceeded that of their coreligionists in the city.[52]

Data points for the population of the province of Damascus in the sixteenth century reveal similar secular trends. The Ottoman tax collectors recorded in 1543 that Damascus had 7,213 Muslim, 546 Christian, and 512 Jewish households; in 1569, there were 7,054 Muslim, 1,021 Christian, and 546 Jewish households. Significantly, the number of Christian households for the villages in the subdistrict of Damascus, with the exception of the predominantly Christian villages Saydnaya and Maᶜalula, show no corresponding increase.[53] By 1597, Damascus' population growth had apparently peaked, with returns of 6,741 Muslim families, 1,453 Muslim bachelors, 798 Christian families, 264 Christian bachelors, 20 Jewish families and 6 Jewish bachelors. The low return of the number of Jewish households in the 1597 enumeration is obviously anomalous and reminds us yet again of the precarious nature of any population data we might uncover for the early Ottoman period. There was a general decline in the city's population for at least the first half of the seventeenth century with an apparent rebound at

[49] İsmet Binark (ed.). *Musul-Kerkük ile ilgili arşiv belgeleri* [Archival Documents concerning Mosul and Kirkuk] *(1525–1919)* (Ankara, 1993), pp. 59, 76, 93.

[50] D. Khoury, *State and Provincial Society*, p. 112; Tom Nieuwenhuis, *Politics and Society in Early Modern Iraq: Mamluk Pashas, Tribal Shayks and Local Rule between 1802 and 1831* (The Hague, 1981), p. 73.

[51] Khoury, *ibid.*, p. 29.

[52] Nieuwenhuis, *Politics and Society*, p. 73.

[53] Adnan Bakhit, "The Christian Population of the Province of Damascus in the Sixteenth Century" in *Christians and Jews in the Ottoman Empire*. Edited by B. Braude and B. Lewis (New York, 1982), vol. II, pp. 19–66.

the end of the century.[54] A recent study estimates the city's population was between 60,000 and 65,000 persons in 1700, with 11 percent of the total Christians and 5 to 6 percent Jews.[55]

We have slightly better evidence about demographic trends in Palestine than elsewhere in southern Syria. As was the case in both Aleppo and Mosul, the Christian population of Jerusalem apparently grew between the sixteenth century and the end of the seventeenth century. In 1562–63, there were 315 Christian *jizya* payers enumerated in the city, but by 1690–91, the total had risen to 622. At the same time the number of Christian *jizya* payers in the neighboring villages of Bethlehem and Bayt-Jala had declined, from 149 to 144 and 218 to 143, respectively.[56] This was representative of a demographic trend occurring throughout Palestine over the course of the Ottoman period as Christians left their villages for Jerusalem, or for the larger, predominantly Christian, villages of Bethlehem and Nazareth.[57] In the process, villages in Palestine that had been home to Christians in the sixteenth century became entirely Muslim by the nineteenth century. In 1744, the total number of *jizya* payers in Bethlehem was recorded as 287, supporting the assumption of its continued growth, but 239 adult male Christians were registered as living in nearby Bayt-Jala, an approximate return to the number counted in the sixteenth century. The complaint to the sultan in which these figures were reported, however, stated that the Christians had been moving away from both villages in favor of Jerusalem to the detriment of the pious endowments in Mecca and Jerusalem their *jizya* payments supported.[58] But it is not at all certain that rural flight for Christians was constant over the Ottoman period in all parts of Palestine given the absence of any population data to confirm or rebut the hypothesis.[59]

In contrast to the Christian population, which seems to have remained relatively stable as to its percentage of the total population after the seventeenth century, the Jewish population in Jerusalem fluctuated greatly in the Ottoman period, reflecting major shifts in patterns of immigration. Jerusalem reported 1,194 Jewish *jizya*-payers in 1525–26; the number rose to 1,958 in 1553–54. Thereafter it dropped, reaching an apparent nadir of 690 men registered in 1572–73. The numbers rebounded toward the end of

---

[54] Abdel-Nour, *Introduction*, p. 73.

[55] Establet and Pascual, *Familles et fortunes*, pp. 73–74.

[56] Oded Peri, "The Christian Population of Jerusalem in the Late Seventeenth Century: Aspects of Demographic Development" in *Histoire économique et sociale de l'Empire Ottoman et de la Turquie*. Edited by Daniel Panzac (Paris, 1995), pp. 447–54.

[57] Amnon Cohen, "The Receding of the Christian Presence in the Holy Land: A 19th Century Sijill in the Light of 16th Century Tahrirs" in *The Syrian Land in the 18th and 19th Century*. Edited by T. Philipp (Stuttgart, 1992), pp. 333–40. Chad Emmett, *Beyond the Basilica: Christians and Muslims in Nazareth* (Chicago, IL, 1995), pp. 22–27.

[58] Istanbul, BOA, Ahkâm-ı Şam-ı Şerif, vol. I, p. 86.

[59] Peri, "Christian Population," p. 454.

the century, but never attained the levels that were registered at mid-century.[60] Jerusalem was not the only beneficiary of these migrations. Safed had 233 Jewish households in 1525–26 and 719 in 1555–56; by 1567–68, the number had risen to 945, and almost equaled the Muslim population of the town.[61] That ratio did not remain constant. In the early nineteenth century, Rabbi d'Beth Hillel reported that there were 2,000 Jewish families and 10,000 Muslim families in the town.[62] As the figures from Safed and Jerusalem suggest, the sixteenth century may represent the highest proportion of Jews to non-Jews in the population of Palestine during the Ottoman centuries before the advent of Zionist settlement at the end of the nineteenth century.[63]

Elsewhere in the Ottoman Arab lands, the Jewish population seems to have remained stable as a percentage of the total after the period of immigration of Sephardic Jews came to an end. The exception to this was Baghdad where the Jewish population received two major waves of migrants from Iran in the seventeenth and nineteenth centuries, largely due to persecution by the Shi$^c$a authorities in their homeland. 1,500 Jewish families were reported in Baghdad in 1824; the estimate of their number in 1908 stood at between 25,000 and 40,000 persons, out of a total population of approximately 100,000 people. The Ottoman census of 1906–07 returned 12,933 adult Jewish males for the entire Baghdad province, in addition to 1,511 adult Christian males and 109,568 adult Muslim males.[64] Both the Jews and Christians were overwhelmingly urban while the Muslims were disproportionately rural in their distribution.

In summary, demographic data on the Christians and Jews of the Arab lands in the first three centuries of Ottoman rule remain sparse and problematic. Estimates given by European visitors could vary wildly. Worse, once a travel writer had set a figure to paper it was accepted and repeated by those who came later. Ottoman sources are not much better, even if they carry a seductive impression of accuracy with their seemingly exact counts. Not only is there the question of whom was actually counted but all too often, the actual entries do not add up to the total calculated by the enumerator. In other cases, tax collectors simply repeated totals from earlier years.[65] As a result, we cannot be certain how many non-Muslims there actually were. But we lack reliable counts for the Muslim population as well. We can establish broad patterns both of settlement and migration in

---

[60] A. Cohen, *Jewish Life under Islam*, pp. 34–35.
[61] Cohen and Lewis, *Population and Revenue*, p. 161.
[62] Hillel, *Unknown Jews*, p. 59.
[63] Barnai, *Jews in Palestine*, pp. 14, 32.
[64] Nissim Rejwan, *The Jews of Iraq: 3000 Years of History and Culture* (Boulder, CO, 1985), pp. 172, 195; Kemal Karpat, *Ottoman Population, 1830–1914: Demographic and Social Characteristics* (Madison, WI, 1985), p. 165.
[65] Peri, "Christian Population," p. 448.

the period, however. These inform us that there was a movement of Christians away from rural areas, with the possible exception of Mount Lebanon, and a transformation of the Christian population in the region from a largely rural one to one that was increasingly urban. Flight from the land was a reality for Muslim peasants of the Fertile Crescent as well, as the countryside became unstable in the seventeenth and eighteenth centuries due to tribal incursions into formerly agricultural lands. There was a difference, however. The Muslim population was still overwhelmingly rural at the end of the nineteenth century; the same could not be said for the Christians. Everywhere in the Fertile Crescent, the Christians were becoming, like their Jewish neighbors, an urban population, leaving only pockets of Christian villagers scattered across the rural landscape. This pattern of an increasing urbanization contrasts sharply to that which occurred in the same period in Egypt where the Copts were underrepresented in the population of Cairo in the eighteenth century and were still largely rural in their choice of settlement.[66]

It is not clear why Christians of the Fertile Crescent left their villages at a much higher rate than Muslims. Perhaps, it was due to persecution by their Muslim neighbors.[67] The Polish-Armenian traveler, Simeon, reported that political unrest in Anatolia in the early seventeenth century had sent large numbers of rural Armenians to Aleppo and the cities of Anatolia.[68] It is conceivable that predatory tribesman targeted Christian villages as easier prey than Muslim villagers who were more likely to be armed. Such was the pattern of Kurdish incursions against Armenian, Jacobite, and Nestorian villages in the nineteenth century and it is probably safe to assume that similar depredations had occurred earlier. When asked, however, seventeenth-century Christian migrants to Aleppo said they had left because their villages could no longer sustain them or their families.[69] There is probably not one causal explanation that would explain every individual peasant's decision to leave. But there can be little doubt that the collective weight of their decisions set in motion a significant demographic shift. As an unintended result, the region's Christians, having become a predominantly urban population, would be in a disproportionate position to participate in the economic, political, and cultural changes that were to come than were their former Muslim neighbors who had remained on the land.

66  André Raymond, *Artisans et commerçants au Caire au XVIII<sup>e</sup> siècle*, 2 vols. (Damascus, 1973–74), vol. II, pp. 456–59.
67  A. Cohen, "Receding Christian presence."
68  Polonyalı Simeon, *Polonyalı Simeon'un seyahatnamesi* [Travelogue of Polonyalı Simeon] *1608–1619*. Translated by Hrand Andreasyan (Istanbul, 1964), p. 93.
69  Damascus, Aleppo Court records, vol. II, p. 234; vol. XXIV, p. 160.

## *Ta'ifa* or *millet*?

Having surveyed the distribution of the non-Muslim communities in the Ottoman Arab provinces, we need now to turn briefly to their internal governance in the early Ottoman period. Official Ottoman correspondence dealing with the non-Muslims of the empire in the early nineteenth century consistently affirmed that non-Muslims were organized into three officially sanctioned *millet*s: Greek Orthodox, Armenians, and Jews. The bureaucrats further asserted this had been the "tradition" since the reign of Sultan Fatih Mehmed (second and decisive reign, 1451–81). The *millet*s as constituted in the nineteenth century were hierarchically organized religious bodies with a decidedly political function. Each was headed by a cleric (patriarch or chief rabbi, known in Ottoman Turkish as the *millet başı*) who was appointed by the sultan and resident in Istanbul but who was largely free to order the affairs of his community as long as he remained loyal to the sultan. More importantly as an officially sanctioned bureaucracy, the *millet*'s leadership could command the civil forces of empire, i.e. governors and qadis, to implement its will over an errant flock. Without questioning the nineteenth-century bureaucrats' appeal to an unbroken tradition, the pioneering study of the empire by H. A. R. Gibb and Harold Bowen asserted that the paradigm of the *millet* was "traditional" for the non-Muslim communities within the Ottoman Empire. This was, unfortunately, echoed by many subsequent studies. Recent scholarship has shown it was, in fact, a relatively latecomer to the Ottoman political scene, even if its workings were always cloaked in the rhetoric of an ageless tradition.[70]

The non-Muslim communities in the Arab provinces were accorded a degree of internal political autonomy by the Muslim authorities in the centuries leading up to the emergence of *millet* politics in the eighteenth century. The Arabic form of the word (*milla*) was used in the court records of Aleppo in the seventeenth century to designate Christians or Jews generically (*millat al-Nasara*, "Christians"), but it lacked the precise meaning it would later acquire. If the recording bureaucrat wanted to signify a particular sect in his document, another expression, *ta'ifa*, was invariably used. That term could be translated as "group" or "party" and was liberally assigned to almost any collective social or economic group: craft organization, merchants, tribals, residents of a particular quarter, or even foreigners (*ta'ifat al-afranj*, "the Franks"). The same bureaucratic

---

[70] Sir Hamilton Gibb and Harold Bowen *Islamic Society and the West: A Study of the Impact of Western Civilization on Muslim Culture in the Near East*, 2 parts (London, 1950, 1957), part II, pp. 207–61. For a critique, Amnon Cohen, "On the Realities of the *Millet* system" in *Christians and Jews in the Ottoman Empire*. Edited by B. Braude and B. Lewis (New York, 1982), vol. II, pp. 7–18.

practice prevailed throughout the empire.[71] The importance of this linguistic excursion comes from the underlying political and legal understanding the Ottoman bureaucrats attached to the social construction of a *ta'ifa*, with its accompanying liberties and limitations.

The membership of any *ta'ifa* established its own rules for inclusion, chose its leadership, and promulgated its internal regulations. The members then affirmed these before the chief qadi and the rules were registered. Once this was done, the *ta'ifa*'s regulations received official sanction and its membership could appeal to the court to enforce its rules. The state's interests were served by creating collective entities that would be responsible for tax collection. But the autonomy was not absolute. The Muslim courts were ultimately obliged to insure that a *ta'ifa* lived up to its own rules, thereby providing the state with a mechanism with which it could intervene both in internal disputes of the *ta'ifa* and in disputes between *ta'ifa*s which might otherwise threaten the established order.

The standard practice in Aleppo in the seventeenth century was for large delegations of Christian laymen, consisting at times of over one hundred individuals, to affirm before the qadi their choice of lay representative (*koca başı*) and of their metropolitan (the Eastern-rite equivalent of bishop). Alternately, such a delegation could affirm that they no longer recognized the authority of the men holding high ecclesiastical office. Evidence from Damascus in the same century suggests councils of laity and clergy in that city elevated, or dethroned, the men holding the office of the Patriarch of Antioch without reference to clerical synods, the Patriarch of Constantinople, or the sultan.[72]

Similarly, the Jews of Jerusalem routinely chose their rabbis internally in the sixteenth century and those men would then be registered by the city's chief qadi as the community's political and religious leaders.[73] By the eighteenth century, that internal cohesion had unraveled. The wealthy Sephardic community in Istanbul took over the responsibility of the community's governance through the institution of the Istanbul Committee of Officials for Palestine, and it appointed the men who would represent the community locally.[74] That situation was, however, apparently unique to Palestine with its diverse Jewish communities. Elsewhere, the Jews of Basra elected a man to serve as *nasi*, or secular leader. The men holding the office might also be rabbis, but their function as office holders was primarily to represent the secular interests of the community to the Muslim authorities. With recognition from the state, they wielded considerable political

---

[71] Daniel Goffman, "Ottoman Millets in the Early Seventeenth Century" *New Perspectives on Turkey* 11 (1994): 135–58.

[72] J. M. Neale, *A History of the Eastern Church: The Patriarchate of Antioch* (London, 1873), pp. 180–84.

[73] A. Cohen, *Jewish Life under Islam*, pp. 48–49.

[74] Barnai, *Jews of Palestine*, pp. 109–46.

authority in their own community.[75] In Baghdad, a prominent Jewish banker who had ties to the city's Muslim governors usually occupied the position of *nasi*, apparently without the consent of those he governed. That office remained central in the administrative life of Baghdad's Jews until the reforms of the Tanzimat, when the office of *nasi* disappeared as the rabbis in the city reasserted their authority to govern and speak for their community.[76] The rabbis were aided in this by the importation of the office of *haham başı* (chief rabbi) to Baghdad, a reflection of the newly constructed hierarchy of the Jewish *millet* that was only established empire-wide in 1835. Following the end of the Egyptian occupation of Syria in 1840–41, the office of *haham başı* also appeared in Aleppo and Damascus from where we have little evidence as to how the Jewish communities governed themselves internally before the Tanzimat reforms.

Once a religious *ta'ifa* was registered with the qadi, its leadership could call on the Muslim authorities to enforce its own internal discipline. This principle is illustrated by a case, involving members of the tiny Nestorian community in Aleppo, which eventually reached the attention of the Porte in 1721. Although previously the Nestorians had been registered as belonging to the Jacobite *ta'ifa*, the Jacobite metropolitan complained that they had begun taking communion with the Maronites. The Jacobite hierarchy in the city was concerned over this and petitioned the Porte to return the community to its proper fold. Reading between the lines, the Nestorians had apparently become Catholic and had chosen to worship with the Maronites rather than with the Jacobites who in the 1720s were experiencing a heated contest between "Catholic" and "traditionalist" factions. But this was stated neither in the complaint nor in the response ordering the Nestorians back to their "traditional" church. Rather what was appealed to was the internal regulations of the Nestorian *ta'ifa* itself, which had been mutually agreed upon by the lay membership previously. These stated that they would worship with the Jacobite clergy in the absence of their own.[77] The state had intervened, but only to the extent that internal rules of the *ta'ifa* required it to do so.

Another example of the official inattention to Christian religious differences also comes from the records of Aleppo's courts. In a testimony registered in September, 1642, representatives of the Greek Orthodox, Armenian, and the Jacobite *ta'ifa*s in the city agreed that all taxes, whether required by shari‘a or imperial decree, levied on the Christians of Aleppo

[75] Rejwan, *Jews of Irak*, pp. 177–84; David Sassoon, *A History of the Jews in Baghdad* (Letchworth, 1949), pp. 113–16. Avigdor Levy "*Millet* Politics: The Appointment of the Chief Rabbi in 1835" in *The Jews of the Ottoman Empire*. Edited by A. Levy (Princeton, NJ, 1994), pp. 425–38.

[76] Shlomo Deshen, "Baghdad Jewry in Late Ottoman Times: The Emergence of Social Classes and Secularization" in *Jews among Muslims: Communities in the Precolonial Middle East*. Edited by S. Deshen and W. Zenner (London, 1996), p. 189.

[77] Damascus, Aleppo Awamir al-sultaniyya, vol. II, p. 3.

would be evenly distributed among them. But if taxes were levied on a particular community, it alone would bear the responsibility for their collection and payment.[78] Curiously, no representation from the Maronite community was present. They would be present at all such subsequent registrations. There are two points to be made here. The government officials left it to the Christians to decide the fair distribution of the tax burden. They did not care whether the Christians formed a single collectivity for the purpose of taxation, the option exercised by the city's Jewish community, or were divided into smaller sectarian groups, as long as they paid what was owed. The sectarian divisions which were recognized by the governor and the qadi were those upon which the Christians themselves insisted. The Muslim authorities thus continued to treat Christians as constituting one "nation" (milla) even while recognizing what were to them the undoubtedly irrelevant, and most probably capricious, divisions upon which the Christians had insisted.

The question of what constituted a fair distribution of taxes in Aleppo did not end there. In 1754 the schedule by which the various communities paid their fair share of the total levied on the millat al-Nasara was in question. By that date, the established formula had the Rum paying 46.7 percent of the total levied on the Christians; the Maronites 23.3 percent; the Armenians and Jacobites, each 15 percent. The judge ruled the division of fiscal responsibilities should reflect the jizya totals for each community rather than being based on conflicting claims offered by the squabbling communities of their ability to pay.[79] The communities came back three years later represented by Hanna w. Shukri ᶜA'ida (see below in chapter 3) who was identified as the "chief deputy of the four communities" (tevaif-i erbaa baş vekili). ᶜA'ida stated under oath that the city's judges had ruled in 1720 and again in 1754 that the distribution of the tax burden should be based solely on the number of jizya payers in each community. This position was supported by fatwas issued by Sayyid Yusuf Efendi in Istanbul and al-Sayyid Ahmad al-Kawakibi in Aleppo. All four communities now agreed to the following distribution: Rum, 42.5 percent, Maronites 31.5 percent, Armenians 16 percent, Jacobites 10 percent. But in deference to the opinion of the muftis, the communities acceded that in the next and all subsequent years the percentages levied on each community would reflect the actual number of jizya payers.[80]

This haggling over the distribution of communal fiscal responsibilities suggests that the new ordering of the religious communities as millets was not enforced in the middle of the eighteenth century in Aleppo. But that should not surprise us as the distinction between ta'ifa and millet was still

---

[78] Damascus, Aleppo Court records, vol. XXIII, p. 147.
[79] Ibid., vol. LXXXV, pp. 130–31.
[80] Ibid., vol. LXXXVII, pp. 216–17.

not at all certain in Istanbul either.[81] Further evidence that the articulation of the *millet* system was still evolving came three years later in a case again involving ᶜA'ida. An order issued in response to a request (*arz-ı hal*) from the Armenian Patriarch in Istanbul 1757 dismissed "a certain Maronite (sic) named Hanna" from the post of the representative of the four Christian communities in Aleppo (*dört milletler vekili*). Significantly, *millet* had replaced *ta'ifa* in ᶜA'ida's title. According to the Patriarch's complaint, ᶜA'ida had used his position to lead the Armenians, who were a community "both small in number and impoverished" to the "religion of the Franks." The Patriarch asked that the post be given to Arakil Malkumoğlu, an Armenian presumably still loyal to orthodoxy. Bowing to the Patriarch's wishes, the order revoked Hanna's authority and established Arakil in his place.

The order reflects the existence of an Armenian *millet* with a patriarch resident in Istanbul able to effect some measure of political control over his flock in distant Aleppo. But it also explicitly acknowledged that the Jacobites and Maronites were independent communities, confusingly called *millet*s in the order and not subsumed into the Armenian *millet* as they would be by the end of the century. Furthermore, despite the patriarch's charge that ᶜA'ida had turned Armenians into "Franks," it was his financial malfeasance and political intrigues, not his Catholicism, which were cited in the Porte's orders for the revocation of his patent of office.[82] In short, the order indicates confusion over the full prerogatives of the *millet* system in the minds of the bureaucrats who had written it. This point is important to remember as we proceed to discuss the struggle between Catholics and Orthodox factions in the next chapter. It was that very inattention to internal differences among Christians by the Muslim governing elite in the Arab east that allowed the Unia (the acceptance of the spiritual primacy of the Latin Pope) to take root.

## Conclusion

The non-Muslims of the Ottoman Arab provinces represented a heterogeneous mix of sects and traditions that confused and confounded the Ottoman authorities and European visitors alike. But that heterogeneity was not nearly as pronounced as could be found elsewhere in the empire where language often served additionally to demarcate sectarian communities. In Istanbul, the Armenian *millet* spoke Armenian, the Orthodox *millet* Greek or Slavic tongues, the Jews *Judezmo* or Greek, and most Muslims spoke Turkish. By contrast, the communal identities in the Arab

---

[81] Paraskevas Konortas, "From Taife to Millet: Ottoman Terms for the Ottoman Greek Orthodox Community" in *Ottoman Greeks in the Age of Nationalism*. Edited by Dimitri Gondicas and Charles Issawi (Princeton, NJ, 1999), pp. 169–79.
[82] Istanbul, BOA, Ahkâm-ı Halep, vol. II, p. 203.

provinces, as was the case in Bosnia where a common Slavic dialect prevailed or parts of Anatolia where Orthodox and Armenian Christians had adopted Turkish as their mother tongue, arose from history and tradition. There were, of course, the obvious linguistic exceptions: Armenians, Sephardim, and Aramaic-speakers among the non-Muslims, Kurds and Turkomans on the cultural periphery of an Arabo-Muslim world. But the overwhelming majority of those living in the Fertile Crescent and Egypt spoke Arabic and shared a remarkably similar culture, regardless of their faith, even if "Arabness" (ᶜUruba) as a cultural and political identity had not as yet been articulated. Despite their cultural affinities, however, the various religious communities in the Arab world at the time of the arrival of Sultan Selim lived in a world governed by a tradition, which was imagined to be centuries old, that held the various religious communities should remain separate.

But it should be evident to the reader by now that "tradition" was a porous fabric in the first two centuries of Ottoman rule in the Arab lands rather than a barrier to change. True, the shariᶜa served as an anchor for those who would appeal to the Tradition of the Prophet (Sunna). But even that Tradition might be interpreted in seemingly contradictory ways, or even subverted, if the authorities felt it necessary. That is not to say the Ottoman state was a regime without a strong commitment to law. Indeed, few of their Muslim predecessors had been so scrupulous in drawing up law codes and posting them for all to read, as had the descendants of Osman. Rather, what was appealed to as tradition could change all the while those who were reshaping it insisted nothing had changed. A good example of that seeming conundrum was the creation of the millet system itself which ran counter to the well-established Islamic legal position that the communal affairs of the non-Muslims were of no consequence to the people of Islam.

Although many contemporary Western observers described the implementation of Ottoman justice as arbitrary and capricious, the authorities in Istanbul had an ordered universe in mind when they issued their writs and decrees. In that universe, the affairs of non-Muslims were important only if they impinged on the state's sovereignty or its revenues. This attitude worked to the advantage of some of the empire's Christians who would seek to propose an alternative "tradition." The primary policy concern of the Ottoman bureaucrats between the sixteenth and the eighteenth century was to maintain the status quo. With that rationale, most laws came as an ad hoc reaction to either external or internal threats.[83] Nevertheless, when framing a policy or issuing an edict, Ottoman officialdom had still to justify their decisions within an ordered universe governed by laws. Beginning in the

---

[83] See Rifa'at Abou-El-Haj, "Power and Social Order: The Uses of the Kanun" in The Ottoman City and its Parts. Edited by I. Bierman, R. Abou-El-Haj and D. Preziosi (New Rochelle, NY, 1991), pp. 77–99.

eighteenth century, the administrators of the Ottoman state could no longer ignore the changing social dynamics within the empire caused by contact with Europeans. Their understandable reaction was to seek to regulate what appeared to be subversion of the established social or economic order. The Europeans rarely mastered what the Ottomans had in mind as constituting that *status quo* (read "tradition"). They were, therefore, continually baffled and perplexed by Ottoman reactions to European pressures.[84] The non-Muslims of the empire, by contrast, understood fully the weight of "tradition" in Ottoman legal arguments and how it might be manipulated to their advantage.

[84] G. R. Bosscha Erdbrink, *At the Threshold of Felicity: Ottoman–Dutch Relations during the Embassy of Cornelis Calkoen at the Sublime Porte, 1726–1744* (Ankara, 1975); Daniel Goffman, *Britons in the Ottoman Empire 1642–1660* (Seattle, WA, 1998).

# CHAPTER 3

# Merchants and missionaries in the seventeenth century: the West intrudes

The Christian migrants to the Ottoman Arab cities in the sixteenth and seventeenth centuries were unlikely aware of the possibility of contact with their coreligionists from the West when they left their native villages. But the effects of the interaction between the two would be profound. At the start of the Ottoman period, the Europeans resident in the Arab cities of the Levant were few in number and resigned to trade within the framework of the existing political and commercial institutions. The majority of these early traders were Italians, but Frenchman, Catalans, and even an occasional German also found their way to the Muslim port cities of the Mediterranean Sea.[1] The centuries-old rhythms of the Levant trade began to change, however, as a result of Ottoman policies that reflected shifts in the sultan's geo-political ambitions. No one, not the Ottomans, nor the Europeans, and least of all the local non-Muslims, could have anticipated how those changes would eventually subvert the social hierarchy governing the relations between Muslims and non-Muslims in the Ottoman Arab world.

The Ottoman sultans were aware that trade might enrich the state's coffers, but they were also attuned to its possible use as a diplomatic weapon. Venice, the leading European trading nation in the Levant at the start of the sixteenth century, was often a rival to Ottoman ambitions in the eastern Mediterranean. To counter the longstanding commercial dominance of the "Most Serene Republic," the sultans sought to gain potential allies among the other Western powers by proffering special dispensations for trade, usually in the form of a lower rate of tariffs. Sultan Süleyman issued the first of such treaties (known as Capitulations in the West and İmtiyâzat in Ottoman Turkish) to France in 1535. Similar treaties with the Netherlands, England, Venice, and Austria followed. By the end of the eighteenth century, almost every European nation held a capitulatory treaty.[2] These treaties permitted European merchants to reside in specified Ottoman cities

---

[1] The most accessible account of the preOttoman trading world of the Levant remains Eliyahu Ashtor, *Levant Trade in the Later Middle Ages* (Princeton, NJ, 1983).

[2] Necdet Kurdakul, *Osmanlı devleti'nde ticaret antlaşmaları ve kapitülasyonlar* [Commercial Treaties and Capitulations in the Ottoman State] (Istanbul, 1981).

and to conduct trade with minimal tariffs and interference. This policy was not an innovation as Muslim rulers had long granted foreign non-Muslims the right to reside within their realms (*isti'man*), but the Ottomans, as was their wont, transformed what had been informal practice into an institution. The resident Europeans were not subject to the *jizya*, nor were they compelled to abide by Islamic law in issues of their personal status. They were, however, enjoined by the earliest treaties to conduct their business according to the precepts of Holy Law and to take all commercial cases involving Ottoman subjects, Muslim and non-Muslim alike, to the shari$^c$a courts.

The conduct of trade was becoming more complicated in the Levant by the close of the sixteenth century, even if on the surface little seemed changed from the Mamluk commercial regime. The most important challenge to the *status quo* originated in northwestern Europe, where merchants and bankers created joint-stock trading companies. Once established, these held a monopoly over their countrymen's participation in the region's trade. This development would eventually undermine the preexisting patterns by eliminating many of the old family trading houses and by providing those European merchants so organized with a potentially unified voice at the Ottoman court. The first of these joint-stock trading companies, the Turkey Company of Merchants (reorganized as the Levant Company in 1592), received its charter from Queen Elizabeth I in 1581 to represent English commercial interests exclusively in the Ottoman Empire. It was followed in 1625 by the Netherlands Directorate of Levant Trade and of Navigation in the Mediterranean (*Directie van den Levantschen Handel en de Navigatie op de Middellandsche Zee*). The French were slower to follow suit. But by 1666, Prime Minister Colbert had empowered a trading company with similar functions, granting it a monopoly over French trade in the Levant.[3] These companies proved remarkably resilient in sustaining a prolonged presence in the Ottoman trading cities, despite occasional disastrous downturns in the markets. In the process, they forever altered the practice of trade in the eastern Mediterranean.

Crucial to the European traders' commercial success was the willingness of the home governments to exert diplomatic pressure on their behalf in Istanbul. This change did not come easily and the merchants would suffer a century of trial and error in working out their relationship both to the sultan's divan and their own governments.[4] By the late seventeenth century, the confluence between national interests and company interests was finally recognized in northern Europe. Company stockholders often recommended who would serve as their country's ambassador to the sultan's court and as

---

[3] Niels Steensgaard, "Consuls and Nations in the Levant from 1570 to 1650" *Scandinavian Economic Review* 15 (1967): 13–55.
[4] Goffman, *Britons in the Ottoman Empire*.

consuls in the various treaty ports. What was good for the company was good for the nation. As every local commercial dispute between those who had such representation and the sultan's subjects became a diplomatic issue, the companies afforded their factors an instrument of political pressure and influence not available to individual merchants, whether Ottoman or European. The existence of resident European merchants and a network of diplomats to support them not only provided an unequal basis on which commerce in the Arab Levant would be conducted, it created opportunities for those Ottoman subjects who would collaborate with the company factors. Additionally, the presence of the European merchants, backed by treaty, opened the door to the Catholic missionary enterprise.

The Roman Catholic Church had maintained spotty correspondence with all the churches of the East in the aftermath of the Crusades. But with the Protestant Reformation threatening the "true faith" on the European continent, Rome began to expend efforts to convince the hierarchies of the Eastern churches to enter into communion with the Holy Father. To further that end, the Maronite College was established in Rome in 1584 to train seminarians from the Ottoman Arab lands to spread the Roman version of Christian dogma back home. The establishment of the Congregation *De Propaganda Fide* by Pope Gregory XV in 1622 further invigorated the mission to the East. The Congregation's objective was to extend Catholicism to the peoples of the lands newly encountered by European explorers and conquerors, as well as to bring already believing Christians into accordance with Roman doctrine and practice. Roman Catholic clerics and religious from Europe began to proselytize openly in the Ottoman Near East in the seventeenth century behind the protective wall of the Capitulations. They came with an invigorated sense of mission that had transformed their established, and more circumspect, role as guardians of the holy places in Palestine. That right had been negotiated from a position of political, if not moral, weakness by St. Francis of Assisi from the Ayyubid sultan al-Kamil in the thirteenth century and was honored by his Mamluk and Ottoman successors. The newer, more aggressive mode of attack in the seventeenth century arose out of Rome's perception that the balance of military power in the eastern Mediterranean had shifted with France now in the ascendancy.

Despite French diplomatic support, and initial Ottoman indifference, there were limits to the scope of missionary efforts. The Latins were well aware that attempts to convert Muslims would result in the execution of the converts and proselytizers alike and so concentrated their efforts among the empire's diverse Christian peoples. There would also be continued, if haphazard, efforts to evangelize Jews and the Yazidis, the latter whom Muslim jurists deemed to be outside the pale of the people of Islam.[5] But

---

[5] Damascus, Aleppo Court records, vol. XX, p. 375.

both peoples proved sterile ground for cultivation by the Catholic mission-aries. With non-Christians either inaccessible or stubbornly resistant, the full impact of the Catholic missions fell upon the region's Christians. The missionaries' goal in the Near East was to woo the hierarchy of the Eastern-rite churches into acceptance of the Pope's ultimate authority, thereby preempting any threat of the Protestant contagion.[6] It was a top-down strategy similar to the one that had been employed without success a century earlier with the Patriarch of Constantinople. That attempt had come to an abrupt end with the fall of the city to Sultan Fatih Mehmed in 1453 and the Latins discredited by their inaction in the collective memory of the Greek clergy and laity alike.

The ecumenical dialogue initiated in Syria was begun solely between clerics. But the unanticipated result was the emergence of a populist, reform movement with strong localist tendencies among Arabic-speaking Chris-tians in Syria. Nowhere in the Ottoman Arab lands was the influence of Europe on the native Christian population more visible in the seventeenth and eighteenth centuries than in the city of Aleppo. With the continual presence of both Western missionaries and merchants, the city served as the backdrop for most of the major skirmishes fought between the defenders of the old religious dispensation and those who would welcome the new. Aleppo's central position in the trade networks of the Levant also made possible the rise of the region's first Christian mercantile bourgeoisie. The two developments were, in fact, closely linked.

## Trade and the creation of a Christian bourgeoisie

Aleppo was at the end of the sixteenth century the leading commercial entrepôt linking the Fertile Crescent with Western Europe. With few other competitors, it would remain so until the rise of Beirut in the nineteenth century. Damascus, Aleppo's regional rival, lost its earlier preeminent role in East–West commerce with the collapse of the pepper trade. Increasing insecurity along its caravan route to Baghdad in the latter half of the sixteenth century also diminished its attraction to the Europeans. In their absence, a myth developed among the Muslim Damascenes that no Europeans had ever been suffered to reside there. Those Europeans who did find their way to the city had to do so circumspectly, donning eastern dress and forgoing the riding of horses. Elsewhere, European merchants might visit Cairo, Mosul, or Baghdad, but few were resident until the nineteenth century. The inhabitants of Aleppo, alone among the fabled caravan cities of the interior Fertile Crescent, had prolonged experience of Europeans living among them. That reality created both opportunities and challenges

---

[6] Bernard Heyberger, *Les chrétiens du proche-orient* and his "Le Catholicisme Tridentin au Levant (XVII<sup>e</sup>–XVIII<sup>e</sup> siècles)" *Mélanges de l'École Française de Rome* 101 (1989): 897–909.

which gave the city's Christian inhabitants a historical trajectory unique among the Ottoman Arab cities until the nineteenth century when European influences became pervasive everywhere.

From its beginning, the fate of the Catholic enterprise in Aleppo was tied to the emergence of a Christian mercantile class that would prove receptive to the new dispensation. Western visitors to Aleppo in the late sixteenth and early seventeenth centuries were fascinated by the multiplicity of Christian sects that they encountered there. They were, however, not impressed with the economic conditions of the local Christian Arabs. William Biddulph, an English visitor to the city in 1600, wrote:

The Greeks in Aleppo are very poore, for they are there, for the most part, but Brokers or Bastages, that is, Porters; and many of their women are light as water, maintayning their husbands, themselves, and their families, by prostituting their bodies to others. And their own husbands are often times their Pandars or procurers to bring them Customers.[7]

Five years after Biddulph, Pedro Teixeira visited Aleppo and concurred about the impoverished state of the local Christians.[8] Both Biddulph and Teixeira contrasted the poverty of the Syrian Christians with the wealth of Aleppo's Jewish community. But they were even more impressed by the affluence of, and influence wielded by, the Armenian merchants from New Julfa in Iran who were resident in the city.

The Iranian Armenian merchants held a monopoly over the export of their nation's silk to the Mediterranean and their entrepôt of choice in the late sixteenth and early seventeenth centuries was Aleppo. Enjoying their patronage, Armenian miniaturists, artisans, and architects in the city produced a cultural renaissance that was unequaled elsewhere among Ottoman Armenians. Azariya, the Catholicos of Sis (1581–1601), moved his see from Cilicia to Aleppo in the year before his death, emphasizing the city's growing importance to the spiritual and cultural life of Ottoman Armenians. The transfer of the see of Sis to Aleppo transformed the city into a potential, ecclesiastical rival to Istanbul as the spiritual heart of the western Armenian diaspora and provided a major boost to the civic pride of the city's Armenians.[9] In gratitude, the Armenian merchants financed the construction of the Church of the Forty Martyrs (*Surp Karsunk*) in 1616 to house their catholicos.[10] The construction of new churches was, of course, a violation of the Pact of ᶜUmar and we have a hint that it cost the Armenians dearly to build their cathedral. The Polish-Armenian traveler Simeon, who visited Aleppo shortly after it was consecrated, reported that the merchants

[7] Purchas, *His Pilgrimes*, vol. VIII, p. 275.
[8] Pedro Teixeira, *Travels of Pedro Teixeira* (London, 1902), vol. IX, p. 116.
[9] Kevork Bardakjian, "The Rise of the Armenian Patriarchate of Constantinople" in *Christians and Jews in the Ottoman Empire*. Edited by B. Braude and B. Lewis (New York, 1982), vol. I, pp. 89–100.
[10] Sanjian, *Armenian Communities of Syria*, p. 261; Taoutel, "Watha'iq" vol. 42, p. 219.

of Aleppo had recently provided their catholicos with the princely sum of 40,000 *ghurush* in order to provide government officials with gifts.[11] Although he did not specify why the Armenians needed to win the approval of the authorities, buying their acquiescence in the building of the cathedral seems a plausible explanation.

As important as the Julfa Armenians were in the silk trade of the seventeenth century, Christians of all sects were establishing a niche for themselves in Aleppo's commerce. Large-scale trade, whether local or long distance, had been at the start of the seventeenth century in the hands of prominent Muslim traders and the Julfa Armenians. Armenians whose names identified them with Ottoman towns, for example Arapgiri, Vanlı, Erzurumlu, also appeared as traders in the court records of Aleppo as the century progressed. In addition to the traveling merchants who required some capital to operate, individuals could make a start in trade by acting as commercial agents in partnership agreements, known as *mudaraba*, in which one person would supply the capital for the venture and the other would do the actual trading.[12] By the middle of the seventeenth century, Christian Arabs began to appear with frequency in the registration of *mudaraba* contracts as agents. By the start of the eighteenth century, they had largely supplanted Ottoman Armenians in that role.[13]

Dr. Russell wrote in the eighteenth century that only Christians would travel from Aleppo on trading ventures, as Muslims preferred to stay at home.[14] The court records show that Muslims continued to travel with the merchant caravans during the period when he was resident in the city, but the number of cases involving Christians traders financed by Muslim investors suggests the foundation for Russell's stereotype. Unfortunately, these early commercial adventurers were registered typically only with a patronymic in the court records and without the family name that would be the norm for most entries from the eighteenth century onward. We cannot be sure, as such, if the Christian Arab agents active in the seventeenth and early eighteenth centuries were the founders of the merchant dynasties that dominated Aleppo's commerce in the latter half of the eighteenth century. But it is tempting to speculate that they were.

Before the Christian merchants could break into the east–west trade in a significant way, they needed patrons more powerful than their Muslim partners. That would not be possible until the Ottoman sultans modified the conditions under which their subjects might serve the European merchants as their translators and agents. Throughout the seventeenth century, the European consuls in the Levant had utilized several strategies to create a

11 Polonyalı Simeon, *Seyahatname*, pp. 134–35.
12 Bruce Masters, *The Origins of Western Economic Dominance in the Middle East: Mercantilism and the Islamic Economy in Aleppo, 1600–1750* (New York, 1988), pp. 50–53.
13 *Ibid.*, pp. 62–63.
14 Russell, *Natural History*, vol. II, p. 56.

pool of translators who would facilitate their dealings with local government officials and merchants. The first was to employ either Sephardic Jews
or Levantine Catholics (i.e. descendants of Venetian, Genoese, or Cypriot
merchant families who had resided in the Muslim world for generations).
The Ottoman authorities generally recognized individuals from these two
groups as being subjects of European powers, even if that connection were
historically remote, with the rights of extraterritoriality that entailed. The
alternative to hiring these dubious Europeans was to send out boys from
the home country who would be "raised in the trade" and learn the
prerequisite local languages – Arabic, Armenian, and Turkish. These
youngsters, nicknamed *"Giovanni di lingua"* by factors of the English
Levant Company, would then be expected to serve out their lives in the
employ of the sponsoring trading companies. Recruitment proved difficult,
however, and many of the boys who did arrive failed to master the necessary
languages despite periods of prolonged residence in the Levant.[15]

A third alternative was to hire locals, but these rarely won the Porte's
acquiescence to their claim to foreign protection. Without such a refuge,
local non-Muslims were subject to the vagaries and extortion of often-venial
provincial administrators. Saddled with that liability, the Europeans were
extremely hesitant to employ them. This situation changed for the better, at
least as far as Ottoman Christians and Jews were concerned, with the
sultan's commercial treaties with France in 1673 and with England in 1675.
In these, and in all subsequent treaties negotiated with the Ottomans, the
Europeans were permitted to designate Ottoman subjects as translators
("dragoman" in English/ *tercüman* in Ottoman Turkish). While that in itself
was not new, these treaties explicitly gave rights to the translators comparable to those the Europeans enjoyed, even while asserting that they were to
remain the sultan's subjects. These included exemptions from the *jizya* and
the irregular taxes imposed either by the central treasury or the local
governors on the dragoman's confessional community. Furthermore, the
treaties established that those individuals holding the *berats* (patents) of
office would pay the same customs duties as their European patrons.
Ottoman customs regulations routinely stipulated that Muslims be charged
3 percent of the value of the goods they were transporting while *dhimmi*s
had to pay 5 percent. European merchants from favored nations such as
England and France, and their dragomans, paid the same rate as
Muslims.[16]

The Anglo-Ottoman Treaty of 1675 also entitled dragomans, as was the
case with the English merchants, to take any commercial dispute with
ordinary Ottoman subjects involving money or goods worth over 4,000 *akçe*
(the equivalent of between 33 and 40 *ghurush*, depending on the date) to the

[15] London, PRO, SP 105/117, p. 41, November 16, 1731.
[16] Istanbul, BOA, MM 3462, p. 281.

Porte. There the case would be heard in the presence of the ambassador of the country who had issued the dragoman's *berat*. As this was a relatively small sum, the treaties ensured that almost any commercial dispute involving the merchants or their dragomans would end up in Istanbul. Having extended this right to those who were still legally Ottoman subjects, Ottoman judges and bureaucrats consistently tried to limit the commercial activities of the dragomans to insure that the privilege was not abused. But as W. Pollard, the British consul, wrote from Aleppo in 1754 it was impossible to find anyone competent to serve as dragoman who would willingly give up the opportunities of trade to become a full-time employee of the consulate.[17]

The promise of the coveted patent of a dragoman is often cited as being one of the key inducements for Orthodox Christians to apostatize to Catholicism.[18] This was perhaps true in the coastal towns of Sidon and Tyre where the French trading presence predominated. But even there, the French generally preferred to employ Maronites who did not need to be bribed into Catholicism. The largest trading presence in Aleppo from the second half of the seventeenth century to the mid-eighteenth century, however, was the English Levant Company. There was a half-hearted attempt by some of the English factors to introduce Protestantism into the religious mix of Aleppo in the late seventeenth century.[19] Afterwards, the English remained largely indifferent to their employees' religion, unless they perceived some conspiracy arising from a specific ethnic group against Company interests. They were particularly suspicious of Jews in this regard, but they accused Armenian merchants of conspiring on occasion in underhand commercial deals as well.[20]

Sephardic Jews and Levantine Christians provided the majority of the dragomans in the Levant Company's employ in Aleppo in the years leading up to the treaty of 1675. But due to their connections to trading diasporas outside the Levant, the English merchants viewed them warily as potential competitors. An alternative after 1675 could be found in the local Christians who – thanks to the Catholic mission schools – had the prerequisite technical skills of a competent dragoman: Italian, Arabic, and bookkeeping. A *berat* issued in 1688 established that Ilyas walad Jirjiz would henceforth serve as the dragoman of the English consul in Aleppo, replacing Pietro who had died. This Ilyas, his sons, and servants (*hizmetkâr*) were from that time on exempt from all regular and irregular taxes. Unfortunately, no family name is given for either man but their Christian names suggest a Christian Arab replaced a Levantine. Ilyas died in 1720 and was

17 London, PRO, SP 110/29, p. 116, May 2, 1754.
18 Haddad, *Syrian Christians*, pp. 32–38.
19 Holt, *Egypt and the Fertile Crescent*, p. 245.
20 London, PRO SP 110/20 p. 89, July 5, 1696; SP 110/23, p. 98, June 22, 1704; SP 105/116, p. 3, December 20, 1710, p. 89, February 25, 1713, pp. 225–26, July 23, 1718.

replaced by Yorgaki veled Ceraki. He is identified elsewhere in Ottoman documents as Androniko-oğlu Yorgaki veled Ceraki and was presumably the son of Signore Gerasimo Andronico, a Levantine of Cypriot origin, who appeared regularly in the Levant Company's correspondence in the first two decades of the eighteenth century as its chief dragoman.[21]

The Levant Company's factors were hesitant initially to employ local Christian Arabs with "papist" leanings for "fear that the Romish Church will give sanctuary to those villains."[22] Nonetheless, Elias Facher (Ilyas Fakhr) was hired as "second dragoman" to replace Giuseppe Pisani in 1724. Fakhr became chief-dragoman (baş tercüman) for the British consul in Aleppo in February 1727 with the death of Gerasimo Andronico. Ilyas Fakhr was originally from Tripoli where his uncle was the Greek Orthodox Metropolitan and he had two brothers active in trade in Alexandria and Leghorn (Livorno). All three brothers were also deeply committed to the Catholic cause as was their uncle.[23] Catholic Arabs would dominate the post of dragoman in Aleppo throughout the remainder of the eighteenth century. There were simply few other options as most of the city's Christian merchants had become Catholics, loyal to one or the other of the various Uniate rites in the city. Catholic young men were also typically better educated than their Orthodox contemporaries and even the wary Britons realized the benefits of employing them.

In addition to the Fakhrs, the ʿA'ida clan was one of the earliest, and most prominent of the Aleppo Catholic merchant families to emerge into the light of the extant historical record. Shukri ʿA'ida first appears in the records of the Levant Company in 1734.[24] Following that entry, he is mentioned frequently as one of the leading local middlemen engaged in the sale of Syrian silk to the company factors. Shukri entered the Company's employ sometime before 1753. In that year, he lost his patent as dragoman after moving to Istanbul, where the Ottoman authorities charged he was engaged solely in trade. Shukri returned to Aleppo in 1756, and again entered the service of the British consul as his dragoman – a post he held until his death in 1760.[25] Shukri ʿA'ida's son, Jirjis, was registered as a dragoman of the British consulate in Aleppo in 1747.[26] He was not able to enjoy his position for long as Aleppo's governor arrested him in 1750. Consul Pollard wrote that Jirjis had been falsely charged with conspiring with the governor of Baghdad to sell in Aleppo goods that had been appropriated illegally from the customs house in Baghdad. Pollard sus-

[21] Istanbul, BOA, Ecnebi vol. XXXV, pp. 57, 70.
[22] London, PRO, SP 105/116, p. 119, June 9, 1715.
[23] London, PRO, SP 105/116, p. 480, November 17, 1724; Istanbul, BOA, Ecnebi vol. XXXV, p. 76; Heyberger, Les chrétiens du proche-orient, p. 133.
[24] London, PRO, SP 110/118, p. 46, September 18, 1734.
[25] Istanbul, BOA, Ecnebi vol. XXXV, pp. 95–103.
[26] London, PRO, SP 110/29, p. 116, n.d.; Istanbul, BOA, Ecnebi vol. XXXV, p. 89.

pected that the instigator behind the arrest was Yusuf Dib, another Aleppo merchant serving as dragoman for the Levant Company. Dib, who remained loyal to orthodoxy, had been able to effect the arrest of several members of the city's Catholic clergy and laity in 1749. Pollard had reprimanded Dib for doing this, but he had been warned, in turn, by Sir James Porter, the British ambassador in Istanbul, not to intervene in internal Christian affairs. Nevertheless, Pollard persisted and after he paid a bribe of seven thousand, five hundred *ghurush*, Jirjis was released from prison in 1751.[27] Shortly thereafter, he was again enrolled as a dragoman for the British and became their chief translator.

The rivalry between the ʿAʾida and the Dib families, undoubtedly, had economic as well as theological roots. Members of both families continued in British service well past 1751, with Jirjis' brothers, Antun and Mikhaʾil serving as dragomans until their deaths, respectively in 1760 and 1762. Jirjis' son, Ilyas, assumed the role of chief dragoman for the British consul after his father's death in 1777. Jirjis' grandson, Ilyas Antun, in his turn, later held the post of dragoman at the British embassy in Istanbul.[28] The ʿAʾida family amassed a considerable fortune as Shukri ʿAʾida appears in the court records as a prominent and frequent investor in real estate in Aleppo in the decade of the 1750s, as did his son Jirjis in the 1760s.[29] The Dib family also dabbled in many other financial activities besides translating. Yusuf subleased the *malikâne* (tax-farm) for the village of Batiyya for a number of years in the 1750s.[30] Yusuf's son, Mikhaʾil, served as dragoman for the British until his death in 1758.[31] After that date, the Dib family fortunes seemed to have declined precipitously as they vanished from the extant documents, British or Ottoman, from the last decades of the century. Members of the family reappeared in the historical record in the nineteenth century when Jirjis Dib (alternately written Adib) served as the dragoman for the British in 1836. Hanna Dib, his brother, was consul for the Greek Kingdom during the period of the Egyptian occupation in the 1830s.[32] The possession of the latter post suggests that the family remained loyal to orthodoxy. If so, they were one of the few Christian merchant families in Aleppo to do so.

Twentieth-century Turkish scholars have often characterized the protégé

[27] Istanbul, BOA, Ecnebi vol. XXXVI/2 , p. 7; London, PRO, SP 110/29, pp. 25–29, April 18, 1749; p. 34, September 25, 1749; p. 40, June, 3 1750; pp. 49–51, June 11, 1750, p. 86, June 14, 1751.
[28] Istanbul, BOA, Ecnebi vol. XXXV, pp. 91, 94, 104, 109, 110, 113, 118, 123, 127; Ali İhsan Bağış, *Osmanlı Ticaretinde Gayri Müslimler* [Non-Muslims in Ottoman Commerce] (Ankara, 1983), p. 128.
[29] Abraham Marcus, *The Middle East on the Eve of Modernity: Aleppo in the Eighteenth Century* (New York, 1989), p. 366.
[30] Damascus, Aleppo Court records, vol. LXXVIII, p. 108; vol. LXXX, p. 162.
[31] Istanbul, BOA, Ecnebi vol. XXXV, p. 113.
[32] Naʿum Bakhkhash, *Akhbar Halab* [The Events of Aleppo]. Edited by Fr. Yusuf Qushaqji, 3 vols. (Aleppo, 1987–92), vol. I, pp. 45, 79, 151.

system as an iniquity which soured Christian–Muslim relations by alienating Christians from their status as the sultan's subjects and providing
them with unfair trade advantages over their Muslim competitors.[33] Many
of the critics of the protégé system also point to its wholesale abuse for
either monetary or political gain by the European consuls who obtained
*berat*s far in excess of the numbers to which they were entitled. The
Ottoman bureaucrats were well aware of these potential inequities inherent
in the institution, however. To counter the possibilities of abuse, they
consistently invoked two principles: the banning of *beratlı*s (those holding
patents) from trade and the enforcement of the limit placed on the number
of individuals who could legitimately be employed by a European consul.

The first issue was stressed in repeated orders to governors and judges
throughout Syria. When Jirjis ʿAʾida was arrested in 1750, the official
charge was that he had engaged in trade in contravention of Britain's treaty
with the sultan. In another suit involving ʿAʾida in 1758, the judge in
Aleppo was again reminded by the sultan's divan that trade was off limits to
someone holding an imperial patent for translating.[34] There was, however,
a conundrum in the state's policy; the ban on trade was never formally
incorporated into the language of the treaties, despite the frequent assertions by Ottoman officials that it had been.[35] Furthermore, the right to
appeal to Istanbul all commercial disputes involving sums greater than four
thousand *akçe* seemingly served as an invitation to trade. Nevertheless, in
such cases brought on behalf of dragomans in various Syrian cities by their
sponsoring consuls in the middle of the eighteenth century, the authorities
in Istanbul often turned them back to the local courts to be administered by
the qadis under the regulations of the shariʿa. This practice saw a dramatic
reversal in the second half of the century when imperial orders routinely
reminded the local governors in Syria of the dragomans' right of appeal to
Istanbul.[36] It was undoubtedly European pressure at the Porte that effected
a stricter adherence to the treaties and there are numerous indicators that
Ottoman officialdom deeply resented the interference. In 1809, Ottoman
negotiators finally managed to have a clause inserted in a draft of a secret
protocol with the United Kingdom that dragomans could not engage in
trade, even while acknowledging the seemingly contradictory point that all
the provisions of the treaty of 1675 were still in effect.[37] It was, however,

---

[33] Bağış, *Gayri Müslimler*; Gülnihâl Bozkurt, *Gayrimüslim Osmanlı vatandaşlarının hukukî durumu* [The Legal Status of Non-Muslim Ottoman Citizens] *(1839–1914)* (Ankara, 1989); Salâhi Sonyel, *Minorities and the Destruction of the Ottoman Empire* (Ankara, 1993).

[34] Istanbul, BOA, Ecnebi vol. XXXVI/2, pp. 7, 64–65.

[35] Bruce Masters, "Ottoman Policies toward Syria in the 17th and 18th Centuries" in *The Syrian Land in the 18th and 19th Century*. Edited by T. Philipp (Stuttgart, 1992), pp. 18–21.

[36] Istanbul, BOA, Ahkâm-ı Halep, vol. III, pp. 46, 56; vol. VI, pp. 54, 73.

[37] Istanbul, BOA, Ecnebi vol. XXXV, pp. 154–56; English translation in J. C. Hurewitz, *Diplomacy in the Near and Middle East: a Documentary Record: 1535–1914* (Princeton, NJ, 1955), pp. 81–84.

never ratified by parliament, having been acceded to by Britain only as a temporary exigency of the Napoleonic Wars.

The Porte, having granted extraordinary privileges to the dragomans, showed an ongoing concern to enforce the limit on the number of those enjoying them as stipulated by treaty, i.e. four dragomans for each consul, with each dragoman given the right to employ two "servants" (*hizmetkâr*). These "servants" were, in effect, commercial agents who might be entitled by their own patents to take up residence in another city. Provincial governors were periodically required to make a survey of the protégés and to forward the names of all those holding *berats* to Istanbul where they would be checked against the registers for each individual country. In 1743, such a census reported 7 *beraths* working for the British consul in Aleppo, 4 with the French, and 6 with the consul of the Netherlands. The governor's response to an order in 1795 for yet another tally of those protected in Aleppo recorded for Britain 13 dragomans, Netherlands 10, France 6, Sicily and Sweden 5 each, Prussia, Spain, and Dubrovnik 2 each, Denmark 1. Additionally, there were 69 individuals listed by name in the document as being *hizmetkâr*s to the dragomans, for a total of 115 individuals holding *berats*.[38] Although the number of dragomans in the case of most of the nations represented exceeded the limit set by the treaties, the total did not approach the figure of 1,500 persons often cited by later historians as being enrolled as European protégés in Aleppo at that date.[39]

The majority of those who held the post of dragoman in Syria in the eighteenth century were Catholics. It is misleading, however, to suggest that they became Catholics in order to win the *berat* of the dragoman. It clearly was not a prerequisite for the job as there were other dragomans who were Jews or adherents to the orthodox factions. While the French had used the promise of protection as an inducement to conversion in the seventeenth century, many of their most prominent protégés in eighteenth-century Syria were Maronites. Although some Melkite/Rum Catholics would enter into French service, the majority of those from that community in Aleppo who obtained *berats* derived their protégé status through service to the consuls of Britain and the Netherlands, two nations with little interest in cultivating Catholics. Other opportunities were presented by newer arrivals on Syria's diplomatic scene: Austria, Prussia, Sweden, Sicily, and Spain. Sephardic Jews typically represented these latter countries in Aleppo and it is unlikely whether they cared which theology their dragomans espoused.

[38] Istanbul, BOA, Ahkâm-ı Halep, vol. I, pp. 41–42; Rhoads Murphey, "Conditions of Trade in the Eastern Mediterranean: An Appraisal of Eighteenth-Century Documents from Aleppo" *Journal of the Economic and Social History of the Orient* 33 (1990): 38; Istanbul, BOA, Cevdet Hariciye, 7670.

[39] Kamil al-Ghazzi, *Nahr al-dhahab fi ta'rikh Halab* [The River of Gold in the History of Aleppo] 3 vols. (Aleppo, 1922–26), vol. III, p. 311. Halil İnalcık, "Imtiyazat" in *Encyclopedia of Islam*, 2nd edn.

It would also be wrong to assume that these men became rich solely through their dragoman connections as we learn of dragomans who never emerged as prominent merchants. Rather, as Christian or Jewish merchants became wealthy, they sought to secure that wealth by enrolling as a dragoman for a foreign consul. This strategy among the non-Muslims paralleled the attempts by the newly emerging Muslim elite in Aleppo to be registered as *ashraf*, a status that also conferred certain political and economic advantages.[40] A dragoman's patent enhanced the financial position of those who succeeded in obtaining one by giving them a legal defense they would not otherwise enjoy. But the position in itself did not ensure financial and commercial success. Although the *beratlı*s were important in both the economic life of the region and the internal politics of their communities, it is erroneous to focus on them alone. The late eighteenth century saw the emergence of a Christian mercantile bourgeoisie in Aleppo and the Syrian port cities who were not connected directly to a foreign power. Many actually replaced the European merchants as their presence in the Arab Levant contracted in the latter part of the eighteenth century. But whether they worked hand in glove with the Europeans or not, almost all of these merchants were Catholics. To understand how trade and Catholicism became so closely intertwined, we need to survey briefly the fate of the Catholic enterprise in the Ottoman Arab lands.

## Between Constantinople and Rome: the emergence of a Catholic Arab people

The capitulatory treaty signed between France and the Ottoman Empire in 1604 granted Roman Catholic pilgrims and priests the right to visit the holy places in Palestine and permission for French clerics to take up residence in Jerusalem. The Ottomans had routinely renewed the privileges negotiated by St. Francis, but the insertion of France as the guardian of the holy places was an innovation. The treaty of 1673 extended diplomatic status to priests and religious serving the French consuls in "Galata, Izmir, Sidon, Alexandria and wherever else Frenchmen resided" under the terms of the capitulatory treaties.[41] These agreements provided the legal pretext under which Latin priests would enter the sultans' realms, openly wearing their clerical garb. France was recognized in these protocols as enjoying pride of place among the Christian nations represented at the Porte. It would persist in its role as the official protector of the Empire's Christians, and especially Catholics, until Russia challenged that preeminence and claimed the right to

---

[40] Jean-Pierre Thiecke, "Décentralisation ottomane et affirmation urbaine à Alep à la fin du XVIIIe siècle" in *Passion d'Orient*. Edited by Gilles Kepel (Paris, 1992), pp. 165–69.
[41] Kurdakul, *Ticaret antlaşmaları*, pp. 68–83.

protect the empire's Orthodox Christians after the treaty of Küçük Kaynarca in 1774.[42]

Beyond French intentions and papal ambitions, a necessary condition for the success of the missionary effort was the official Ottoman attitude toward the transfer of loyalties by the *dhimmi* population from patriarch to pope. Initially, the authorities had no clear intent to limit the missionaries' activities other than to be wary of any change in the status of a non-Muslim which might undermine either the sultan's sovereignty or his tax base. As noted above, the established Muslim legal tradition recognized no distinction between the Christian sects. Rather the prevalent response of Muslim religious scholars to cases involving the defection of an individual Christian from one sect to another was to invoke the saying ascribed to the Prophet, "Unbelief constitutes one nation" and dismiss the complaint.[43] The officials in the sultan's entourage in Istanbul, in contrast to the nonchalance of the Islamic legal establishment, had to be more keenly aware of the internecine nature of Christian communal politics. They had little other choice with the Orthodox Patriarchate (*patrikhane*) figuratively, if no longer literally, on their back doorstep. But for most of the seventeenth century, the Porte remained neutral in Christian squabbles and at times even moved to stop Orthodox harassment of Catholic priests in Palestine and the Balkans.[44]

Abetted by this official ambivalence, the Latin Catholics established Aleppo as their headquarters for the Syrian mission after initially considering Damascus. That choice was conditioned in no small part by the fact that there was no consul resident in the latter city. The first Catholic missionaries to take up permanent residence in Aleppo arrived in 1627. They found their warmest response from the Armenians. In the late sixteenth century, the Catholicos of Sis, Azariya, received Leonardo Abel, the emissary of Pope Gregory XII, and signed a profession of the Catholic faith. His reign set in motion a tradition of Armenian hospitality toward the Catholic missionaries in Syria that would last throughout the seventeenth century.[45] The ranking Greek Orthodox clergyman in Aleppo, the Metropolitan Meletius (Malatyus) Karma, also initially welcomed the Roman Catholics. Karma allowed the Jesuit, Jérôme Queyrot, to open a school in his residence in Judayda in 1629. When Meletius was elevated to the patriarchate of Antioch in 1634, he invited the missionaries to establish a second school in Damascus.[46]

There are signs not all the Christians of Aleppo greeted the Catholic

---

[42] Roderic Davison, "Russian Skill and Turkish Imbecility: The Treaty of Kuchuk Kainardji Reconsidered" reprinted in *Essays in Ottoman and Turkish History, 1774–1923*. Edited by Roderic Davison (Austin, TX, 1990), pp. 29–50.

[43] Damascus, Aleppo Court records, vol. XX, p. 28 and vol. LXXX, p. 179.

[44] Goffman, "Ottoman *millet*s," pp. 139–41, 144–46.

[45] Taoutel, "Watha'iq" vol. 42, p. 220.

[46] Heyberger, *Les chrétiens du proche-orient*, pp. 391–92; Frazee, *Catholics and Sultans*, pp. 132–33.

missionaries with open arms. Several Latin priests were arrested in 1633 by the city's governor for holding religious services in their residence, a charge which could only have been initiated by their fellow Christians. The priests were soon released after the European consuls in the city protested their arrest. They resumed administering the sacraments to the city's Christians in the Armenian cathedral. Following this incident, France's ambassador in Istanbul succeeded in convincing the Porte to issue a *berat* naming the Catholic priests in Aleppo as chaplains to the consul.[47] The number of those claiming to be chaplains must have raised more than a few eyebrows in the governor's *saray* (seraglio), however. In 1680, the French consul, the chevalier Laurent d'Arvieux reported that there were twenty-four Latin Catholic priests and friars in the city but only fourteen resident French merchants.[48] It would seem that the French merchants' spiritual needs in the city were extremely well attended.

French activism in support of the missionary activity substantially increased with the consulship of François Picquet in Aleppo (1652–62). Picquet was the first to link France's economic and political interests in the Ottoman Empire directly to the Catholic cause. His consulship also coincided with a growing interest among the leadership of all the Eastern churches for dialogue with Roman Catholic clerics.[49] In 1647, a council of Damascene laity and clergy elected an Aleppine, Makarios (Makaryus) III al-Za°im, as Patriarch of Antioch. He had previously served as metropolitan in Aleppo where he often hosted the Latin missionaries. Although he publicly made no move to confirm it, the Latin priests were confident of his support, as well as that of Khachadur, the reigning Armenian Catholicos of Sis. Consul Picquet boasted in his dispatches to Paris that all three senior clerics of the Eastern churches in Aleppo, i.e. Orthodox (*Rum*), Armenian, and Jacobite (*Suryani*), were now "Catholic."[50] It is, however, not at all clear that he was correct in his assessment.

The Latins' greatest success in terms of numbers of converts came among the Jacobites. By the end of the seventeenth century, one missionary source estimated that three-quarters of the community in Aleppo were Catholics.[51] The lists kept by the missionaries of their converts also indicate that the Jacobites accepted Catholicism in numbers disproportionate to their share of the total Christian population in the city during the first century of Catholic missionary activity. We can speculate that the Jacobites, who were largely a community of recent migrants, might have been more open to a

[47] Frazee, *ibid.*, p. 133.

[48] Warren Lewis, *Levantine Adventurer: The Travels and Mission of the Chevallier d'Arvieux, 1653–1697* (New York, 1962), p. 41; Heyberger, *Les chrétiens du proche-orient*, pp. 285–94.

[49] Georges Goyau, "Le rôle religieux du consul François Picquet dans Alep (1652–1662)" *Revue d'Histoire des Missions* 12 (1935): 160–98.

[50] Frazee, *Catholics and Sultans*, pp. 133–36.

[51] Antoine Rabbath (ed.). *Documents inédits pour servir à l'histoire du Christianisme en Orient*, 2 vols. (Paris, 1905–10). Reprinted (New York, 1973), vol. II, pp. 87–88.

new spiritual dispensation as they were physically in new surroundings and far removed from their traditional hierarchy. A Catholic faction emerged among the Greek Orthodox community in Aleppo and Damascus as well, but it is tempting to see the Rum's interest in the Catholic option as coming at least initially as an expression of a strong localist sentiment, rather than an ideological shift to the Latins. The Aleppo community was much wealthier than their Damascene counterparts and they must have resented the preponderant voice the laity and clergy of Damascus exercised in choosing those who would sit on the throne of Antioch. That rivalry surfaced in 1672 with the death of Patriarch Makarios III al-Za'im.

Initially, things went well for the Aleppines as the Orthodox of Damascus elected as patriarch, Makarios' grandson Qustantin who took the patriarchal name of Kyrillos (Kirilyus), even though he was, according to some accounts, still a minor.[52] Kyrillos' opponents feared the growing assertiveness of the Catholic party among the Rum of Syria and appealed to the Patriarch of Constantinople to nullify the election as they argued Kyrillos was too immature to contain the Latin contagion. In response, Constantinople replaced Kyrillos with Neophytos (Nawifitus), the nephew of Euthymios (Ifthimiyus) al-Saqizi who had preceded Makarios III on the patriarchal throne. This action which marked the first direct intervention of the Ecumenical Patriarch into the affairs of the see of Antioch was not without irony, as it was Neophytos who would turn out to have Catholic sympathies. The struggle between the two men did not end there as Kyrillos al-Za'im had strong support among the Rum merchants of Aleppo and their money was freely expended on his behalf in both Damascus and Istanbul. Unable to compete financially in what had become a bidding war for the office of patriarch, Neophytos abdicated in Kyrillos' favor in 1681. All was not completely secure, however, as Kyrillos' opponents were able to effect his dismissal twice more during a reign which lasted until 1720.[53]

In the opening salvo of the campaign to depose Neophytos, a large delegation, identified simply as belonging to the *ta'ifat al-Rum*, affirmed before the chief qadi of Aleppo on September 3, 1678 that Neophytos, whom they acknowledged as their reigning patriarch, was ignorant of the rules of their faith and did not understand Arabic. Citing affidavits registered at court in the previous year, they claimed he had also taken money from the community illegally. The Rum then attested that their true patriarch was Kyrillos who was present at court. The delegation added for good measure that Kyrillos knew all the rules of their faith, spoke excellent Arabic, and possessed outstanding morals.[54] The registry of their affidavit is

[52] Neale, *History of the Eastern Church*, p. 183.
[53] *Ibid.*, pp. 183–84; Heyberger, *Les chrétiens du proche-orient*, p. 85; Robert Haddad, "Constantinople over Antioch, 1516–1724: Patriarchal Politics in the Ottoman Era" *Journal of Ecclesiastical History* 41 (1990): 217–38.
[54] Damascus, Aleppo Court records, vol. XXXIV, p. 39.

significant on several counts. Firstly, the fact that it took place at all indicates that the representative of the Ottoman state, the chief qadi of Aleppo, was still unconcerned as to the process by which the Christians chose their leaders. If the Rum of Aleppo were willing to assert that Kyrillos was properly their patriarch, he was. It did not seemingly matter that another man had been confirmed in that position by an imperial patent. Secondly, among Neophytos' more telling alleged failings was his ignorance of Arabic. This was undoubtedly an exaggeration. Although his family was originally from Chios, (hence his designation in Arabic *Saqizi*, or *Sakızlı* in Turkish) he had grown up in Damascus where he was educated by the Jesuits. It is doubtful that they would have neglected training such a potentially prominent protégé as the nephew of the patriarch in proper Arabic. Nevertheless, the charge served to accentuate the fact that Neophytos was an outsider in the eyes of his flock in Aleppo.

For the community in Aleppo, it was undoubtedly more significant that Kyrillos was an Aleppine than that he was an Arab. We know from a case initiated in 1679 by his brother Hananiyya that the family maintained a residence in the city. Furthermore, both brothers were actively engaged in the silk trade and had ties to many of Aleppo's newly emerging Christian commercial elite.[55] Finally, it is significant that the Aleppines voiced their choice for a man who was at that time a confirmed "traditionalist" while Neophytos tentatively was in the Catholic camp. Their choice of candidate for the patriarchal see is perhaps an indicator that the Catholic party among the Rum was weak in the city. It is more likely, however, that Kyrillos' place of birth and continuing connections in the city, rather than his theology or mother tongue, provided the motivation for Aleppo's Rum merchants to support his claim.

Despite Kyrillos' triumph, the Catholic party throughout the empire was given a major boost in February 1690, when the French ambassador in Istanbul obtained an imperial decree, directed to the governors of the provinces of Egypt, Aleppo, Damascus, Tripoli, Diyarbakır, Mosul, Raqqa, Baghdad, Erzurum, and Cyprus, informing them that the Jesuits and other French priests who were teaching the principles of the Christian faith to the people of the Rum, Armenian, and Coptic sects (*mezhebler*) were to be left alone. Neither government officials nor members of the other Christian religious communities would be suffered to interfere with their work. Not only was the term *millet* absent from the order, but the French were implicitly given the right to "convert" members of the Eastern-rite churches to Catholicism.[56] The order came in the wake of a major Ottoman defeat at the hands of the Hapsburgs and, undoubtedly, reflected an attempt by the sultan to curry favor with France. Although this was the first time that the

---

[55] *Ibid.*, vol. IV, p. 89.
[56] Istanbul, BOA, Ecnebi vol. XXVIII/3, p. 32.

Catholic missionaries were given explicit permission to proselytize openly, it is also clear that there was concurrently an awakening concern in Istanbul that the Catholics were indeed subversive.

That fear was substantiated in 1695 when the Venetians attempted to capture the island of Chios. Chios had been home to a relatively compact Roman Catholic community whose autonomy from the Greek Orthodox Church had been recognized by the Ottomans when they seized the island from Genoa in 1558. But the Catholics on the island became suspect as a potential "fifth-column" in the aftermath of the failed Venetian assault when their leading clergy on the island decamped with the invaders. This provided the Greek Orthodox Patriarch in the capital, who viewed the island as falling within his proper sphere of influence, with the weapon he needed to lash out against the Latin missionary movement.[57]

The Orthodox clergy pointed to the intrinsic "foreignness" of Catholicism, invariably labeled in their polemic as *Firenk Dini* ("the religion of the Franks"). They, in turn, emphasized their own loyalty to the sultan. Perhaps more significantly given the conservative nature of Ottoman public policy, the Orthodox polemic stressed that they were the true heirs of the Christian tradition in the East, while the Catholics represented the sin of innovation. The sultan ultimately agreed with the Orthodox whichever argument he found the more compelling. He could not expel the Latin priests, however, as the treaties with France provided for their presence. But he, and his successors, would make sure that their contacts with local Christians were curtailed. Periodic orders followed over the next century which forbade Latin priests to educate, treat the sick, or offer sacraments to Ottoman Christians in Syria, in what was a stunning reversal of the freedoms granted in 1690.[58]

These actions did little to halt the spread of Catholic practices. By 1700, a cadre of Syrian seminarians from all four *ta'ifa*s – Rum, Jacobite, Maronite, and Armenian – had been sent to Rome, trained and ordained there, and were now back in their homeland ready to offer the sacraments to any who would take them. These Latin-trained clergy physically occupied some of the churches maintained by their communities in Aleppo, Damascus, and the Lebanese port cities of Sidon and Tripoli. As most of the communicants seemingly approved of, or at the least were indifferent to, their tilt toward Rome, the Orthodox clergy could only fume from afar. The Catholics were subverting the community of Rum from within by winning over their best and brightest.

In Aleppo, this group was represented by Athanasios (Athanasiyus) Dabbas who was ironically given the community's established preference for one of its own, a native of Damascus. In 1685, the French had succeeded

---

[57] Heyberger, *Les chrétiens du proche-orient*, p. 368.
[58] Istanbul, BOA, Ahkâm-ı Şam-ı Şerif, vol. II, pp. 28–29; 98.

in buying the approval of the sultan for the investiture of Athanasios as Patriarch of Antioch, temporarily unseating Kyrillos al-Za'im. A year later, he secretly made a profession of faith to the Pope. Kyrillos did not give up easily, however, and in 1687 the sultan again invested him as patriarch. The skirmishing between the two was settled finally in 1694 when Athanasios gave up his claim in return for Aleppo's metropolitan see. Significantly given their earlier support for Kyrillos, it was an assembly of merchant notables from Aleppo that effected the compromise. Rome, however, continued to recognize Athanasios as the true Patriarch of Antioch, creating for the first time a Catholic "shadow patriarch" claiming to be the spiritual head of all the Rum in Syria.[59]

The accession of Athanasios Dabbas as metropolitan served as a watershed in the process of Catholicization of the Rum in Aleppo. For the next twenty-five years, the leading cleric in the city encouraged the movement of his priests and laity toward the Unia. The reasons for the attraction of the Uniate communion for Aleppo's Christians can only be speculated upon, however. Two twentieth-century historians offer divergent opinions; Robert Haddad presents a material cause for the switch, while Bernard Heyberger prefers a spiritual one. Haddad sees the promise of French protection for Catholics as a compelling incentive. But more importantly, the availability of fraternal contacts with the Europeans that Catholicism offered provided a compelling inducement for the Christian merchants in Syria to embrace the Catholic option. Haddad also cites the more lax requirements in the Catholic faith, both towards fasting and the definition of consanguinity for canonical marriage over Orthodox practice as being persuasive to those who would apostatize. Contemporary Orthodox commentators also preferred that explanation.[60]

Citing Catholic sources, Heyberger argues that Orthodoxy in Syria had become a moribund tradition that no longer satisfied the spiritual needs of the faithful. Catholicism, by contrast, engendered a spiritual rebirth among Syrian Christians. The Catholic option offered to the faithful pastors who were dedicated, educated, and amenable to the spiritual needs of their community in place of the nepotism and corruption previously prevalent among the Orthodox clergy. Heyberger's explanation is supported by the periodic complaints about the abuse of power by their clergy registered in the Aleppo courts by the Orthodox laity in the seventeenth century.[61] These disappeared in the eighteenth century after the Catholic triumph. Equally important for Heyberger, the Uniate movement did not require that Syria's Christians give up their traditional liturgy, their feast days, or their icons for

---

[59] Haddad, "Constantinople over Antioch," pp. 230–34; Neale, *History of the Eastern Church*, pp. 184–85.

[60] Neale, *ibid.*, p. 186.

[61] Damascus, Aleppo Court records, vol. XXXIV, p. 12.

Latin imports. They could retain what was comfortable from their tradition and still embrace reform.[62]

Heyberger also suggests that the special appeal of Catholicism to the Christian women of Syria was another inducement that led the formerly Orthodox faithful to embrace the Catholic option. The Orthodox tradition in Syria had borrowed much from the Islamicate culture in which it survived. This included the segregation of women in churches, behind curtains and lattices.[63] By contrast, the Catholic missionaries made a direct appeal to Christian women in Syria and were rewarded. Supporting this assertion, seventeenth-century lists of converts, kept by the missionaries, show individual women accepted Catholicism in acts of conscience, independent of their husbands, fathers, or brothers, at a rate higher than that of Christian males.[64] It is easy to see why Christian women in Syria might choose Catholicism. The Catholic missionaries were willing to educate girls as well as boys, an option previously not widely available to Orthodox girls. Women were encouraged to participate in religious services and processions by the missionaries. The Catholics also introduced separate religious orders for women, whereas the Orthodox monks and nuns had occupied the same physical space. Furthermore, the post-Tridentine emphasis on the Marian cult must have seemed emotionally empowering to some formerly Orthodox women. The greater freedom that Catholicism offered Aleppo's Christian women served to attract converts, but it also led to problems with the Muslim community. On several occasions, Muslims prevented Catholic women from going to the Shaybani Khan, the residence of the French consul in Aleppo and a site of an officially sanctioned chapel, to worship on the grounds that they were unaccompanied by male relatives.[65]

Both Haddad and Heyberger agree that the pull of localism was also a strong factor in the Syrian Christians' choice of the Catholic option.[66] The Uniate churches allowed their congregations to participate in the mass through the medium of Arabic, replacing the traditional Greek and Syriac. As the result of their linguistic choice, Arab nationalist historians have often represented the Uniates as being in the vanguard of a nascent Arabist movement. Although ethnically based antagonisms could color the polemics of schism, the contemporary sources do not support the supposition that Arabist sentiments were at the core of the reasons why Aleppo's Christians chose Rome. In that regard, it must be remembered that Armenians and Jacobites in Aleppo also chose the Catholic option and neither of these

[62] Heyberger, *Les chrétiens du proche-orient*, pp. 149–53.
[63] Neale, *History of the Eastern Church*, p. 227.
[64] Bernard Heyberger, "Les chrétiens d'Alep (Syrie) à travers les récits des conversions des missionaires Carmes Déchaux (1657–1681)" *Mélanges de l'Ecole Française de Rome* 100 (1988): 461–99.
[65] Heyberger, *Les chrétiens du proche-orient*, pp. 344–45.
[66] Robert Haddad, "Conversion of Eastern Orthodox Christians," p. 454.

communities was plagued by the linguistic dysfunction between hierarchy and laity that could afflict the Orthodox Church in Syria. But a strong mercantile middle class dominated all three sects and a locally based hierarchy would serve best its political interests. The Rum had already stated their clear preference for one of their own to be metropolitan, if not patriarch. For Aleppo's Armenians, a Catholic Catholicos of Sis might be able to resist the centralizing push initiated by the Gregorian Patriarch in Istanbul. For the Jacobites, a Catholic Patriarch or at the least a metropolitan of their own seated in Aleppo would be unfettered by interference from the traditionalists in Dayr Za῾afaran. In all three cases, the Pope in Rome was ready to sanction the choice of a local to head the new Uniate churches in Aleppo. The patriarchs in Istanbul or Dayr Za῾afaran were not willing to accede to this and as a result lost the battle for the loyalty of the faithful in the city.

For many Syrians, however, the reasons for conversion were probably simpler. The nineteenth-century chronicler, Mikha'il Mishaqa gave an account of his great-grandfather's conversion to Catholicism which was conditioned by his desire to marry a woman from a Catholic clan. In order to learn what Catholicism was, he agreed to stay in a Catholic monastery in Lebanon where he observed that the monks used Greek in their services, wore Greek Orthodox vestments and robes, and conformed to rites he had known in his former church. Saying that the Catholics had simply changed their name and nothing else, he declared himself to be a Catholic and married the sister of Hajj Musa Mansi.[67] Obviously, not all converts were aware of the subtle theological differences that were, in fact, emerging between Orthodox and Catholic doctrines. But the point about the similarity between the old and new dispensations was well taken. Syrian Christians, whether Jacobite, Armenian, or Orthodox, could embrace Catholicism without making a clear break with the past. They could pick what was useful about the Catholic option – political autonomy, reform, and links to the West – while retaining what was comfortable from their traditions.

## The traditionalist "counter-reformation"

Despite the popularity of Catholicism in Aleppo and the Lebanese port cities, the "traditionalist" camp could increasingly call on the authorities in Istanbul in its attempt to suppress Catholicism. The sultans had been ambivalent about Catholic influence in the seventeenth century and had granted imperial *berat*s for the offices of patriarch and metropolitan to partisans of both the Orthodox and Catholic factions. Their decision in any particular case was based on the size of the gifts on offer from the interested

---

[67] Mishaqa, *Murder, Mayhem, Pillage and Plunder*, p. 10.

parties. But a fear of political meddling by the Europeans in the affairs of their subjects led the sultans in the eighteenth century to side with the traditionalists in the hierarchies of the Eastern-rite churches. Slips in that affirmed policy could still occur when large gifts were on offer, but whenever a position was articulated in writing by the state's bureaucrats, it invariably supported orthodoxy as representing "tradition."

The Latin challenge in the see of Antioch resurfaced in 1720 when Kyrillos V al-Zaᶜim, died. Despite his earlier opposition to the Catholics, Kyrillos had moved tentatively toward full communion with Rome in his later years, an act he finally acknowledged in a written profession of faith to Clement XI in 1716. His drift toward Rome was bitterly opposed by the "traditionalist" faction in the church hierarchy who, ironically, chose as his successor Athanasios IV Dabbas. Maybe they knew what they were doing. As a part of the compromise that led to his elevation as Patriarch of Antioch, Dabbas was required to go to Istanbul to consult with the Patriarch of Constantinople. Following the meeting in Istanbul, an order was sent, at Patriarch Athanasios' request, to the governors of Damascus and Aleppo in 1723 to arrest a certain Damascene priest named Khalil Suhuri and two unnamed laymen in Aleppo. They had, reportedly, "gone over to the Franks' religion and caused great harm to the *ta'ifa* of the Rum."[68] It is not clear why Dabbas, who up until his investiture had been in the Catholic party, now chose to pursue a traditionalist path. Constantius, Patriarch of Constantinople in the middle of the nineteenth century, offered the following explanation:

He lived four years longer in sorrow and repentance because that, through his friendship and toleration towards the popish fathers, he had become the cause that many of the orthodox in Damascus and Aleppo had revolted from the sacred traditions of their fathers and embraced Roman doctrines: miserably beguiled by the popish fathers – who in the name of the Pope granted indulgences and relaxations of the fasts to those who were by their nature slaves of their bellies, and everything else besides which was forbidden by the orthodox Church of the East.[69]

An open struggle for the Patriarchate erupted upon Athanasios' death in 1724, resulting in what would become permanent schism. The clergy and laity in Damascus initially elected Kyrillos VI Tanas, but his legitimacy was not recognized by the Porte, which invested in his stead Sylvestros, a monk originally from Cyprus and the candidate favored by the Patriarch of Constantinople. Facing arrest, Kyrillos VI fled to Shuwayr in Mount Lebanon, where the Pope named him the Patriarch of Antioch in 1729. The Catholics among the Rum laity and clergy in Aleppo had originally supported Sylvestros' candidacy, apparently out of anger at not being consulted in the election of Kyrillos, or alternatively, simply because he was

---

[68] Istanbul, BOA, Cevdet Adliye 3570.
[69] Neale, *History of the Eastern Church*, p. 185.

a Damascene. That support evaporated with Sylvestros' visit to Aleppo in 1726. In advance of Sylvestros' entry into the city, the governor registered on March 24, 1726, a list of men from the Armenian, Jacobite, and Rum *ta'ifa*s who were accused of worshipping with the Frankish priests and a number were imprisoned.[70] Despite this attempt to cow the Aleppines into obedience before his arrival, Sylvestros' mission fared miserably. An Orthodox version of the events offered the following explanation:

But this blessed man on arriving at Aleppo from Constantinople on a Wednesday, and seeing fish on the table which had been prepared for his reception outside the city by the principal Christian inhabitants of Aleppo in an ungovernable fit of passion upset the table and violently reproved those leading Christians who had come out to meet him; paying not the slightest attention to their explanations – that in consequence of the lack of fast meats in those parts, the patriarchs, his predecessors, had by way of ecclesiastical condescension, granted this indulgence. On his entrance into Aleppo, he not only shewed himself unbending to their earnest appeals on this subject, but excommunicated them in the churches as being guilty, through gluttony, of eating fish on fasting days. Not satisfied with this, he further accused them to the pasha of Aleppo as Franks and infidels.[71]

There were obviously deeper divisions between the Rum of Aleppo and their new Patriarch than the question of whether or not it was permissible to eat fish on Wednesday. But that dispute emphasized the desire of the Aleppine community to maintain their religious traditions as they under-stood them and not to conform to "tradition" as it was understood in the see of Constantinople. A copy of Sylvestros' complaint against Aleppo's laity was recorded on July 1, 1726 in the central court of Aleppo and contained a list of over a hundred names of men from among the Rum whom he charged had "turned Frank" in their religion. Unfortunately, no family names were given in his deposition and we are, therefore, deprived of knowing the identities of the Catholic families in Aleppo in this period.[72] The Ottoman governor responded to Sylvestros' complaint; arrests and deportations of members of the Catholic faction followed. The Catholic party did not give up easily, despite this heavy-handed intimidation. On August 24, 1726, a delegation, consisting of those who, apparently from the ordering of their names, were the same individuals previously denounced by Sylvestros, registered a complaint against the "priest" Sylvestros; they had refused to grant him even the title of Patriarch. He had stolen vestments and ornaments from their churches and had requested illegal taxes and gifts from the laity. They further charged that when they failed to pay what Sylvestros demanded, he had enlisted government officials to collect the money for him by force. They concluded their deposition by saying

[70] Damascus, Aleppo Court records, vol. LI, p. 34.
[71] Neale, *History of the Eastern Church*, p. 186.
[72] Damascus, Aleppo Court records, vol. LI, p. 95.

Sylvestros' actions had been unjust and immoral. As a result, they claimed many Christians had fled the city.[73]

This was the first recorded use of the threat of flight should the Catholics not be allowed to practice their faith. It would reappear in all Catholic depositions to local officials over the next century. It was a somber reminder to the city's governors of the wealth held by the Catholics. It also carried an unspoken promise of financial rewards that might come their way should they accede to the Catholics' wishes. Strengthening their argument, a number of prominent Muslims affirmed before the qadi that the Catholics' account of the events was true. The support of prominent Muslims would also be a continuing weapon in the Catholics' arsenal against orthodoxy in the city. Later that year, a complaint registered by the French ambassador at the Porte detailed roughly the same charges against Sylvestros as the earlier Catholic deposition in Aleppo. In response, the Porte sent a certain Ahmed Çavuş from the capital to investigate.[74] Unfortunately his report seems not to have survived, but the counter-charges, coupled with French diplomatic pressure and gifts dispensed at the Porte, gained the Catholics of Aleppo a respite.[75] Several years followed in which the situation remained muddled in Aleppo allowing the partisans of the Catholic cause to buy a limited degree of autonomy from the local authorities. But they had failed to achieve legal recognition from their sultan.

The schism left rancor on both sides of the divide. Mikha'il Burayk, an Orthodox chronicler in Damascus, accused the Aleppines of having poisoned Athanasios and added that they had purchased their independence with bribes to the Porte so that they might remain "heretical Catholics."[76] The latter charge was undeniably true. The split also had an ethnic dimension in that a Greek had been chosen over an Arab to fill the see of Antioch. In pleading their case to the Pope for recognition of Kyrillos Tanas' investiture, his partisans stated that the Greeks were the enemies of the "True Church." In contrast, the Arabs had remained loyal to the successors of Peter from the earliest days of the Church, prefiguring the myth of the "Melkite church" which would infuse the debate over origins in the nineteenth century.[77]

It is uncertain if that rhetoric represented any deeply held feelings of

---

[73] *Ibid.*, vol. LI, pp. 149–51.

[74] A copy of the document preserved in the record books of the French Consulate in Istanbul, dated awa'il Rabiᶜ al-akhir 1139/ November 1726. My thanks to Ethem Eldem for making it available to me.

[75] A slightly different version of these events is given in Cyril Charon (Korolevsky), *History of the Melkite Patriarchates, Vol. I Pre-modern period (869–1833)*. Translated by John Collorafi. Edited by Bishop Nicholas Samra (Fairfax, VA, 1998), pp. 35–37.

[76] Burayk, *Ta'rikh al-Sham*, pp. 3–6; on Burayk, see Masters, "View from the Province," and Joseph Nasrallah, "Historiens et chroniqueurs melkites du XVIIIe siècle" *Bulletin d'Études Orientales* 13 (1949–51): 145–60.

[77] Heyberger, *Les chrétiens du proche-orient*, p. 399.

ethnic identity among the Catholics of Syria as the ethnic labels "Greek" and "Arab" were absent from their chronicles. Individuals from both peoples were simply subsumed under the category of "Rum," without further differentiation as to ethnicity and only their religious faction was seemingly important enough to be recorded. As an alternative to the suggestion that the schism was the result of ethnic tensions, we should remember that the antagonism had a distinctly regional flavor to it. Although there would continue to be Catholic partisans among the laity and clergy in Damascus, they would remain a minority among the city's Christians until at least the twentieth century. By contrast, a large majority of Aleppo's Christians had accepted the Pope as their supreme prelate, creating a religious/political basis for the interurban rivalries that already existed between the Christians of the two metropolitan centers of inland Syria. The battle was not won, however, and the position of the Catholics in Aleppo would remain precarious as long as they did not win official recognition from Istanbul.

Although his Arab flock may have seemed remote to the Patriarch of Constantinople, he undoubtedly understood that the capture of the see of Antioch by properly Orthodox clergy was an important objective in the war to keep the Catholic contagion away from the Orthodox faithful. It was equally imperative for the new Catholics of Syria to secure positions within the church hierarchy, recognized by the state. Central to both parties' ambitions was the contested metropolitanate of Aleppo. The Catholics found their champion in Maksimos al-Hakim, a cleric of an illustrious family that had long served Aleppine interests in the church. Ironically, the patriarch in Istanbul had first elevated Maksimos to his see. The Catholic missionaries were, therefore, initially dubious as to his true loyalties. He surprised them, however, by making a profession of faith to the Pope and was consequently named as the Catholic metropolitan of Aleppo in 1730, thereby forfeiting the support of the patriarch.[78] Nonetheless, the sultan reissued a *berat* to Maksimos naming him as metropolitan of the Rum in Aleppo, after a reputed gift of forty-five sacks of silver coin (22,500 *ghurush*) was offered.[79] Istanbul had experienced a palace coup in 1730 and political unrest in the capital probably provided an increased appreciation for the cash the Aleppines were willing to expend for their candidate's investiture. The Orthodox faction did not concede this point easily, however.

Their version of the events was presented in an undated memorandum to the sultan bearing the seals of the Patriarchs of Constantinople, Antioch, and Jerusalem.[80] In blunt terms, the three patriarchs informed the sultan of the various nefarious activities that had recently occurred in Aleppo. They

[78] Rabbath, vol. II, pp. 380, 390–94.
[79] The account of the Aleppine priest, Niᶜmat ibn al-Khuri Tuma al-Halabi, contained in Burayk, *Ta'rikh al-Sham*, p. 133.
[80] Istanbul, BOA, Cevdet Adliye 516.

charged that an unholy alliance of Druze rebels, France, and the Pope supported the Catholics in Aleppo in their rebellion against the sultan and the church. The latter two, it was charged, had provided over a hundred sacks of silver to the local Muslim officials in Aleppo so they would not enforce the sultan's orders banning Catholic worship. The deposition of the patriarchs further claimed that the core of committed Catholics in the city consisted of only fifty individuals, with perhaps another hundred or so more who were marginally complicit in the heresy. The silent majority of the community, who were "by nature loyal to the true church and their sultan," were forced into their state of rebellion by threats of economic boycott from the hard core of heretics. Thus, the link between disloyalty to the patriarch and state treason was not so subtly invoked. The situation was further aggravated, the letter claimed, by the presence of "thirty to forty Frankish priests" who actively subverted the "true faith" and the sultan's commands in Aleppo while under the protection of the French consul. The vehemence manifested in this letter was extraordinary. Among the charges was that the Catholics had built a church in the Druze country in violation of shari‘a. This was, in fact, true as the Rum Catholic Church standing in Shuwayr attested. But the fact that one group of Christians would make such a claim to the Muslim authorities indicates the depth of the anger present in the see of Antioch.

A counter document from the Catholics dated December 3, 1732, provided their version of the situation.[81] The "priest" Sylvestros had falsely accused them of practicing the "Frankish" rite, they wrote, when they were simply following the faith received from their fathers and grandfathers, an appeal to the authority of "tradition" even if that claim were historically suspect. Furthermore, they asserted that the Rum of Aleppo were no longer subject to the Patriarch of Antioch, having switched their allegiance to the *patrikhane* in Istanbul in 1726. Sylvestros, whom they charged gratuitously as being a thief, was illegally trying to replace Maksimos with a man they did not want. Finally, the Catholics – never, of course, self-identified as such, but simply called the sultan's humble subjects among the Rum (*ehl-i zimmet-i Rum reayaları fukarâsı*) – pointed out that Maksimos was a native Aleppine. Here, the comfortable, colloquial Arabic phrase, *Halabi al-asl*, slipped into the formal Ottoman Turkish text. For the Aleppines, this was perhaps the most important qualification for the man who would be their spiritual leader. As early as 1721, they had demanded assurances from Patriarch Athanasios that the metropolitan in the see of Aleppo would always be a native of the city.[82] Although the desire for local control over their church was not the only reason the Rum of Aleppo chose the Catholic option, it is noteworthy that they chose to make the point of identifying

[81] *Ibid.*, 6212.
[82] Burayk, *Ta'rikh al-Sham*, p. 128.

their choice as metropolitan as being one of their own. Significantly as a counter-point to those who would posit a nationalist sentiment as underlying the struggle, no mention was made in the deposition of Maksimos' Arab identity. For good measure, the Catholics ended their deposition by stating both the qadi in the city and the governor of Aleppo had confirmed Maksimos al-Hakim in his position.

This last statement proved the linchpin for winning their case. On the margin of the Catholics' petition is a report prepared by an anonymous Ottoman bureaucrat who checked the documentation in the case and wrote to the sultan that the Catholics (identified again simply as the "Rum in Aleppo") were correct in their assertions. The chief-judge of Aleppo had written to confirm Maksimos as metropolitan in 1729 and again in 1731. He had also affirmed that the Aleppo community had effected secession from the see of Antioch with their submission to the authority of the Patriarch of Constantinople. To smooth the transfer, the community had paid a "gift" of 3,600 *ghurush* to the Porte.[83] That was all it took. Although the sultan warned that unsubstantiated charges of thievery against Sylvestros should not go unchallenged, Sylvestros was informed he had no authority to try to reverse a decision made by two of the sultan's trusted servants, i.e. the judge and the governor. With this decision, Maksimos was confirmed with an imperial order as Aleppo's metropolitan. Aleppo's Catholics had circumvented the traditional church hierarchy by appealing to both the religious and secular arms of the Ottoman state. The fact they could do so successfully indicates that a fully articulated *millet* system was not yet in place.

Armed with the sultan's approval, a large delegation of the Rum declared in a deposition registered with the chief-judge of Aleppo in early October 1733 that Maksimos was their legitimate Metropolitan and head of the *ta'ifa* of the Rum in Aleppo. They stated that the attempt by Sylvestros, Patriarch of Antioch (now acknowledged by them as holding that post), to depose Maksimos was illegal as the metropolitan see of Aleppo had been transferred from Antioch to Constantinople in 1726.[84] This tactic was designed to place an even greater physical distance between Aleppo and the patriarch who had presumed authority over it. It also sought to remove the Damascenes from interfering in the Aleppines' choice of the man who would serve as their spiritual guide. This was not to say Catholicism's triumph would go unchallenged. As the Patriarch of Constantinople had rightly pointed out, there was an inherent flaw in the argument articulated by the Rum of Aleppo. He, after all, was *the* Patriarch of Constantinople, the very man the Aleppines said to whom they were loyal, and he had not approved Maksimos' investiture. That argument, coupled with hefty gifts

---

[83] Damascus, Aleppo Awamir al-sultaniyya, vol. III, p. 39. The account of Niʿmat ibn al-Khuri Tuma, recorded that the Catholics paid the judge 8,500 *ghurush* for his *arz-ı hal* (petition) on their behalf.

[84] Damascus, Aleppo Awamir al-sultaniyya, vol. III, p. 39; Rabbath, vol. II, pp. 378–89.

from the Orthodox, eventually carried the day. At the Patriarch's request, the sultan reversed himself and revoked Maksimos' patent in late 1733 and the metropolitan went into exile at Shuwayr.[85] Maksimos was, however, able to return to the city in 1734 after a gift of 7,500 *ghurush* was given to Aleppo's chief qadi. With that, Aleppo's Rum sank happily back into their "heresy," unimpeded for the next twelve years.[86]

## Conclusion

The mission begun by the Latin clerics in Syria in the seventeenth century had reached full maturation by 1750. The overwhelming majority of Aleppo's Christians and many of those in Damascus and the coastal cities of greater Syria had embraced one form or another of the Catholic faith, although the reasons for that success are not completely transparent. Catholic missionaries actively sought converts in all of the Ottoman cities. But by the end of the eighteenth century, only two major cities, Istanbul and Aleppo, could boast sizable Uniate populations. The Latin success in the capital had come among the Armenians. Despite active intervention by the state in support of the Gregorian Patriarch in the city, a determined core of faithful believers was established among the wealthy Armenian merchants and these would eventually win the right to an officially sanctioned *millet* of their own in 1831.[87] But in Istanbul, those accepting the Pope's authority were a tiny, albeit influential, minority of the city's Christian population.

In contrast, most European observers agreed that by 1750, the majority of Aleppo's Christians were Uniates. Faced with the anomaly of Aleppo's case, we must ask why? The two conventional explanations posit the presence of European merchants in the city and the option Catholicism provided for Syria's Christians to have a clerical hierarchy who reflected the laity's ethnic identity, i.e. Arabs. Both of these explanations have merit, but neither seems to be totally satisfactory. Izmir, after all, had a much larger Western commercial presence in the eighteenth century than did Aleppo. Although the Catholic missionaries made some inroads there, the overall percentage of Greeks and Armenians who embraced Catholicism was dwarfed by the rate of conversion to the Unia in Aleppo. When we compare the fate of the Catholic experience in Aleppo to that of Damascus, however, it is clear that the presence of a French consuls was a necessary condition for Catholicism to flourish. In their absence Latin priests could offer the sacraments in Damascus only intermittently after the debacle of Chios.

The Arabist argument also has merit. The Christians of the *ta'ifat al-Rum*

[85] Heyberger, *Les chrétiens du proche-orient*, pp. 400–01.
[86] Burayk, *Ta'rikh al-Sham*, p. 133.
[87] Kemal Beydilli, *Recognition of the Armenian Catholic Community and the Church in the Reign of Mahmud II. (1830)* (Cambridge, MA, 1995).

in Aleppo resented the hegemony of the clergy in Istanbul over the see of Antioch. But it is not at all clear that Arabist sentiments permeated the consciousness of all of the Rum of Syria in the eighteenth century. The Aleppo Catholics would most probably have chafed under the rule of men who were Damascenes as well those who were Greeks. Further undermining a possible Arabist interpretation, Fr. Burayk in Damascus praised the ʿAzm governors for being Arabs (*awlad al-ʿArab*), but he did not seem to mind the fact that the Patriarch Sylvestros was not. He did write disapprovingly of the table manners of his successor Philemon in 1766, after having labeled him as a "proper Ottoman."[88] But Philemon was a Phanariot Greek and it was probably his effete Istanbul manners rather than his mother tongue to which the provincial cleric objected as Patriarch Philemon shared Greek as his mother-tongue in common with Patriarch Sylvestros, the undisputed hero of Burayk's narrative. More importantly, the linguistic explanation does not explain why the Rum in Aleppo embraced Catholicism while their more conservative brothers and sisters in Christ in Damascus did not.

We also need to remember that the Catholic option was equally attractive to Armenians and Jacobites in Aleppo and neither group suffered from a linguistic divide between laity and church hierarchy. In trying to explain the appeal of Catholicism to all three Christian sects, a desire for local control seems the crucial factor. The Christian merchants of Aleppo were prospering in the eighteenth century and they wanted a church attentive to their political interests. The presence of activist Latin clergy in the city, providing education and other services, must have led the secular merchants working for, and with, the Europeans to question the efficacy of the traditional churches in their lives. But more importantly, Catholicism offered a vehicle for the Aleppines to seize control of their church, the only political arena open to Christians in the preTanzimat period. Catholicism met the political, cultural, and spiritual needs of an emergent Christian mercantile bourgeoisie and they embraced it with enthusiasm.[89] Put simply, the Christians of Aleppo had two options in the eighteenth century as the *millet* wars unfolded. They could remain in the Orthodox *millet*s and forfeit their say in who would head their communities or they could switch their allegiance to Rome and retain local autonomy. Unlike some Protestants in Europe during the Reformation who were content to do away with hierarchical religious authority altogether, the religious world-view of Syrian Christians, and that of the Ottoman state, demanded that they remained governed by a hierarchy. Faced with accepting the authority of either patriarch or the Pope, they chose the latter.

By 1750, the Catholics of Syria had experienced an unprecedented economic and cultural transformation. With the contraction of European

[88] Burayk, *Ta'rikh al-Sham*, pp. 84–85.
[89] Thomas Philipp, *The Syrians in Egypt, 1725–1975* (Stuttgart, 1985), pp. 18–20.

interest in the Levant trade at the end of the century, Catholic merchants were prepared to move into the niche formerly filled by Europeans. Their doctrines and practices had been subtly altered to conform to those of Rome. In the process, Syria's Catholics could begin to feel that they were part of a wider world of Catholics that extended beyond their sultan's realm. But along with their acceptance of elements of a Western world-view, arising out of their conversion and education by the Latins, Syria's new Catholics retained a sense of their old identity, preserving what was comfortable from the older traditions. The Uniate churches kept their former liturgies (albeit translated into Arabic), their calendars, and holidays while adding Latin ones. Their clergy retained the right to marry, and their communion host (*qurban*) remained leavened bread rather than the unleavened wafer of the Latins. But there was also a major psychological transformation that was inherent in their conversion. The Catholics had retained what was comfortable from their past while gaining a collective input into the political life of their churches and a spiritual link to the West through Rome. They were protected behind that all-important façade of tradition, while committing themselves to a place in a new economic and political world-order, increasingly dominated by the West.

# CHAPTER 4

# New opportunities and challenges in the "long" eighteenth century

The Ottoman Empire came perilously close to political implosion in the transition from the eighteenth to the nineteenth century. Warlords challenged the hegemony of the House of Osman on the empire's periphery and the dynasty's destiny seemed doomed to follow that of its rivals, the Safavids in Iran. More threatening to the empire's long-term survival, the sultan's Christian subjects in the Balkans were increasingly restive as some began to dream of independence. In the Arab lands, the military rulers of Egypt moved toward full autonomy and the followers of the religio-political dynasty founded by the alliance between Muhammad ibn Sa$^c$ud and Muhammad ibn $^c$Abd al-Wahhab mounted an ideological and military challenge to Ottoman hegemony in the desert borderlands of the Fertile Crescent. When compared to these formidable military threats, the chronic political instability and corruption in the core Arab provinces were understandably far down the list of the priorities facing Sultan Mahmud II (1808–39) when he activated the machinery of state to preserve his patrimony. If the Ottoman eighteenth century were to be characterized by the contestation of the Porte's authority by local political elites, then it did not come to an end in the Arab provinces until the restoration of Ottoman authority in Syria in 1840–41 and even later still in Iraq and Arabia. Egypt was never restored to Ottoman sovereignty. The uncertainties of the political outcome of the struggle between center and periphery in this "long" century provided opportunities and challenges for the non-Muslims of the Ottoman Arab provinces.[1]

## *Millet* wars: from repression to establishment

The Catholics among the Rum in Syria were in a precarious legal position after 1725 as the sultan and his bureaucrats increasingly sided with the Greek hierarchy in the capital. The alarm at the Porte over the possible

---

[1] Albert Hourani, "The Changing Face of the Fertile Crescent in the XVIIIth Century" *Studia Islamica* 8 (1957): 89–122.

spread of Catholicism among the sultan's subjects had not arisen from a sea change in Ottoman attitudes toward doctrinal differences among the *ahl al-dhimma*. Rather it reflected the shifting dynamics of politics as played out at the Ottoman court, coupled with the Porte's annoyance at the Catholic powers' meddling into the religious affairs of the empire. The intervention by the Patriarch of Constantinople into the selection of those who would occupy the see of Antioch in 1720, and then again in 1725, signaled the start of a campaign to consolidate the religious affairs of all the sultan's Orthodox subjects under one ecclesiastical office. The Greek merchants and bankers of the Phanar/Fener district of the capital were essential in that scheme as influence at court came at a high price. Their silver enabled the Patriarch of Constantinople to counter the gifts that the Latins were offering and suggest to the sultans the parameters of an emerging *millet* system.

Key to the legitimation of the patriarch's ambitions was the invention of a myth of origin that posited the establishment of the *millet*s with Sultan Fatih Mehmed. Like many myths, this one had an element of historical truth embedded within it. Fatih had established the anti-Latin Gennadius as Patriarch and *millet başı* of the Orthodox community in 1453 after the conquest of Constantinople. Later, he ordered the subordination of the Southern Slavic churches to the Patriarchate of Constantinople as a part of his ambition to centralize all political authority in his new capital. The patriarchate of Peć regained its autonomy in 1557, however, thanks to the intervention of the grand vizier Sokollu Mehmed Paşa. His brother, who had remained Christian, was not coincidentally then elevated as patriarch of the Serbian church.[2] There is little evidence to suggest that the sultans after Fatih cared much about the political organization of their non-Muslim subjects until the eighteenth century. In the vacuum, traditions of local ecclesiastical autonomy prevailed almost everywhere outside of Istanbul. Fatih's action had nonetheless established the legal precedent for the *millet*s and it would only take the nudging of the Ecumenical Patriarch of Constantinople, backed by Phanariot wealth, to convince the sultans in the "long" eighteenth century that they were only returning to the traditions of their noble ancestors.

The willingness of the sultans to abet the myth of the *millet*s by empowering the patriarchs was helped, no doubt, by their growing appre-hension that the Catholics indeed represented a potential "fifth column" that might be manipulated by the European powers at the Porte's expense. The sultans must have also appreciated that the consolidation of church affairs into the hands of patriarchs, who were physically proximate to the palace, might make the governing of their non-Muslim subjects easier at a

---

[2] Bozkurt, *Gayrimüslim durumu*, p. 12.

time when so much of their political authority was slipping away.[3] Basking in this newly configured relationship with the Porte, the Patriarch of Constantinople suppressed the Patriarchate of Peć for a second time in 1766 and the Archbishopric of Ohrid in 1767. These two actions effectively brought the Southern Slav Orthodox ecclesiastical hierarchies in the Balkans under Constantinople's control, much as earlier interventions had succeeded in subordinating the see of Antioch to the Patriarch's ambitions in the 1720s.

Spurred on by the success of the Orthodox Ecumenical Patriarch, the Armenian Gregorian patriarchate in Istanbul, which also could claim a dubious legacy dating back to Fatih Mehmed, conspired in the early eighteenth century to reduce the see of the Catholicos of Sis to its will. This came despite a lack of a tradition of a centralized hierarchy in the Armenian church. The catholicos of Ečmiadzin (near Yerevan) historically had held the pride of place among the church's clergy, but there had been historically no equivalent of pope or patriarch. But with that see falling outside Ottoman control in the eighteenth century, the Armenian Patriarch in Istanbul, whose title was borrowed from the Greeks, could rely on the sultan's bureaucrats to help establish his monolithic spiritual and political control over the sultan's Armenian subjects everywhere in the empire. This represented a conscious replication of the organized hierarchy and prerogatives of the emerging Orthodox *millet*, whose agents typically supported the Gregorian Armenian Patriarch at the sultan's court as natural allies against the Catholic contagion.[4]

As noted previously, the Ecumenical Patriarch's ambitions for greater centralization of his authority in the Arab lands centered on the metropolitan see of Aleppo. With properly Greek patriarchs enthroned at the see of Antioch, whoever controlled Aleppo would determine the fate of Catholicism among the Rum of Syria for better or for worse. Since 1730, that man had been the Metropolitan Maksimos al-Hakim. Although challenged in the early 1730s by the Orthodox, the Catholics had won the first round in the battle by convincing the government that the see of Aleppo had never truly been subordinate to the Patriarch of Antioch. Rather, it rightly lay within the jurisdiction of the Patriarch of Constantinople. The stratagem had reduced the pressure Damascus could exert in Aleppo's religious politics, but had afforded the patriarch in Istanbul with a new legal tool with which to extirpate Catholicism from the city and to enlarge the prerogatives of the *patrikhane*.

Although Catholic resistance in Aleppo continued to thwart the Ecumenical Patriarch's ambitions, the stalemate broke first in Damascus.

---

[3] Halil İnalcık, "The Status of the Greek Orthodox Patriarch under the Ottomans" *Turcica* 21–23 (1991): 407–36.

[4] Kevork Bardakjian, " Rise of the Armenian Patriarchate," pp. 89–100.

Displaying a rare flash of defiance, Catholics there succeeded in convincing the local authorities in 1745 to evict the Orthodox clergy from their churches and hand them over to clergy loyal to the Catholic Patriarch Kyrillos, still ensconced in exile in the mountain fastness of Shuwayr. The Catholics maintained their occupation for thirty-two days until the Orthodox faction obtained an imperial order restoring their proprietorship.[5] That order reminded the city's governor of an earlier order issued in 1141 (1728–29) which had banned Frankish priests from visiting the homes of the Rum, or teaching their children. Furthermore, it informed the governor that no Frankish priests could reside in the city, in the absence of a capitulatory treaty permitting them to do so.[6]

But with a change in governors, the Jesuits returned to Damascus in 1747. They seemingly reinvigorated the Catholic cause, claiming in 1750 that the city was home to 9,000 Catholics. That number was undoubtedly inflated but even if only partially true, it stood as testament to the resistance of the Catholic Rum of Damascus to an outsider patriarch for a quarter of a century.[7] The Catholics' triumph was momentary and was soon reversed, however, with the foreign priests once again expelled from the city. Without a senior cleric sympathetic to their cause, or foreign consuls to protect them, the Catholic faction soon shrank to a small nucleus of beleaguered believers. That quick turn around in their fortunes provides proof, if any were needed, that the actual presence of European consular protection was a necessary condition if Catholicism were to take root in an Ottoman environment. Latin priests would return to Syria's unofficial capital later in the century, but their previous freedom of action was greatly curtailed under the watchful eye of a properly orthodox patriarch.

In the aftermath of the attempted coup in Damascus, the Patriarch of Constantinople directed attention to his wayward flock in Aleppo. At his behest, an order calling for the arrest and imprisonment of twelve priests for practicing the "Frankish rite" (*ayîn-i Firenk*) arrived in the city in 1746.[8] Their arrest was not accepted peacefully, however. There was bloodshed in the streets of the city's Christian quarters between adherents of the old rite and the new. Eventually, the European consuls protested to the governor, bribes were paid, and the clergy were released. Not willing to risk remaining in the city, the Metropolitan Maksimos al-Hakim again fled to Lebanon to join his patriarch.[9] His flock in Aleppo did not forget him in his exile. After handing out a reputed total of 210,250 *ghurush* as gifts in both Istanbul and Aleppo, the Catholics succeeded in obtaining an imperial *berat* once again

[5] Burayk, *Ta'rikh al-Sham*, pp. 12–13.
[6] Istanbul, BOA, Ahkâm-ı Şam-ı Şerif, vol. I, p. 150. Burayk, *ibid.*, p. 19.
[7] Charon, *History of the Melkite Patriarchs*, vol. I, p. 38.
[8] Istanbul, BOA, Ahkâm-ı Halep, vol. I, p. 182.
[9] Heyberger, *Les chrétiens du proche-orient*, pp. 400–01.

naming Maksimos as their Metropolitan in 1748.[10] There was undoubtedly some exaggeration in that total as reported by Ni'mat ibn al-Khuri Tuma, a Catholic chronicler. For if true, it would have represented well in excess the total revenues from the province sent to the Porte in that year. What is not clear is why the Porte acceded to Maksimos' investiture, given its definitive tilt toward Orthodoxy. Apparently no Ottoman documentation for this reversal of policy has survived, but we may speculate that the sultan's resolve to support the institution of the *millets* could be subverted temporarily with the offer of ready cash. His acceptance of the gifts in this case was made all the easier by the array of Muslim officials and scholars in Aleppo who weighed in with written petitions and *fatwas* on the side of the Catholics, obtained according to our chronicler with generous gifts as well.

Maksimos' reinstatement was immediately challenged by the long-suffering Orthodox Patriarch of Antioch, Sylvestros, who attempted again in 1749 to place his nominee – this time a priest named Sophronios – in the metropolitan see of Aleppo. Yusuf Dib, whom we have met before, proved an important ally in effecting this reversal due to his personal contacts with the city's judiciary. His efforts brought success for the Orthodox as ibn al-Khuri Tuma succinctly opined, "the Ottomans can never get enough money but neither do they allow bloodshed."[11] The chronicler had rightly surmised that the governor and qadi could not permit sectarian tensions to explode into violence on the city's streets, whichever faction they might have favored. Sophronios' *ferman* of appointment from the Porte was accompanied by a letter addressed to the people of Aleppo from Kyrillos, Patriarch of Constantinople, in which he appealed to his flock to embrace Sophronios and to resist the "false" (*bâtil*) Metropolitan Maximos who sought "to turn them into Franks."[12]

Unfazed by the reprimand, the Catholics managed to avert the enthronement of Sophronios by presenting gifts to the Porte, to the governor, and the local judiciary, following a now well-trodden course of action. With treasure and persistent argument, they effected the arrest and imprisonment of the once, and future, Orthodox metropolitan in 1752 as a usurper. According to Hypsilantis, an Orthodox chronicler in Istanbul, the Catholics were aided in their counter-attack by a friend at the Porte who was the brother of Maksimos, a Muslim convert, and physician to the sultan.[13] Ibn al-Khuri Tuma, the Catholic chronicler, did not mention the name of his faction's agent in Istanbul. But he noted with a certain wonderment that the Catholics' agent was often able to get the better of the Ecumenical Patriarch

[10] Burayk, *Ta'rikh al-Sham*, p. 135.
[11] *Ibid.*, p. 137.
[12] Theodore Papadopoullos, *Studies and Documents Relating to the History of the Greek Church and People under Turkish Domination* (Brussels 1952), p. 188.
[13] *Ibid.*, pp. 224–25. Heyberger, *Les chrétiens du proche-orient*, p. 502.

and his Armenian ally, despite having less money to dole out as gifts.[14] The Catholic's celebration was short lived as Phanariot money soon won Sophronios' release and his investiture by imperial patent as metropolitan once again.

With their patriarchs and metropolitans so frequently absent from the city, Aleppo's Catholics became adept at finding alternate strategies that would allow them to practice their faith as they pleased. The orders emanating from Istanbul may have caused temporary disruptions of their religious life, but they did little to eradicate Catholic loyalties. When the provincial governors cooperated with the "traditionalist" factions and ordered the churches turned over to them, the Catholics would employ alternative strategies. These included taking communion with the Maronites, or celebrating the mass in their own homes as many of the houses of the Christian elite had elaborate chapels within their walls and outside the public gaze of the Muslim authorities.[15] That the Uniate Catholic clergy openly offered the sacraments in Aleppo, with only temporary interdictions, is a testimony both to the steadfastness of the local Catholic clergy and the willingness of the Christian merchants to expend their treasure in the Catholic cause. This created a simmering contest between the two factions, with the Porte typically supporting orthodoxy, while the city's governors and qadis sided with the Catholics. Weighing the availability of ready cash against the sultan's possible displeasure at their noncompliance with his orders, the governors opted for the cash.[16] The qadis' rationalizations were undoubtedly more complicated as they balanced what took precedence, the shariᶜa or the sultan's writ.

The benign neglect that Syria's Catholics enjoyed at the end of the eighteenth century did not signal their victory in the *millet* wars. But the patriarchs in Istanbul had learnt that if they were going to bring their wayward flock back to orthodoxy they would need the complicity of a strong state. That was lacking until Sultan Mahmud II was able to subdue the various warlords who had contributed to the instability that brought down the reign of his uncle, Sultan Selim III in 1807. The opening bow-shot of the Porte's offensive against the Catholics of Syria came in an order issued in January 1818, directed to Hürşid Paşa, governor of Aleppo. It informed him of the various misdeeds of the Rum's clergy in his city; they had seized churches and forbidden others from the Rum (i.e. the Orthodox faction) from using them; they had built new churches; they had persisted in leading their congregations in the practice of the Frankish rites. Furthermore in defiance of an imperial order issued in 1732, Frankish priests were educating the children of the Rum in Aleppo and ministering to their infirm.

---

[14] Burayk, *Ta'rikh al-Sham*, p. 135.
[15] Istanbul, BOA, Ahkâm-ı Halep, vol. II, p. 203.
[16] ᶜAbbud, "al-Murtadd," pp. 46–47.

The order went on to state that similar abuses had occurred in Jaffa and Acre. But there, the Patriarch of Jerusalem had acted vigilantly to stop them. The metropolitan of Aleppo was, in contrast, aiding the Catholics in violation of an imperial edict issued in 1757. In conclusion, the order stipulated that the governor was to expel from the city any of the priests of the Rum who were in violation of the imperial orders and to act vigilantly to prevent the Latin priests in the city from ministering to the sultan's subjects.[17] The governors of Izmir and Damascus received similar orders. Bloody sectarian rioting between Catholics and Orthodox Christians broke out in the former in May 1818 while Catholic clergy and laity were arrested in the latter.[18]

A bona fide Orthodox metropolitan, Gerasimos al-Turkuman, arrived in Aleppo from Istanbul on March 14, 1818. He presented to the governor an imperial decree requiring the Rum in the city to accept the authority of the patriarch in Istanbul and of himself as the patriarch's representative.[19] Gerasimos was a native of Aleppo and it appears that the Ecumenical Patriarch had finally conceded to the strong preference of the city's laity for a local man to fill the post. This was a bold step as there had been apprehension in the century before among the leading Greek clerics that Arabs could not be trusted to fill any high posts in Syria, given their propensity to heresy.[20] It was a gesture much too late to win Aleppo's Rum back to Orthodoxy, however. Hürşid Paşa, temporized over the implementation of the imperial order and did not call the prominent members of the community to his residence until March 30. The assembled Catholics, numbering in the hundreds, were told that mass could no longer be celebrated in private homes. Frankish priests could not enter the homes of members of the *millet-i Rum*. Any priest of the Rum who did not acknowledge the authority of the patriarch in Istanbul would be banished from the city. Only the last of these was an innovation from the many similar orders received, and ignored, over the course of the eighteenth century. It hit, however, at the very heart of the Catholic movement among the Rum by requiring the obedience of the very clergy who had been in the vanguard of the Uniate movement.

According to accounts penned by Catholic authors, Gerasimos called the Rum Catholics to the metropolitan's residence on April 17, 1818. Several thousand Catholics showed up to hear the patriarch's order read aloud. Not willing to accept the conditions set by the Porte, they approached the governor's palace and asked for an audience. The governor agreed to meet with a delegation, including three Turkish-speaking merchants. He asked them if they weren't "Rum." They replied that they were, but that "Rum"

[17] Istanbul, BOA, MD vol. CCXXXVII, p. 205.
[18] Sonyel, *Minorities* p. 161; Mishaqa, *Murder, Mayhem*, pp. 118–20.
[19] Damascus, Aleppo Awamir al-sultaniyya, vol. XLII, pp. 53–54.
[20] Neale, *History of the Eastern Church*, pp. 193–94.

had split. The governor responded that neither in Anatolia nor in Istanbul had such a thing been heard. The delegation then tried to explain the tortuous logic of the apostolic succession from St. Peter. Apparently frustrated with their theology, the governor reportedly asked, "Well, if you are not Christians, have you become Muslims or Jews? If you are still Christians, you have to be obedient to the head of the *millet-i Rum*." The Catholics left undeterred by the governor's incomprehension of their theological arguments. They proceeded to Gerasimos' residence and from there to the central court to where he had fled once he heard the angry Catholics were returning to confront him. The governor called out his troops to forestall injury to the cleric and in the melee that ensued, eleven Catholics were killed/martyred.[21]

The official Ottoman recounting of the events, as might be expected, differs from that of the Catholics. In a lengthy commentary sent to the sultan dated April 23, 1818, Hürşid Paşa reported on his meeting with the Catholic delegation. They had told him their fathers had followed the same rites for centuries; if the sultan tried to force them to attend Orthodox services they would leave the city. This was the justification and the threat that had worked so well in the past to deflect the Porte's orders. The Rum were obdurate, the report continued, and refused to end their state of rebellion to both the Patriarch and the sultan. In the governor's mind, the two were inextricably linked. He wrote that he reminded the community's representatives that Catholics did not exist as a *millet* in the sultan's "protected domains." Despite his best efforts to dissuade them, the Christians would not listen to reason. They departed and soon attacked the residency of the patriarch's representative in the city. Faced with anarchy and rebellion, he called out his troops to restore order. Hürşid Paşa acknowledged the death of some of the "rebels," but he noted that force had been necessary to end the state of rebellion in the city. He concluded that Aleppo was at peace and that the Rum were attending services administered by Orthodox clergy.[22] The governor's account indicates he had fully assimilated the parameters of the *millet* system and the necessity to enforce it.

The account of the incident penned by Aleppo's Maronite metropolitan, Bulus Arutin, and the diary of the Carmelites reported that this incident inaugurated a period of persecution of the Rum Catholics, resulting in their outward migration to Lebanon and Istanbul. While it is clear, some of the

---

[21] Bulus Arutin, *Ahamm hawadith Halab fi nifs al-awwal min al-qarn al-tasi^c ^cashar* [The Important Events in Aleppo in the First Half of the Nineteenth Century] (Cairo, 1933), pp. 12–25; Rabbath, *Documents inédits* vol. II, pp. 57–59. Cyril Charon, citing missionary sources, claims the men were executed by the governor. *History of the Melkite Patriarchates*, vol. I, pp. 139–45; Hidemitsu Kuroki, "The Orthodox–Catholic Clash in Aleppo in 1818" *Orient* 29 (1993): 1–18.

[22] Istanbul, BOA, HH 36231.

Catholic clergy fled to the security of Mount Lebanon, both claims of extended persecution and the magnitude of outward migration of the laity are exaggerated. Rather than leave the city, the same strategies that had protected the community from earlier bouts with the Orthodox were activated. By Palm Sunday, April 19, those arrested in the disturbances had been released and representatives of the Catholic community publicly attended services in the Orthodox churches. In May, they paid a large fine to the governor and apologized for the trouble they had caused. But concomitant with that apology, the governor told the qadi that the Catholics did not have to obey any orders issued by the Orthodox metropolitan that were contrary to the shari‘a. So while the qadi forbade the Rum Catholics to attend services in other churches in the city, under pain of death for the poor and confiscation of wealth for the rich, he also prevented Metropolitan Gerasimos from compelling the Catholics to pray in his church. Rather than take communion with the Orthodox, many of the Rum Catholics simply chose to stay at home on Sundays and feast days and prayed in their private chapels as they had done in similar periods of persecution in the eighteenth century.[23]

A hint of the political maneuvering that led to this partial relaxation of the restrictions on the Rum Catholics is found in a letter written in 1841 by a group of American Protestant missionaries to the US consul in Beirut. They cited as the legal justification of their own mission among the empire's various Christian and Druze communities a *fatwa* from Istanbul that the Catholics of Aleppo had succeeded in gaining in 1819. It affirmed an earlier *fatwa* issued to the Catholics of Aleppo in 1761–62 "that if a Christian embrace the religion of a Jew, or a Jew the religion of a Christian, or of a Frank, it should not break his covenant of protection."[24] In short, the Catholics of Aleppo were free to follow the rites of the Franks, as long as they paid their taxes and were content to remain *ahl al-dhimma*. Neither *fatwa* broke new ground with the established Islamic legal tradition in respect to non-Muslims, but simply stated the old axiom "unbelief constitutes one nation" in a more explicit formulation. With his ruling, the *mufti* had implicitly rendered the ideological underpinning of the *millet* system illicit as an innovation. He did not, however, press the issue with the sultan.

The Catholics among the Rum in Syria received a reprieve in 1821 when the Greeks of the Peloponnese rose in rebellion. In retaliation, a Muslim mob lynched the Ecumenical Patriarch from the gate of the *patrikhane* in Istanbul. Sultan Mahmud, outraged by the effrontery of the rebellion, and the massacre of Muslim civilians in the Peloponnese which accompanied it, ordered that Orthodox Christians throughout the empire be humiliated and

23 Kuroki, "The Orthodox–Catholic Clash," pp. 7–8
24 ABCFM, Harvard University, microfilm 538, letter signed by E. Smith, S. Wolcott, W. Thomson, N. Keyes, and L. Thompson to J. Chapeaud, US consular agent Istanbul, dated Beirut, 20 July, 1841.

prominent members of the community executed in reprisal. In Beirut, the Orthodox clergy were imprisoned along with any of the laity who knew Greek. Abdullah Paşa, governor in Sidon, required the wealthy Orthodox Christians of the city to pay extra taxes and to be publicly slapped on the back of the neck, as a symbol of their political subordination. When the order requiring the execution of prominent Orthodox Christians reached Damascus, the governor held a council of the Muslim notables of the city to ask them how to proceed. They asserted that the Christians of the city were loyal; they had paid their taxes; the Qur'an forbade that their lives be forfeit without cause. The notables sent a petition to that effect to the sultan and the city's Christians were spared any physical punishment. The governor did command the Christians to return to wearing the dark-colored clothing, required by the local interpretation of the Pact of ʿUmar. But after a gift of 50,000 *ghurush* was proffered, that obligation was quietly dropped.[25]

The humiliation of the Orthodox hierarchy provided the Rum Catholics with the opportunity to reassert their autonomy. The Catholics of Damascus, who had been in hiding in Lebanon or keeping a low profile at home since the decrees of 1818, began to practice their rite openly in the city again.[26] A large delegation of Catholics appeared before the chief qadi in Aleppo on April 16, 1821, a mere three weeks after rebellion had broken out in the Balkans. They stressed their loyalty to the sultan in a deposition in which they emphasized that while they were indeed *Rum*, they were not *Yunan* – a name revived from antiquity to signify Greeks as an ethnic community rather than a religious one. Soon thereafter, the governor of Aleppo issued a decree recognizing the legitimacy of the Rum Catholic community, now called simply the *Katolik taifesi*.[27]

Sultan Mahmud followed suit and issued an imperial order in October 1821, acknowledging the loyalty of the Rum Catholics of Aleppo.[28] Despite this recognition, the community had still not become a *millet*, only a *ta'ifa* in a curious juxtaposition of the earlier and contemporary categories. The loyalty of the Catholics was contrasted in the imperial order to the perfidy manifested by the *millet-i Rum* whose patriarch had engaged in insurrection and treason. In reward for their steadfastness, the Catholics of Aleppo were now to be left alone in their religious practices. The *status quo* that had reigned for almost a century before 1818 returned. The difference was that the community had now won its autonomy with the sultan's sanction, making it *de jure* as well as *de facto*. As significant as that recognition was, however, no formal break in tradition had yet occurred. The Catholics were simply to have local autonomy under the rubric of their constituting the

---

[25] Mishaqa, *Murder, Mayhem*, p. 121.
[26] Kayat, *Voice from Lebanon*, p. 26; Mishaqa, *ibid.*, pp. 121–22.
[27] Kuroki, "The Orthodox–Catholic Clash," pp. 10–11; Damascus, Aleppo Awamir al-sultaniyya, vol. XXXVIII, p. 74.
[28] Damascus, *ibid.*, vol. XXXVIII, p. 141.

*millet-i Rum* in Aleppo, without the recognition that Catholics formed a *millet* in their own right in the empire at large. But the prerogatives of the Patriarch of Constantinople, inherent in his role as political head of the *millet-i Rum*, had been successfully subverted in Syria.

The sultan's good faith with the Rum Catholics of Aleppo held even after the disastrous battle of Navarino in 1828 when France and Great Britain sank the Ottoman fleet, thereby ending their neutrality in the Greek War for Independence. Enraged at Frankish duplicity, Sultan Mahmud retaliated with the arrest of Armenian Catholics throughout the empire. He had been facing intense pressure from the Gregorian Armenian Patriarch to move against the Armenian Catholics, but had held off any action for fear of alienating France. That restraint now removed, a period of persecution and arrests of Catholic Armenians followed in the capital.[29] Although all Catholics had become suspect, similarly repressive measures were directed at the Armenian Catholics alone in Aleppo in a clear signal that the trust established between the sultan and his Rum Catholic subjects had not changed.[30] At the end of the Greek War in 1829, the Armenian Catholics arrested were released. Bowing to French pressure and oiled by generous gifts from the Armenian Catholic merchants of Istanbul, the sultan recognized an Armenian Catholic *millet* in 1831. That precedent opened the way for the Syrian Catholics to press their case for similar recognition.

## The Melkite Catholic *millet*

The claim of the antiquity of the Catholic Church in Syria lay at the heart of the argument for the creation of a *millet* for the Melkite Catholics. This was underscored by the revived use of the name *Malikiyyun* for the formerly *Rum Kathulik*. Both *Malikiyyun* and *Kathulik* had been employed in internal Arabic-language Catholic documents in the eighteenth century, but neither was utilized when appealing to the Ottoman authorities for the obvious reason that the Catholics had to establish themselves in the minds of the Ottoman authorities as the "authentic" *Rum* in Syria. This would be subverted if they identified themselves with some other communal designation, especially one that linked them to the Europeans. Although *Rum Kathulik* continued to appear in Arabic documents in the nineteenth century, the word Rum was conveniently dropped from the correspondence in Ottoman Turkish in favor of the neologism *Melkit* (derived from the French) *Katolikler*.

The reason for this linguistic convention is obvious. The Greeks had become anathema in the capital and the Ottoman officials and Melkites alike could appreciate any semantic designation that might serve to

[29] Beydilli. *Recognition of the Armenian Catholic Community*, pp. 8–20.
[30] Taoutel, "Watha'iq," vol. 42, p. 403. Frazee, *Catholics and Sultans*, pp. 223–24.

distinguish the Catholic Arabs from the rebellious Greeks, for whom the Ottomans continued to employ the collective Rum. Even so, it is not entirely certain that all Ottomans appreciated the distinction between the Rum in Syria and the Rum of Rumeli (the European portions of the empire). In 1828, the authorities in Aleppo were told to confiscate all the weapons held by the Rum in Aleppo lest they rise up in support of their brethren in Greece. Similar orders went to Anatolian cities that had Greek Orthodox residents. Although it is doubtful that Aleppo's Rum had any sympathy for their erstwhile namesakes in the Balkans, the authorities in Istanbul must have been relieved to learn that they possessed a paltry 92 muskets, 62 pistols, 29 sabers (*kiliç*), and 52 long swords (*yatağan*).[31] These were hardly the stores needed for rebellion. Later in the century after it became clear to most Ottoman officials that the Rum of Syria were not Greeks, the term *Rum Katolik* could be safely used as a self-identifying label for the community in its correspondence to the Porte, without a whiff of treason.

Leaving aside the question of whether or not Syria's Christians had an unbroken historical tradition of calling themselves Melkites, the more historically suspect part of their claim was the assertion that the Syrian Christians had always called themselves "Catholics." This implied that they, unlike their Orthodox Byzantine counterparts – now labeled *Yunan* in their polemic, pointedly the same appellation used for the newly constituted Kingdom of the Hellenes – had never doubted the apostolic succession from Peter claimed by Rome. Indeed, they claimed that they had always been in communion with Rome. No historical documentation was ever produced in support of this claim but that did not stop the Melkite apologists from invoking it. Their rendering of the past further tied the group's fortunes to the foundation myth of the *millet* system. When the Ottomans conquered Syria, the patriarchs in Constantinople using the authority granted to them by Fatih Mehmed began to whittle away at the traditional autonomy of the Patriarch of Antioch. That intervention culminated in the capture of Antioch by Constantinople in 1725. This latter assertion was, of course, true, although actual interventions by the patriarchs had only begun in the late seventeenth century rather than at the time of Syria's conquest. In another claim of even more dubious historical authenticity, the Melkite polemicists asserted that all five patriarchs who had preceded Kyrillos Tanas had accepted the supremacy of the Pope in Rome and made professions of faith as Catholics.[32] Their *apologia* did not seemingly deem it important to identify the ethnicity of those five men.

In fact, an explicit claim that the Melkite Church was Arab was never forwarded at all. Rather, it was asserted that the church was "Syrian" with

---

[31] Damascus, Aleppo Awamir al-sultaniyya, vol. XLV, p. 4; Istanbul, BOA, Cevdet Dahiliye 8316.
[32] Introduction by Qustantin Basha to Mazlum, *Nabdha ta'rikhiyya*.

the newly configured Melkites contending that they were the heirs to the original Church of the Rum in Syria. The Melkite apologists asserted that the Syrian church hierarchy followed in a direct line of descent established in Antioch by the apostles Peter and Paul and was fully autonomous from the Greek Church from the Arab conquest of Syria until the eighteenth century. This was true, but for geopolitical rather than theological reasons. Following this line of defense, the faction loyal to Constantinople represented the sin of innovation, not the Catholics as the latter were simply following the "traditions of their fathers and grandfathers." Amidst this account of origins were liberally interspersed references to the unquestioned and continuous loyalty of the Catholic people of Syria to the sultans. This was a not so veiled appeal to the perception prevalent in official Ottoman circles that the "true" Rum, i.e. Greeks, were guilty of perfidy and rebellion and could no longer be fully trusted.

Armed with these arguments and the financial backing of wealthy Syrian Catholic merchants, Maksimos Mazlum, who had been elevated as the Catholic Patriarch of Antioch by Rome, set off in 1837 to Istanbul. Once there, he was presented to Sultan Mahmud, through the mediation of the Armenian Catholic Patriarch and Yusuf Hajjar, a prominent Aleppo Catholic merchant long resident in Istanbul. The intercession, cash, and the arguments for separation were ultimately successful. An order sent from the Porte to "our loyal governor of Egypt, Mehmed Ali" in April 1841, announced that the Melkite Catholics had separated from the "old" Rum (*Rum-i atik*). However, the order went on, the Orthodox were not turning over churches to the Catholics as ordered. It further cited an earlier document preserved at the Porte from June 1838 recognizing Maksimos Mazlum as the Catholic Patriarch of Antioch.[33] That recognition did not constitute the establishment of a *millet*, however. Rather, using the model of the Orthodox Ecumenical Patriarch in Istanbul, with subordinate patriarchs of Antioch and Jerusalem, the sultan's bureaucrats constructed the Melkite Catholics as being a subgroup of the Armenian Catholic *millet*. With that paradigm in mind, the Melkite Patriarch of Antioch was simply the junior partner to the Armenian Catholic Patriarch in Istanbul, in effect creating a multi-ethnic Catholic *millet* to stand as a mirror image of the one controlled by the Ecumenical Patriarch. This was a start, but obviously not enough for Mazlum.

He resumed his lobbying efforts in Istanbul following the Ottoman reoccupation of Syria in 1841. Finally in December 1845, Maksimos Mazlum received an imperial decree stating his church was no longer part of the Armenian Catholic *millet*. This document still did not establish a separate *millet* for the Melkites, but simply affirmed that his patriarchate was independent from the three established Christian *millet*s, i.e. the Greek

---

[33] Istanbul, BOA, Cevdet Adliye 5029.

Orthodox, the Armenian Gregorian, and the Armenian Catholic, while not constituting a formal fourth Christian *millet* in its own right. That recognition of a Melkite *millet* finally came on May 23, 1848, when an imperial order named Maksimos as Patriarch of the Melkite Catholics with authority over that community's churches in the patriarchal sees of Antioch, Jerusalem, and Alexandria. The document went on to state that although many previous imperial orders had established the Melkite Catholics as an independent church – as had been the case for the Nestorians, Maronites, and Jacobites – there had been as yet no official elevation of any of these communities into a *millet*. All metropolitans, priests, and religious of the Melkite Catholic *millet* were henceforth to submit to Maksimos Mazlum as their spiritual leader. No one else was to interfere in the free practice of their faith, under pain of prosecution by the shariʿa courts.[34] Syria's Catholics had finally achieved their own *millet*. This new church was to be as hierarchical as the Orthodox one from which they had long sought autonomy. The difference was that Syrians were now in charge.

A summary of Ottoman census data compiled in 1914 returned a total of 62,468 Greek Catholic adults – of whom 8,182 lived in Aleppo province, 27,662 in Suriye (Damascus) province, and 24,210 in Beirut province – out of total adult population for the empire of 18,520,016.[35] The Melkite Catholics were a small minority within the Christian minority of the Ottoman Arab provinces on the eve of the First World War. Although the Melkite Catholics of Aleppo had been their patriarch's most ardent supporters in his attempt to gain recognition from the sultan, his flock were by 1914 much more numerous in Syria's southern provinces, a result of revived proselytism in the nineteenth century. Nonetheless, the history of the Catholic enterprise in Aleppo – from the arrival of the Latin missionaries in Aleppo in 1627 to the establishment of the Melkite *millet* in 1848 – provides an example of an incorporation of European intellectual influences by Christian Arabs. It also demonstrates their successful political mediation between the European powers, especially France, and the Ottoman state, as well as a cultural mediation between the Latin West and the traditions of Christian Syria.

## Becoming Catholic, remaining Syrian: the case of Hindiyya ʿUjaymi

The Catholics of Syria did not embrace everything Roman with equal enthusiasm. The Latin clergy reciprocated their ambivalence, often characterizing their native brothers and sisters in Christ as ungrateful pupils. The initial ambition of the Latin Catholic missionaries was to bring the Middle

---

[34] Mazlum, *Nabdha ta'rikhiyya*, p. 120; Arabic translation of this document is contained in *ibid.*, pp. 305–13. A copy of the Turkish original is preserved in Istanbul, BOA, Gayri Müslim Cemaat series, "Melkit Katolikler," pp. 11–12.

[35] Barkan, *Ottoman Population*, pp. 188–89.

Eastern Christians into full communion with the Holy Father as proper Roman Catholics. Over the course of the eighteenth century, the policy was modified to eliminate simply those doctrines or practices which ran counter to the true Christian faith, as defined in Rome. The compromise maintained the hierarchies of the traditional churches with their offices of metropolitans and patriarchs as well as many of the cultural trappings of the Orthodox churches. The physical external façade of the church in the East had not changed. Latin plaster statues did not replace icons; the local clergy proudly retained the clerical garb and "stove-pipe" headgear of the orthodox tradition and were even joined by the Jesuits who appropriated the cassocks and black turbans of the Maronite clergy as their own.

In a bow to Syria's cultural identity, however, Arabic began to replace the older liturgical languages – Greek and Syriac, and even in some cases Armenian in the Uniate churches. This concession to localist sentiments enabled Catholics in Syria to receive the sacraments in their own tongue two centuries before the Vatican would allow most of their coreligionists elsewhere to do the same. A similar linguistic dispensation was granted to the Ukrainian Uniate Church, founded at about the same time. As an unintended result, the Catholic movement in Syria was closely associated with the Arabic language from the start. To spread the new dogma, the Metropolitan Athanasios Dabbas established in Aleppo the first Arabic printing press in the Ottoman Empire, in 1706. The press was subsequently moved to Lebanon in 1720 after his elevation to Patriarch, due to opposition from the Orthodox faction in the city to this "innovation." The press continued to print catechisms, selected books of the Bible, and hagiographies in Arabic throughout the century contributing both to greater literacy and a more informed understanding of the dogma of their new creed for Syria's Catholics.[36] These books circulated in Syria, adding the crucial dimension of the "print revolution," as delineated by Benedict Anderson,[37] to the possibility of an "imagining" of a collective identity for Syria's Catholics. This cultural "Arabism" was expressed in the church in other ways as well. The liturgical music composed by the Catholics in the Ottoman period reflected the aesthetic tastes of Arab Syria, rather than those of the Latin West or Byzantine Constantinople, even as Western religious imagery was appropriated into the hymns' lyrics.[38]

The need to work within the established churches became even more expedient for the Latins after the debacle of Chios when it became clear that the Ottoman authorities would not acquiesce to *dhimmi*s becoming Roman Catholics. In the case of the Rum, Armenians, Jacobites, and Nestorians, the goal of the Latins was to convince the local clergy to choose pope over

[36] Muhammad Raghib al-Tabbakh, *I'lam al-nubala bi-ta'rikh Halab al-shahba'* [Notices on the Nobles in the History of Aleppo, the Milky-White] (Aleppo, 1923–26), vol. III, pp. 247–48.
[37] Anderson, *Imagined Communities*, pp. 44–46.
[38] Sr. Marie Keyrouz, *Chant traditionnel maronite*, compact disc (Arles, France, 1991).

patriarch, and more ideally, that the patriarch himself would seek communion with Rome, as in the case of Kyrillos al-Zaᶜim. With the Maronites,
however, it was felt that a more activist stance should be advanced as the
hierarchy of that church had accepted papal authority. The missionaries
should, therefore, work to bring the Maronites into full conformity with
Latin practice and beliefs. The policy ran into problems, however, as some
of the Maronites refused to conform to Latin norms.

The tension between embracing the new and retaining the old crystallized
in the controversy surrounding Hindiyya ᶜUjaymi. Hindiyya was undoubtedly one of the most extraordinary individuals to emerge out of Catholic
Syria in the eighteenth century. She was born into a wealthy Maronite
merchant family in Aleppo in 1720. Her family displayed the proclivity for
both trade and holy orders characteristic of Syria's Catholics of all four
sects. Her brother, Niqula, became a Jesuit and Hindiyya was drawn to the
religious life early, reportedly precociously reciting both the *Pater Noster*
and the *Ave* at age three. As an adolescent, she indulged in various forms of
self-mortification and fasting. Then, sometime in her early twenties, she
claimed to have experienced a mystical union with Christ.[39]

From the start of her mystical journey, many Maronites supported
Hindiyya ᶜUjaymi, including Jarmanus Saqr their metropolitan in Aleppo.
She also quickly gained a following among the city's Rum and Suryani
Catholics. At the age of twenty-eight, she left Aleppo for the monastery of
ᶜAyntura in Mount Lebanon. There, she started in 1750 her own holy order,
the Sisters of the Sacred Heart of Jesus which was the first exclusively
women's order in the Maronite church. She later established a convent in
Bkirki where her open proclamations of her mystical experience soon
became a matter of controversy. With Hindiyya's claim that Christ spoke
directly through her after she had been transformed by a shared physical
presence with the Holy Trinity, her Jesuit advisers began to distance
themselves from her. They sent reports of her activities to the Vatican,
expressing the fear that she had crossed into heresy. When the Maronite
Patriarch ᶜAwad heard of this, he threatened to excommunicate any of his
flock who attended services with the Jesuits in retaliation. Pope Benedict
XIV, in an attempt to diffuse the situation, appointed a committee headed
by an Aleppo-born Franciscan in 1753 to investigate Hindiyya's teachings;
it found her blameless.[40] Pope Benedict, sensing conciliation was better than
an open break with the Maronites, recommended Hindiyya's convent be
constructed in the mountains, away from the distraction of the city and not
incidentally, her most devoted supporters.

[39] Hindiyya ᶜUjaymi, *Aqwal al-rahiba Hindiyya ᶜUjaymi al-Halabiyya wa tarjumat hayatiha*
[The Sayings of Sr. Hindiyya ᶜUjaymi, the Aleppine, and her Biography]. Edited by Butrus
Fahd (Jounieh, Lebanon, 1972); see also van Leeuwen, *Notables and Clergy*, pp. 133–38;
Heyberger, *Les chrétiens du proche-orient*, pp. 515–20.
[40] Frazee, *Catholics and Sultans*, pp. 196–97.

The controversy did not go away. When Yusuf Istifan became Patriarch of the Maronites in 1766, his earlier opposition to Hindiyya evaporated. Hindiyya was, after all, still wildly popular in Aleppo and she received moral support from the hierarchies of the other Uniate churches in that city. Perhaps as a result of his support for her, Istifan was relieved of his patriarchal duties by the Pope and ordered to Rome in 1779. In his absence, a council presided over by Fr. Pietro de Moretta, the papal legate to the Maronites, met in Mayfuq in 1780 and abolished Hindiyya's order. From that point on, Hindiyya lived a quiet secluded life until her death in 1798.[41]

Although Hindiyya ʿUjaymi's writings were proscribed in 1780, a manuscript copy, entitled *Kashf al-asrar al-khafiyya mima ra'aytuhu fi al-khizana al-sirriyya* (The Disclosure of the hidden secrets that I saw in the Secret Treasury) and dated 18 August, 1774 with her seal, has survived in the Vatican Library. In an example of the syncretism between East and West that infused so much of the Catholic Syrians' world-view in the eighteenth century, Niqula ʿUjaymi, Hindiyya's Jesuit brother and transcriber, claimed that his sister's poor knowledge of literary Arabic constituted a proof that her inspiration was from Christ. How else could a semi-literate woman produce such an intricate elaboration of her mystical experience? It is an argument that echoes the Muslim tradition of an illiterate Prophet Muhammad. Hindiyya described her experience of unity with the eternal reality of Christ through the medium of the Sacred Heart. In that incarnation, she was able to travel back to the very creation of the universe with stops along the way to the Garden of Eden.[42] Through her union with Christ, she was able to relive Jesus' experiences as a fetus growing in Mary's womb as well as the agony of His death.[43] All the imagery described so far betrays hints of a strong Latin influence in her writings as befits a woman educated by the Jesuits. The very centrality of the Sacred Heart in her cosmology provides evidence of her Western education, as it was an object of religious contemplation and veneration absent in Eastern Christian devotional literature before the arrival of the Latins.

But it was apparently the Eastern elements that led to the banning of her work. These have a remarkable resonance to Muslim mystical writings and lead us to wonder if Hindiyya had actual first-hand knowledge of Sufi texts. Her journey with Christ resembles the *marahil* (stages) of some Sufi accounts of enlightenment and like them she also places a major emphasis on encountering the Tree of Life in paradise. This, in turn, is an image drawn originally from Jewish mysticism. It frequently appears in Sufi texts but is rarely found in Latin Christian mystical writings. Hindiyya's use of

---

[41] Richard van Leeuwen, *Notables and Clergy*, pp. 119–20.
[42] ʿUjaymi, *Aqwal al-rahiba*, p. 26.
[43] *Ibid.*, p. 62.

the theme of the four component elements of the universe – earth, wind, air, and fire – to explore Christ's nature also reminds us of the Sufi embrace of neo-Platonist doctrines in its arguments and imagery. Lastly and most dangerously for Rome, the merger of herself with God through the medium of Christ hints at the sufi concept of *fana'* (the loss of self in God's presence). In short, Hindiyya's mystical vision shows a remarkable assimilation of Western and Eastern traditions. Like her, Syrian Catholics explored the new cultural possibilities inherent in their acceptance of Catholicism but they also sought to retain elements of their traditions that might be judged by the Latins as inappropriate or even heretical. Despite the polemics of their Orthodox antagonists, they had not become "Franks" in all aspects of their culture, but clung ferociously to those elements they deemed culturally significant.[44]

## The ubiquitous Catholic merchant

In seeking an explanation why the Catholics of Syria were able to deflect the attempts by the Orthodox hierarchy to turn them from heresy, eighteenth-century Orthodox chroniclers cited the nefarious hand of the Franks.[45] Fr. Burayk in Damascus reported that a visiting delegation of Orthodox priests from Russia had informed him that France sought to insinuate the Catholic heresy in their land as it succeeded in doing in Syria. But their great queen Catherine was well aware of the danger and was vigilant in her defense of orthodoxy. The implicit subtext was that the Ottoman sultans were impotent to do the same. It should come as no surprise that later in his narrative, Burayk reports Moscow's victories over the sultan's forces with obvious glee, as well as the prophecy that the house of Osman would fall in 1762 with the conquest of Constantinople by some unnamed Christian hero.[46] Russia had emerged, for him and undoubtedly for others throughout Syria who remained loyal to the old dispensation, as that hero ready to defend the flame of the true orthodox faith against a sultan who had been bought with Frankish silver.

The French unquestionably had a hand in promoting Catholicism and supported the Catholic community in Syria diplomatically and financially whenever possible. But the emergent Syrian Catholic commercial bourgeoisie more consistently provided the principal financial support for the Catholic faction as the eighteenth century progressed and the *millet* wars intensified. Their conversion in matters of faith was also emblematic of the Syrian Catholics' awareness of changes occurring globally and their ambi-

[44] Thomas Philipp, "Image and Self-Image of the Syrians in Egypt: From the Early Eighteenth Century to the Reign of Muhammad ʿAli" in *Christians and Jews in the Ottoman Empire*. Edited by B. Braude and B. Lewis (New York, 1982), vol. II, pp. 167–84.
[45] Papadopoullos, *Studies and Documents*, p. 227.
[46] Burayk, *Ta'rikh al-Sham*, pp. 29, 100, 54–58.

tion to profit from them.[47] Perhaps as a result of that newly found connection to a wider world, Catholic Syrians were much more willing than their Muslim or Orthodox neighbors to move from their native cities in search of profit. Catholic merchants from Aleppo and Damascus relocated to the coastal towns of Sidon, Tyre, and Acre and beyond Syria, to Egypt, Izmir, and Istanbul. Their migration to Egypt has been attributed to persecution in the interior cities of Damascus and Aleppo by the Ottoman authorities.[48] But the suggestion that persecution drove the Catholic merchants from Aleppo is not supported by evidence from that city itself. True, the city's prosperous Catholic bourgeoisie often invoked the threat of flight, but they usually found alternative strategies to forestall their actual leaving. There is less evidence that the Catholics of Damascus were able to weather attempts to extirpate Catholicism, especially after the crackdown in 1749–50. But all things considered, the pursuit of profits rather than a fear of persecution would appear to be the major motivating factor for the migration into what were for them new centers of commerce.

Christians from interior Syria began to migrate to the coastal towns of Lebanon and Palestine where the French had relocated much of their trade in the late seventeenth century even before the open rift in the Syrian church occurred. Sidon was a center of Catholic activity almost from the start of the Latin missions to the Levant and continued to attract Catholics as the French diplomatic presence in the city afforded them some protection. Elsewhere in Lebanon, the Catholics could count on Druze protection or Shica indifference to the open practice of their faith. They built their first church in the village of Zahle on the edge of Lebanon's Biqca valley in 1740.[49] The valley was the domain of the Shica Harfush clan who rarely followed Istanbul's dictates on anything and they undoubtedly welcomed the wealth the Catholics brought within their grasp. By the middle of the nineteenth century, Zahle had become a prosperous market town with the largest concentration of Melkite Catholics in Lebanon.[50] Elsewhere, Jirjis Mishaqa built the first church in Tyre, where before his arrival in 1750 no Christians had lived.[51]

The authorities in Istanbul were aware of the growing presence of Melkite Catholics in Lebanon and Palestine, prompted by complaints arriving from the Orthodox Patriarch of Jerusalem. The sultan dispatched orders to the governor of Sidon in September 1754, and again in 1767, informing him that Frankish priests were regularly visiting Christian peasants in the Acre

[47] Philipp, *Syrians in Egypt*, pp. 11–18.
[48] Raymond, *Artisans et commerçants au Caire* vol. II, pp. 483–84; Philipp, *ibid.*, pp. 2–24.
[49] Philipp, *ibid.*, p. 21.
[50] Leila Fawaz, "Zahle and Dayr al-Qamar: Two Market Towns of Mount Lebanon during the Civil War of 1860" in *Lebanon: A History of Conflict and Consensus*. Edited by N. Shehadi and D. Haffar Mills (London, 1988), pp. 49–63.
[51] Mishaqa, *Murder, Mayhem*, p. 12; Philipp, *Syrians in Egypt*, pp. 11–12.

region. The Christians claimed in response that they were simply following the same rites as had their forefathers since the "time of the conquest" and occupying churches, which were built by their ancestors. The sultan was not moved by their appeal to tradition. His order further stipulated that only clergy approved by the patriarch could minister to "Arab peasants" (*reaya-ı fellah-ı Araban*, literally, "peasants of the Bedouin") and any of the clergy who did not submit to the patriarch's authority would be exiled.[52] The curious use of "Arab" in the document was taken from the patriarch's original complaint and suggests that the patriarch, at least, was aware of a possible ethnic subtext to the Catholic–Orthodox struggle in Syria. It is not clear that either order was actually implemented. But we may surmise there was even less of an inclination on the part of the local authorities to obey the Porte's writ in Lebanon or Palestine than there had been in Aleppo. The threat that they might, however, may have given some Catholic merchants a nudge in the direction of Egypt.

Trade between Syria and Egypt was largely in the hands of Muslims in the early Ottoman centuries.[53] The court records of Aleppo show that Christians from the city began to be involved in the Egyptian trade during the last quarter of the seventeenth century, but there is scant evidence to suggest there was significant migration to Egypt at that time. That would change in the next century. While there had been only a handful of Syrian Christians resident in Cairo in 1730, the *Description de l'Egypte* reported over 5,000 in 1800.[54] More significant than their numbers, was their spectacular success in Egypt's commerce. The community's rising eminence in Egypt was concomitant with the fall of the financial position of the elite of Cairo's Jewish community. Jews had served as the principal money-lenders, customs officers, and masters of Cairo's mint in the first two centuries of Ottoman rule. But Jewish fortunes took a dramatic downturn when Bulut Kapan Ali Paşa emerged as Egypt's strongman in 1768. Following his rise to power, Jews were removed from their positions in the customs office, their wealth confiscated, and several prominent figures in the community were executed.[55] Syrian Catholics quickly took their places and they also began to replace Jews as dragomans working for the European merchants present in Egypt. By the end of the century, most of the coastal trade between Syria and Egypt was in the their hands. They also played a significant role in the marketing of European goods in interior Egypt and

[52] Istanbul, BOA, Ahkâm-ı Şam-ı Şerif, vol. II, pp. 28–29, 323.

[53] Nelly Hanna, *Making Big Money in 1600: The Life and Times of Isma'il Abu Taqiyya, Egyptian Merchant* (Syracuse, NY, 1998).

[54] Raymond, *Artisans et commerçants*, vol. II, p. 492; Edward Lane, *Manners and Customs of the Modern Egyptians* (London, 1908), p. 23.

[55] Raymond, *ibid.*, vol. II, pp. 460–63; Winter, *Egyptian Society*, pp. 203–10; Philipp, *Syrians in Egypt*, pp. 31–34; J. W. Livingstone, "Ali Bey al-Kabir and the Jews" *Middle Eastern Studies* 7 (1971): 221–28.

along the littoral of the Red Sea.[56] The Syrian Catholics continued to play a dominant role in Egypt's economy until the reign of Mehmed Ali (1805–48) when their commercial preeminence was partially eclipsed by migrants from Greece.[57]

The wealth and political success that accrued to Syrian Christians in late eighteenth-century Egypt often came at the expense of Muslim merchants, as well as their Jewish competitors. When Muslim Cairenes rose in rebellion against Napoleon Bonaparte's occupation of the city in 1798, the Syrian Christians bore the animus of the rebels' outrage, while the Jewish population went largely unscathed. The Syrians, and to a lesser extent the Copts, were perceived by the Muslims as collaborators with the French. Despite Napoleon's protestation that he was a friend of Islam and an enemy of the Holy Father, no one in Egypt was fooled. The Franks were still Christians in the eyes of Muslim Egyptians, even if they professed to be Atheists. The opulent life-style of the Syrian Catholics undoubtedly added envy to the insult felt by many in the Muslim community that Christians, whether foreign or domestic, were upsetting the established social order.[58] The Syrian Christians of Cairo had achieved the dubious distinction of being the first victims of what would become a series of sectarian outbursts which would accompany the Ottoman Arab world's troubled transition to a new political and economic order, dominated by the nations of western Europe. By the end of the eighteenth century, few other non-Muslim communities in the Arab Middle East had been transformed so dramatically, or so quickly, by the region's transitional phase into an increasingly global economy. As one of the most obvious beneficiaries of change, they became the most easily identifiable symbols of what had gone wrong for those for whom change did not bode well.

### The changing fortunes of the region's Jewish merchants and the beginning of sectarian dissonance

The economic transitions that accompanied the Ottoman Empire's "long" eighteenth century often generated bitter competition between social groups for resources. That competition helped to intensify the significance of religious identities. Napoleon's occupation of Egypt had set off the first serious outbreak of anti-Christian rioting in Egypt since the sectarian unrest that land experienced in the wake of the Crusades. But animosities were

[56] Raymond, *ibid.*, vol. II, pp. 489–90.
[57] Philipp, *Syrians in Egypt*, pp. 78–95; Alexander Kitroeff, *The Greeks in Egypt: Ethnicity and Class* (London, 1989).
[58] ʿAbd al-Rahman al-Jabarti, *ʿAjaʾib al-athar fi al-tarajim wa al-akhbar* [Curious Impressions from Biographies and Events], 7 vols. (Cairo, 1958–67), vol. IV, pp. 328–40. Philipp, *ibid.*, pp. 48–52; Partial English translation of al-Jabarti, *Napoleon in Egypt: al-Jabarti's Chronicle of the French Occupation.* Translated by Shmuel Moreh (Princeton, NJ, 1993).

also intensifying between Jews and Catholics as the improved position of the Catholic merchants in the Arab Levant often came at the expense of Jewish bankers and merchants, as had occurred in Egypt. Rivalry between individuals from the two communities also flared in Palestine in the eighteenth century. When the shaikh of the Ziyadina clan, Dahir al-ʿUmar, was in political ascendancy in the Galilee, Catholics were favored and he allowed them to build a new church in Nazareth. Dahir's chief financial advisor was Ibrahim al-Sabbagh, a Melkite Catholic, and the two men amassed fortunes in a mutually profitable relationship. When Dahir died in 1775, Ahmed Cezzar Paşa replaced him as the strong man in Acre. His financial advisors and bankers were drawn from the Jewish Farhi family of Damascus who had long been the economic rivals of al-Sabbagh. After Ahmed Cezzar's death, the Damascene Catholic al-Bahri clan would challenge the paramount position of the Farhis in turn.[59] Although the competition between these families was intensely personal, it could easily adapt to the readily available rhetoric of religious difference as each, in turn, sought to rally support from their own sectarian community.

Economic competition between Arabic-speaking Jews and Christians was a relatively recent development. Jewish merchants had successfully established themselves as financiers and bankers throughout the Ottoman Arab lands in the late sixteenth and early seventeenth centuries. Many of these were Sephardim, but in Damascus and the cities of Iraq Arabic-speaking Jews predominated. In the early Ottoman centuries, their main economic competitors had been Armenians. In the Syrian cities, the Jews won the battle for commercial dominance by the middle of the seventeenth century. This symbolically was marked in Aleppo with the capture of the lucrative post of chief customs officer by Musa walad Ishaq al-Khakham from Sanos Karagözoğlu, a Julfa Armenian in 1640.[60] Although Muslims would typically serve as chief customs officers after 1660, Jews continued to dominate the customs bureaucracy in the city, claiming in a petition to the Porte in 1707 that they held their posts by hereditary right. They were finally ousted from that position by imperial decree in 1831 and Armenians regained the dominant position in the city's customs house that they had lost two centuries before.[61] Jews also held a virtual monopoly over the collection of customs duties in Damascus before the mid-nineteenth century when Christian Arabs replaced them.

---

[59] Thomas Philipp, "Jews and Arab Christians: Their Changing Positions in Politics and Economy in Eighteenth-Century Syria and Egypt" in *Egypt and Palestine: A Millennium of Association (868–1948)*. Edited by Amnon Cohen and Gabriel Baer (New York, 1984), pp. 150–66; Amnon Cohen, *Palestine in the 18th Century* (Jerusalem, 1973), pp. 16, 32; Chad Emmett, *Beyond the Basilica: Christians and Muslims in Nazareth* (Chicago, IL, 1995), pp. 22–23.

[60] Masters, *Origins*, pp. 139–43.

[61] Istanbul, BOA, MM 2777, p. 5; Damascus, Aleppo Awamir al-sultaniyya, vol. XLVI, pp. 91–92.

In Iraq, competition among the various diasporic trading communities centered in Basra where the British East India Company established a commanding presence in the latter half of the eighteenth century. Although Armenian merchants held the initial advantage due to their connections to Iran, Jewish merchants were able to displace them as agents and allies of the British factors in the nineteenth century. This came as a sharp reversal of the situation in the eighteenth century when the British had invariably chosen the Armenians as allies as they viewed the Jewish merchants as potential competitors for Britain's trade in the Gulf. The Jewish merchants, in turn, had created alliances with the Mamluk beys of Baghdad who sought to subvert the British monopoly over Iraq's export trade.[62] It is not clear why British commercial and diplomatic interests became so intimately linked to the fortunes of the Iraqi Jews in the nineteenth century, but the growing importance of the Iraq–India trade was clearly a factor.

Jews from Syria and Iraq established a commercial presence in the Indian port of Surat in the seventeenth century, independent of a British connection. But with the rise of Bombay (Mumbai) as an entrepôt of the East India Company, Arabic-speaking Jews, who were indiscriminately called "Baghdadis" in British India, moved their operations to that city. The importance of the community in Bombay was greatly enhanced with the arrival of David Sassoon as a refugee from the tyrannical rule of Daud Paşa, governor of Baghdad (1817–31). Sassoon founded in Bombay a merchant dynasty that by the end of the nineteenth century extended to Calcutta, Singapore, Hong Kong, and Shanghai.[63] Although the "Baghdadi" community of India never equaled the trading diaspora of the Syrian Catholics in terms of numbers, they represented with their East Asian commercial orientation a mirror image of the Syrian Catholics' commercial success. Both communities adapted to, and profited from, an increasing globalization of trade and from an association with a powerful European patron. In the case of the Catholics, that patron was France, for the commercial elite among the Iraqi Jews it was the United Kingdom.

Elsewhere in the Fertile Crescent, Jewish merchants played a prominent role in the caravan trade of the interior. Russell reported that the caravans between Aleppo and Baghdad stopped in their tracks to accommodate the Jewish Sabbath.[64] Jewish merchants were especially conspicuous in Damascus where wealthy individuals built houses the equal, in terms of opulence and grandeur, of those constructed by the Catholic merchants in Judayda in Aleppo. Interestingly, given the rise of the Christian merchants elsewhere in Syria in the eighteenth century, there was no significant

---

[62] Thabet Abdullah, "The political economy of merchants and trade in Basra, 1722–1795" (Ph.D. dissertation, Georgetown University, 1992), pp. 169–77.
[63] Joan Roland, *Jews in British India: Identity in a Colonial Era* (Hanover, NH, 1989), pp. 15–19; Hillel, *Unknown Jews*, pp. 118–20.
[64] Russell, *Natural History*, vol. II, pp. 78–79.

Christian mercantile presence in Damascus until the nineteenth century. But it must be remembered that Damascus had neither European consuls nor resident merchants who might take the city's Christians as protégés until after the Egyptian occupation in 1831.

The contrast in the religious composition of the non-Muslim commercial elites in Aleppo and Damascus is illustrated by a quick comparison of those who enrolled as *Avrupa tüccarıs* in the two cities between 1815 and 1831. The *Avrupa tüccarıs* were non-Muslim merchants who were granted imperial patents allowing them to trade and import goods at the same favorable customs rates granted to the Europeans and their protégés under the terms of the capitulatory treaties. It was thought that such a scheme would encourage non-Muslim merchants to substitute a clientage relationship to the sultan for one to a European power. Sixty-one merchants eventually enrolled in the program in Aleppo: forty-three Christian Arabs (almost all of whom were Catholics), twelve Jews, and six Armenians. By contrast, only eleven non-Muslim merchants appeared to have enrolled in Damascus.[65] Significantly, however, all but one of these were Jews, including Yaᶜqub Abu al-ᶜAfiya, Harun al-Harari, and Yusuf Liniado who would be implicated by Christian informers and arrested during the events of 1840.[66]

Even in Aleppo, the Catholics had not completely supplanted Jewish merchants. This was especially true for the Sephardim who retained foreign citizenship. Such claims for foreign protection usually derived from one of the Italian states or Austria, but others who had family ties to the port of Leghorn could claim French protection.[67] In addition to the Sephardic merchants, some of the Arabic-speaking Jewish community also prospered in this period of transition. Although they reached neither the pinnacles of wealth nor influence attained by the Catholic merchants or their Sephardic coreligionists, Arabic-speaking Jewish merchants were nonetheless active in the specialized trade niche with Baghdad, which they shared with Muslim merchants. John Bowring's report of 1838 mentions only Christians and Muslims as being involved in Aleppo's trade with Iraq, but all the *Avrupa tüccarıs* in Aleppo who received patents for their agents to reside in Iraq were Jews.[68] Furthermore, a list of Aleppine contributors to the sultan's war chest in June 1829, included three Muslims

[65] Bruce Masters, "The Sultan's Entrepreneurs: The *Avrupa Tüccarıs* and the *Hayriye Tüccarıs* in Syria" *International Journal of Middle Eastern Studies* 24 (1992): 579–97.

[66] Damascus, Damascus Awamir al-sultaniyya, vol. II, p. 124; vol. IV, pp. 66–67, 70–71, 86–87. John Bowring, *Report of the Commercial Statistics of Syria* (Reprinted New York, 1973), p. 94.

[67] Thomas Philipp, "French Merchants and Jews in the Ottoman Empire during the Eighteenth Century" in *Jews of the Ottoman Empire*. Edited by A. Levy (Princeton, NJ, 1994), pp. 315–25.

[68] Bowring, *Report*, pp. 44–45.

and four Jews listed under the heading of "Baghdadi merchants," but no Christians.[69]

Given the continued predominance of Jewish merchants in Damascus and the rise of Catholic ambitions throughout Syria in the early nineteenth century, it is not surprising that sectarian dissonance between Catholics and Jews in Syria first occurred in that city. It is also significant that the outburst occurred in 1840 after almost a decade of occupation by the forces of Mehmed Ali. Egypt's war-lord had given free reign to Catholic aspirations under his rule, allowing their clergy to occupy churches formerly held by the Orthodox faction and appointing Catholics to his administration. The Catholics in Damascus were undoubtedly enjoying a triumphalist moment after almost a century of repression by the orthodox clergy. It would also seem they were on a collision course of competing economic ambitions with the city's Jewish merchants. All that was lacking was an incident to bring the tensions into the open.

The flash point came in 1840 when a Latin Catholic priest and his servant went missing, having been last seen in Damascus' Jewish Quarter. Some in the Christian community brought forward the charge that the two had been abducted and murdered by Jews so that their blood might be used in a Passover ritual. The Egyptian military governor moved to arrest several prominent members of the Jewish community; fines were levied; those arrested were tortured to confess to the crime or name those who had committed it. Although the incident did not lead to a widescale pogrom against the Jewish community of Damascus, as has been claimed by some historians,[70] it ushered in a period of heightened tensions throughout Syria between the Christian and Jewish communities. When the reputed bones of the priest were discovered, six prominent members of Damascus' Jewish community were arrested on murder charges, including the three previously mentioned *Avrupa tüccarıs*. Other Jews were arrested when the reputed bones of the servant were uncovered. In the end, four men died from torture endured while in prison, with the remainder released only after a prolonged period of negotiations, accompanied by gifts liberally extended to many in the governor's saray. This incident became known as the "Damascus Affair" in Europe where it served to galvanize newly emancipated Jews to the fate of their coreligionists in the "Sick Man of Europe." In much the same way, the Greek War for Independence had previously focused Western European and North American Christian public attention on the fate of the Christian subjects of the empire. It also revealed the specter of anti-Semitism, especially in France where the popular press played up the lurid side of the case.[71]

[69] Damascus, Aleppo Awamir al-sultaniyya, vol. LXV, pp. 134–37.
[70] Shaw, *Jews of the Ottoman Empire*, p. 199.
[71] Jonathan Frankel, *The Damascus Affair: "Ritual Murder," Politics and the Jews in 1840* (Cambridge, 1997).

If the "Damascus Affair" highlighted the presence of anti-Semitism in Europe, it is less certain what it says about attitudes then current among Syrian Catholics. The accusations leveled by the Christians against Jews were most probably attempts to undermine the community's economic position, rather than arising out of some deep wellspring of religious prejudice. But the question of whether the charge in Damascus echoed some deeper anti-Semitic sentiments among Syrian Christians remains.[72] Russell reported in the eighteenth century from Aleppo that "Some of the ignorant vulgar among the Christian natives, pretend that the Jews have sometimes, on this occasion (i.e. Passover) sacrificed a Christian child stolen from its parents." He further cites William Biddulph as reporting in 1600, based on "some such idle story" that Jews would kill Christians under their care for a Passover sacrifice.[73] If these two English accounts are accurate, the myth of ritual sacrifice had enjoyed some currency among Syrian Christians long before 1840.

Afterwards, the myth became more vividly ingrained in the Syrian Christians' popular imagination with even such an eminent figure as Patriarch Mazlum writing a leaflet in which he charged the Jews had practiced the rite of blood sacrifice for centuries.[74] There are other echoes of the charge. The Aleppo diarist Naᶜum Bakhkhash recorded in his entry for March 28, 1863, that Jews had seized a Greek boy in Izmir whom they later crucified. The boy's father reportedly organized a group of fellow Greeks who invaded the Jewish Quarter and rescued the boy who was still alive. In the melee that followed, the Greeks killed twelve Jews. The Paşa of the city then arrested the men and women of the boy's family in retaliation.[75] Bakhkhash reports the incident without further comment, neither affirming nor questioning its veracity other than to say that he heard the story from an Aleppine Catholic priest resident in Izmir. But elsewhere in his diary, we learn that Bakhkhash regularly taught Jewish students in his classroom, socialized frequently with members of the Jewish community in his city, and often recorded in his diary the occurrence of Jewish holidays with their appropriate Hebrew names and dating. It would seem from such entries, that his attitudes toward his Jewish neighbors were at least ambivalent, if not friendly.

Although he would charge the Jews of Damascus for complicity in the riots of 1860, Mikha'il Mishaqa, the Protestant Damascene chronicler, was far less opaque about claims of blood libel than was Bakhkhash. In his account of the events of 1840, he noted that the Jews were strictly forbidden by their religious law to eat blood so the charge of ritual murder to obtain blood for Passover matzoth was outlandish. He discussed the torture of

---

[72] *Ibid.*, pp. 27–30.
[73] Russell, *Natural History*, vol. II, p. 74.
[74] Frankel, *Damascus Affair*, p. 53.
[75] Bakhkhash, *Akhbar Halab*, vol. III, p. 323.

those who confessed and asserts, "I can state with certainty that the prominent Jews who were imprisoned in this case were innocent . . . no one who knew them could imagine them having the boldness to slaughter a chicken, much less a human being." Although not a ringing endorsement of the character of those arrested, Mishaqa's own view was that a servant of the prominent al-Harari family and a barber had murdered the priest for the money he was carrying, and not out of religious prejudice. The only blame he laid on the leadership of the Jewish community was that they had sought to shelter the real criminals from the authorities out of a sense of communal solidarity when they should have realized "just like all groups, there are good and bad among them."[76]

If we take the accounts of Bakhkhash and Mishaqa to be representative voices of Syria's literate Christians, albeit a rather small group, we are hard pressed to find echoes of the virulent anti-Semitism that was commonplace in nineteenth-century Catholic Europe. Undoubtedly, such sentiments were filtering into the consciousness of Christians in the region and colored how they viewed their Jewish neighbors, accelerated both by economic competition and by the increasing number of Latin clerics in the region. Nonetheless, I would like to suggest that more often than not the attitude of the two communities toward each other was one of ambivalence. In that regard, it was not unlike the attitude of Muslims toward non-Muslims generally. But as individuals from the two religious communities engaged in economic competition with each other, as was the case in late eighteenth-century Egypt or in early nineteenth-century Damascus, that ambivalence could easily give way to anger, rage, and perhaps bigotry. In an atmosphere of growing sectarianism, anti-Semitic rhetoric could be imported whole cloth from Europe and assimilated into the world-view of Syrian Catholics, thereby providing the ideological underpinnings for what was for most an essentially economic contest. Equally, anti-Christian rhetoric could inform the language employed by the region's Jews in a reflection of their alarm at Christian ambitions to displace them.[77]

## Finding allies in the long eighteenth century

A Greek commercial bourgeoisie emerged in the late eighteenth century in a parallel rise to that of the Syrian Christian merchants in the same century or the later success of Jewish merchants in Iraq in the early nineteenth century. Contact with Western Europeans initiated through commerce led individual Greeks to explore new intellectual, and eventually political, possibilities. The world-views of Syrian Christian and Iraqi Jewish elites were evolving in

[76] Mishaqa, *Murder, Mayhem*, pp. 193–200.
[77] Yaron Harel, "Jewish–Christian Relations in Aleppo as Background for the Jewish Response to the Events of October 1850" *International Journal of Middle Eastern Studies* 30 (1998): pp. 95–96.

response to contact with Europeans as well. But there was a major difference between the Greek bourgeoisie and those among the non-Muslims of the Arab provinces in that the former began to dream of an independent Greece.[78] Such an option was unimaginable for the non-Muslim commercial bourgeoisie of the Arab East. Rather their individual ambitions had to be subordinated to the political realities in which they found themselves.

Initially, some Christians and Jews had sought to tie their fortunes directly to the European powers by becoming *beratlıs*. Others would continue to follow that strategy with increasing frequency in the nineteenth century. While there had been no more than a few hundred European protégés in Syria in the eighteenth century, their numbers throughout the Fertile Crescent would swell into the thousands by the mid-nineteenth century. There is little question that protégé status enhanced the political position of those acquiring it. In the Muslim courts, non-Muslim merchants had suffered the disability of their *dhimmi* status, but as dragomans they had the right to petition to have their cases heard in Istanbul where the pitch was decidedly tilted in their favor.

Muslims did not concede that right without complaint, however, as expressed in a petition sent to the sultan by al-Hajj Musa al-Amiri and his sons in 1764. Al-Amiri was a leading Muslim merchant in Aleppo and as such we would suspect that his position in the city's commercial sector was secure.[79] Nevertheless, he claimed that a commercial rival, Antun Sadir, held unfair advantage over him due to his status as dragoman for the British consul. Al-Amiri's petition stated that the legal basis for the *berat* lay not in the shari'a, but in sultanic law (*kanun*). *Kanun* had proven harmful to Muslim interests, he wrote, and should be abandoned. In closing, he urged the sultan to return to the shari'a as the basis for all his policies. The implications of al-Amiri's complaint were clear. When the sultan agreed to the terms of the capitulatory treaty with Great Britain, he had acted against the spirit of shari'a that positioned Muslims in the ascendancy over non-Muslims in terms of their legal and social status. The treaty had reversed that hierarchy and non-Muslims were now superior to Muslims. The Porte responded to al-Amiri's complaint by issuing an order to Aleppo's governor and chief judge simply stating that the shari'a was to be followed when appropriate.[80] With this vague injunction, the question at the heart of the petition was deftly avoided. But the perception on the part of Muslims that the Ottoman sultans had acted to upset the

[78] Richard Clogg, "The Greek Mercantile Bourgeoisie: 'Progressive' or 'Reactionary'?" in *Anatolica: Studies in the Greek East in the 18th and 19th Centuries* (London, 1966), Section X.

[79] Thiecke, "Décentralisation ottomane et affirmation urbaine," pp. 149–50.

[80] Istanbul, BOA, Ahkâm-ı Halep, vol. III, p. 84.

hierarchy established by the shari°a would return to haunt intercommunal relations in the next century.

A hint of the displeasure bureaucrats at the Porte felt at having to extend such freedoms to subject *dhimmi*s is found in orders sent to Aleppo in 1799 to revoke the *berat*s of the dragomans of the French and Dutch Consuls, in the wake of Napoleon Bonaparte's occupation of Egypt. The opening line of one such *ferman* requires little textual deconstruction. It dispenses with the benediction typically found in such imperial orders, choosing in its place "In the name of God who is neither begotten nor did He beget." This invocation of the *Surat al-Ikhlas* from the *Qur'an* was an unambiguous statement of the contempt felt by the drafter of the document for the *beratlı*'s religion.[81] Its use suggests there were Ottoman officials who resented as much as did al-Hajj al-Amiri the privileges available to the dragomans. Furthermore, there was no guarantee that local authorities would implement the provisions of the capitulatory treaties. °Abbud, the chronicler of late eighteenth-century Aleppo, recounted an incident in 1784 when Yusuf Tutunji, a dragoman for the British in Aleppo, pressed the qadi to forward a legal dispute he had with a *sharif* to Istanbul. The qadi refused, saying he agreed with the *sharif* that the matter between them was rightly the provenance of the shari°a. When the British Consul Hess brought the question to the governor, Abdi Paşa promptly threw Tutunji and his brother into prison. The governor announced he would execute them unless 2,300 *ghurush* in "fines" were paid. °Abbud added that the Tutunjis had only 100 *ghurush* cash between them. But after that amount was presented to the governor, they were released. Needless to say, no more was said about forwarding the case to Istanbul, at least as long as Abdi remained governor.[82]

Faced with the reluctance on the part of Muslims to acquiesce to the privileges that were, in theory, to be accorded to the *beratlı*s, other strategies were explored by non-Muslim elites to build bridges to their Muslim counterparts. These could differ dramatically throughout the region, depending on local political conditions. By the end of the eighteenth century, most leading Muslim families in Aleppo had equally prominent Catholic families associated with them in business and politics. The Catholic families supplied the bankers, business partners, and even political agents in Istanbul for the Muslims. The Muslims, in turn, opened up the lucrative business of subletting tax farms to their Christian allies. Aleppo's elite families, whether Muslim or Christian, were often in bitter competition for power with one another. This led them to conclude alliances across sectarian lines. A prominent Muslim family would typically have a Catholic family as

[81] Istanbul, BOA, Cevdet Hariciye 1540; Cevdet Hariciye 6984, °Abbud, "al-Murtadd," pp. 195–96.
[82] °Abbud, *ibid.*, p. 58.

an ally against another Muslim family with its own Catholic supporters. These connections fostered greater cooperation as the political self-interests of Christian and Muslim elites converged in the faction fighting of late eighteenth-century Aleppo.[83] Prominent Muslims could also be frequently called upon to witness before the qadi or to sign petitions to the sultan on behalf of their Catholic allies in the bitter struggle with the Orthodox Christians. The Catholics often gave the Muslim notables handsome gifts for their support. But even so, the intervention of Muslims in internal Christian affairs highlights the existence of a tradition of intercommunal reciprocity in the political life of the city.

The strategy employed by non-Muslims in other Ottoman Arab cities, without a comparable Christian elite as could be found in Aleppo, more typically involved finding a powerful patron, usually the local warlord. The Christians of Mosul found theirs in the al-Jalili family who dominated the politics of that city for most of the eighteenth century. When Nadir Shah, the Afghan strongman of Iran, invaded the region in 1743, he set alight the churches of the large Christian village of Qara Qosh. The villagers fled to the city where they enlisted in the defense forces of Husayn Paşa al-Jalili. In gratitude for the valor they displayed in the city's defense, he later permitted them to rebuild their churches. Thereafter, there was a close relationship between the villagers and the al-Jalili family who acquired the village as their private property. The villagers' patron at the paşa's court was his treasurer, Ishaq al-Halabi, a Catholic from Aleppo, whose family were instrumental in getting permission for Catholic priests to reside in the village, leading to the villagers' eventual conversion to Catholicism.[84] Elsewhere in Iraq, Büyük Süleyman Paşa, governor of Baghdad between 1780 and 1802, was remembered by the Jews and Christians alike as a just and honorable man. This was undoubtedly due, in no small part, to the fact that governors before and after him had used their office to extort large sums from both communities. Süleyman Paşa also sheltered the Catholic Jacobite Patriarch, Mikha'il Jarwah, after he was deposed in 1800 and facilitated his escape from Dayr Za'afaran to Baghdad and from there, eventually to Lebanon. Further endearing him to the Catholic faction in the city, European Catholic priests were free to offer sacraments openly in Baghdad to any who would take them during his reign.[85]

Fr. Mikha'il Burayk, the Orthodox chronicler of Damascus, viewed the ʿAzm dynasty with similar affection as having been the patrons of his faction. He praised Asʿad Paşa al-ʿAzm as the best governor Damascus' Christians had experienced since the city fell to the Muslims in the seventh

[83] Eldem, Goffman, and Masters, *The Ottoman City*, pp. 59–60.
[84] D. Khoury, *State and Provincial Society*, pp. 197–98.
[85] ʿAbbud, "al-Murtadd," pp. 50–51; Stephen Longrigg, *Four Centuries of Modern Iraq* (Oxford, 1925), p. 219; Rejwan, *Jews of Iraq*, p. 167; Joseph, *Muslim–Christian Relations*, pp. 48–49; Frazee, *Catholics and Sultans*, pp. 207–09.

century. As^cad Paşa had allowed Christians to wear any style and color of dress they wished, save the color green; he had granted them the right to build grand, new houses; he had permitted Christian men and women to commingle in the city's gardens on picnics. Perhaps they had taken too many liberties, Fr. Burayk added, as some of the Christian women had drunk ^caraq (distilled liquor made from grapes and flavored with anise) in public and drawn the ire of their Muslim neighbors. The good father did not blame the Muslims, as "There is no evil nor oppression that does not have women as its cause."[86]

The drawback in relying on a Muslim warlord was obvious. When that patron died or fell from power, there was no guarantee his successor would feel the same commitment to the minority community whom he had favored. In fact, there could often be dramatic reversals as was the case in the ongoing rivalries for patronage between Catholics and Jews in Egypt or Palestine. Nonetheless, the unsettled political conditions of the long eighteenth century gave rise to political alliances across the sectarian divide. Muslims realized that non-Muslims' financial assistance was beneficial to their ambitions, while non-Muslims understood that such alliances were essential for their continued economic prosperity and as a potential political alternative to the ephemeral advantages gained by becoming a *beratlı*. It will be important to remember that reality in the context of the sectarian dissonance that emerged in the nineteenth century, to be discussed in the next chapter.

## Conclusion

The Ottoman Empire's seventeenth, eighteenth, and early nineteenth centuries are often consigned to a historical backwater by historians, positioned between the "classical" period and the era of the Tanzimat when the Ottoman regime is depicted as rousing itself to try to stave off the disintegration of empire. While it is clear that by the middle of the eighteenth century, many of the institutions of empire were slowly sinking into a quagmire of corruption and institutionalized inefficiency, that does not mean that institutions were not changing profoundly behind the façade of a timeless "tradition." Egypt achieved *de facto* independence under the rule of Mehmed Ali. Yet Ottoman bureaucrats penned letters to "our loyal governor of Egypt" preserving the myth that Egypt was just one among many of the sultan's "protected domains." The evolution of the religious communities into the Orthodox *millet-i Rum* and its mirror image in the Armenian *millet* provides an example of new institutions that actually emerged in the eighteenth century, but which were provided with properly "traditional" pedigrees to legitimate them. Changes were, in fact,

[86] Burayk, *Ta'rikh al-Sham*, pp. 62–64.

occurring in Ottoman society in the "long" eighteenth century even if it was not obvious to everyone at the time.

The emergence of the politics of the *millet*s was clearly one of the most significant developments for the empire's Christians. It represented an attempt by the church hierarchies in Istanbul to centralize ecclesiastical, hence political, authority in their hands, setting a precedent that would eventually be applied to all the empire's diverse religious communities. This prefigured the sultan's attempts to reestablish his political control over wayward provincial warlords in the nineteenth century. Both attempts would have mixed results. For some of Syria's Christians, the attempt at centralization provided a clarion call for resistance if they were to maintain local control over the one political institution in which they had a voice, their church. Although that struggle was on the surface about local versus centralized control, the reformulation of social community for many of Syria's Christians along what could be interpreted potentially as ethnic lines was significant. Unwittingly, a distinctly Arab church had been born in the guise of the Melkite Catholic Church.

Another arena in which the transformation was particularly of import for non-Muslims was that of commerce. After 1675, the capitulatory regime favored those who would tie their futures to Europe. Due to prejudices held on both sides of the divide between Franks and Muslims, those who benefited locally came almost exclusively from the indigenous non-Muslim elites. The evolution of the commercial economy that the Ottoman Arab world experienced in the eighteenth and early nineteenth centuries was only the first manifestation of much greater social and political transformations which would occur before the outbreak of the First World War. The main competitors for commercial dominance initially were Jews and Christians. As such, the strain of change was first made manifest in communal tensions between those two groups. But as the ripples of change reached further into the general Muslim population, the delicate balance that had governed intercommunal relations throughout the Ottoman period was strained. The social chasm between Muslims and Christians was widening, as Christians with their European patronage and rising economic status represented the most visible manifestations of change. The immediate causes and outcome of that social rift will be the subject of the next chapter.

# CHAPTER 5

# Intercommunal dissonance in the nineteenth century

Change occurred incrementally, and almost imperceptibly, in the first three centuries of Ottoman rule in the Arab lands. This was no longer true in the nineteenth century when the reform of existing institutions and the creation of new ones, mandated from Istanbul, shook the foundations of the social compact between the sultan and his subjects. The unease with which many Muslims viewed an increasing European economic, political, and ideological presence in the empire strengthened their perception that their world was no longer governed by rules they had once believed to be immutable. That sense of loss when coupled with fear of what might come next provided the spark to a series of violent outbursts directed by Muslims against their Christian neighbors. The most tragic, in terms of loss of life, occurred in 1860 with the civil war in Lebanon and the subsequent Damascus riot. But violence aimed at Christians, either foreign or domestic, occurred in Aleppo in 1850, Mosul in 1854, Nablus in 1856, Jeddah in 1858, and Egypt in 1882. Muslim anger could also be directed at Jews, as occurred in the Mosul riot or in Baghdad in 1889. But across the region, the descent into sectarian violence served to segregate Muslims from Christians, rather than pit Muslims against all non-Muslims indiscriminately as the Christians had become associated with the most obvious manifestations of change. Each of these incidents, the *hawadith* ("events") of Arab folk memory, arose from local conditions and was played out in a widely divergent scenario. Nevertheless, an alarm shared by many Muslims throughout the Ottoman Arab world that the old order was under threat of collapse provided the emotional spark to the violence everywhere.

The tragic consequences of that era of increased sectarian tension have colored the ways in which subsequent generations in the region have remembered intercommunal relations in the Ottoman centuries. The question of why the outbursts happened, however, was and remains debated. European observers and commentators in the nineteenth century posited that the violence was simply an expression of bigotry inherent in Islam. This oversimplified causal explanation helped to inflame European public opinion, already conditioned by sensationalist reportage of the Greek War for Independence, against the Ottoman regime and Muslims generally.[1] Closer to the events, the urban Muslim Arab elite at the time blamed "outsiders" – Bedouin, Kurds, peasants, and Druzes – as their world-view could not admit that their poorer, urban compatriots could perpetuate such outrages, however much the Christians might have provoked them.[2] The Ottoman officials on the scene were yet to experience the wrenching sectarian violence of late nineteenth-century Anatolia and often ascribed the outbursts to the historic, and by implication innate, rebellious nature of the inhabitants of *Arabistan*.[3] Some twentieth-century Lebanese historians have, by contrast, characterized the sectarian outbreaks as having resulted either from direct or indirect manipulation by the Ottoman authorities in a "divide and rule" strategy.[4] Other Arab historians have implicated the Europeans in stirring up ethnic tensions to advance imperial ambitions.[5]

Immanuel Wallerstein and others influenced by his theoretical construct of world history have suggested a more complex set of circumstances resulting from a crisis in social discontinuity in the Ottoman Empire, which accompanied its incorporation into the "modern world system" of global capitalism. They posit that the empire's increasingly dependent economic relationship with Europe undermined the regime's political stability by creating competition between social groups that previously had cooperated in loosely defined power coalitions. The shifts in political alignment accompanying the Ottoman restoration in Syria and Lebanon in 1841, for example, marginalized many of the established Muslim and Druze elites. Where once they held political sway, they lost influence as a reformed and newly empowered Ottoman army and bureaucracy displaced them, eliminating the basis of much of their economic and political clout. Further adding to a Muslim sense of discontent, the state had undermined its authority by introducing reforms such as universal conscription and a rationalized tax system that could only alarm Muslim sensibilities by blurring the distinction between Muslims and *dhimmi*s. The reforms proved ultimately ineffective in saving the regime and served only to alienate some

---

[1] Jeremy Salt, *Imperialism, Evangelism and the Ottoman Armenians 1878–1896* (London, 1993), pp. 44–49.

[2] Muhammad Abu Suͨud al-Hasibi al-Dimashqi, "Mudhakkirat" [Memoires] in *Bilad al-Sham fi al-qarn al-tasiͨ ͨashar* [Syria in the Nineteenth Century]. Edited by Suhayl Zakkar (Damascus, 1982), pp. 281–316. See also Kamal Salibi, "The 1860 Upheaval in Damascus as Seen by al-Sayyid Muhammad Abu'l-Suͨud al Hasibi, Notable and Naqib al-Ashraf of the City" in *Beginnings of Modernization in the Middle East*. Edited by William Polk and Richard Chambers (Chicago, IL, 1968), pp. 185–202.

[3] Istanbul, BOA, İ. Dahiliye 13185/14.

[4] Samir Khalaf, "Communal Conflict in Nineteenth-Century Lebanon" in *Christians and Jews in the Ottoman Empire*. Edited by B. Braude and B. Lewis (New York, 1982), vol. II, p. 129; and his *Persistence and Change in 19th Century Lebanon* (Beirut, 1979), p. 69. A. J. Abraham, *Lebanon at Mid-Century: Maronite–Druze Relations in Lebanon 1840–1860* (Lanham, MD, 1981), p. 86.

[5] Abd al-ͨAziz Muhammad ͨAwad, *al-Idara fi wilayet Suriyya* [Administration in the Province of Syria] *1864–1914* (Cairo, 1969), pp. 332–33.

of those who had formerly identified the House of Osman as Islam's protector.[6]

There was undoubtedly also prejudice on both sides of the religious divide separating Christians and Muslims in the Ottoman Arab provinces in the nineteenth century. But as suggested earlier, indifference and an abiding sense of the moral superiority of one's own community as God's true people were more commonly the reigning attitudes toward those outside it. In the rare cases where scholars have uncovered the voices of the rioters, we are confronted not so much with the statements of bigots but of men who felt that their world had turned upside down. Many in the Muslim community felt the Tanzimat regime had abrogated the old laws governing Christian–Muslim relations at the expense of Muslim privilege. This was undeniably true. At the same time, it seemed that the state was continuing to condone Christian economic privilege through the maintenance of the capitulatory regime. Rubbing salt into the Muslims' psychological wound, a community that had once existed largely outside the public gaze of Muslims had become triumphalist – building new churches, holding public religious processions, and vaunting its connections to the militarily dominant Europeans. In the language of the American South in the "Jim Crow" era, the Christians had become "uppity." But more tellingly, the position of Muslims whether on the battlefields of the Balkans or in the marketplace at home was undeniably worsening. It was not so much equality with the non-Muslims that the Muslims were protesting, but their perception that the Christians were now in the ascendancy. The Muslim poor most acutely held these feelings of alienation, but similar echoes could be found among the Muslim elite as well. As such, the possibility of incipient class conflict can explain the roots of the rioters' ennui only in part.

The Europeans were also implicated in helping to deepen sectarian fissures. That is not to suggest sectarian identities were created by the Europeans and foisted upon unsuspecting "natives." It is, however, true that the European diplomats at the Porte privileged religious differences and conflict in their reports and analyses of events in the Ottoman Empire, even if they often used categories which seemed to be national rather than religious, i.e. Turks, Greeks, Armenians. This emphasis on sectarianism, both real and imagined, carried over to the issues their home governments sought to raise with the Porte and contributed to elite Ottoman Christian perceptions, as well of those of Ottoman officialdom, that religious identities were both primary and primordial. But it is questionable whether

---

[6] Huri İslamoğlu-İnan, "Introduction: 'Oriental Despotism'" in *The Ottoman Empire and the World Economy*. Edited by Huri İslamoğlu-İnan (Cambridge, 1987) p. 22; in the same volume, Immanuel Wallerstein, Hale Decdeli, and Reşat Kasaba "The Incorporation of the Ottoman Empire into the World Economy"; Fatma Müge Göçek follows a similar line of argument in her *Rise of the Bourgeoisie*.

ordinary Muslims would have been equally influenced by European constructions of their collective identity.

Europeans did, however, have an indirect, and unanticipated, impact on the political consciousness of Muslim Arabs in the nineteenth century, encouraging them to see the world in terms of a dialectical struggle between Islam and Christendom. Events such as Napoleon's occupation of Egypt, the Greek War for Independence, and the Crimean War reactivated the countervailing imagery and vocabulary of crusade and jihad. Symptomatic of this, the more generic category of "Christian," or worse yet *kafir*, increasingly replaced "Frank" in the political vocabulary of ordinary Muslims when referring to the Europeans in contemporary chronicles and petitions to the Porte. This semiotic shift conflated the identity of local Christians with that of their coreligionists outside the empire's borders. Alarmed that the *Dar al-Islam* was under attack by European powers, which also happened to be Christian, the Muslims of the Ottoman Arab provinces experienced an increasing unease as to the loyalties of their Christian neighbors. Rumors further helped to fuel fears of imminent doom and inflamed Muslim passions with accounts of distant Christian atrocities, while others of Muslim outrages intensified the Christians' darkest suspicions and served to separate them psychologically from their Muslim neighbors. The result was further communal polarization and a deepening mistrust of what the other community might be planning. Fear, in turn, increased the possibilities of preemptive strikes when none were called for and added another layer of complexity to Muslim–Christian relations. It was noticeably absent from Muslim attitudes towards Jews, who held no potential political allegiances to a threatening foreign power until the twentieth century.[7]

There is no question that religion, as a signifier of identity, had become more overtly political in the nineteenth century than it had been in the earlier Ottoman centuries. That does not mean that religious identity had not been important before, but it now intruded into almost every issue. Disputes between individuals of differing sectarian communities could no longer be discretely settled in the governor's saray, or the sultan's divan. Christians were much more confident in pressing their demands to the Porte with the European powers ever ready to intervene to support them. Furthermore, the Ottoman army's ability to keep communities separate and quiet through armed coercion was severely weakened despite its reorganization. Indeed, it had become part of the problem in the Balkans where the imperial *yatağan* (saber) was often wielded indiscriminately against nationalist, and not incidentally Christian, rebels and innocent peasants alike.

---

[7] Moshe Ma'oz, "Communal Conflict in Ottoman Syria during the Reform Era: the Role of Political and Economic Factors" in *Christian and Jews in the Ottoman Empire*. Edited by B. Braude, B. Lewis (New York, 1982), vol. I, pp. 91–105.

The continuation of the politics of the *millet*s into the nineteenth century further encouraged Christian elites to articulate and refine religious identity as a means to obtain political power. The success of the Uniate Armenian and Melkite Catholics in achieving recognition for their respective *millet*s contributed to their increased self-confidence when dealing with other sects and the central and provincial governments. This led smaller and formerly less active Christian sects to seek to emulate their success. In this regard, it is significant that no one thought it necessary to configure Jewish communal organization into a *millet* until 1835, almost as an afterthought to a century of Christian *millet* politics. The century of bitter battles between Orthodoxy and Catholicism had politicized religion for the Christian elites throughout the empire, but most especially in Syria. In reaction, Muslims began to imagine themselves defensively as constituting a *millet* in their own right. The adoption of the phrase *milel-i erbaa*, "the four millets" (i.e. Orthodox Christians, Armenians, Jews, and Muslims) by the state bureaucrats into their political vocabulary could only encourage this trend. With every contestation between the various communities transformed into a "zero-sum" game, Muslims increasingly interpreted any perceived Christian advances as defeats for their own community.

## The Tanzimat and the attempt to create a civic "Ottomanism" (*Osmanlılık*)

Between 1839 and 1876, the driving force for reform in the Ottoman Empire was a small clique of bureaucrats committed to a program of state transformation. They had few viable options if the empire were to survive. The Greek War for Independence (1821–29) and Mehmed Ali's occupation of Syria (1831–40) had demonstrated that the empire required a modern army to stave off its partition. Such an army would depend on a rationalized system of taxation and reformed provincial administration to collect revenues. These, in turn, necessitated educated bureaucrats to carry out the directives of the state planners.[8] Whereas change in the past had always been cloaked in tradition, survival of the empire provided justification for radical change and the wholesale importation of patently Western models. The Ottoman army was to be European in its armaments, organization, and training, even if in a nod to an "invented" Muslim tradition the soldiers would wear fezzes atop their European-styled trousers and tunics. This proposed transformation required a major reformulation of all the institutions of state, as well as the political world-view of its bureaucrats. In this regard, it bore a resemblance to Gorbachev's *Perestroika* of the 1980s beyond the linguistic

[8] Bernard Lewis, *The Emergence of Modern Turkey* (London, 1961); Şerif Mardin, *The Genesis of Young Ottoman Thought: A Study in the Modernization of Turkish Political Ideas* (Princeton, NJ, 1961); Carter Findley, *Bureaucratic Reform in the Ottoman Empire: The Sublime Porte 1789–1922* (Princeton, NJ, 1980).

coincidence that both terms may be translated as "restructuring." Tanzimat and Perestroika each sought to stave off the collapse of a multi-ethnic empire from the double-barreled attack of the forces of the global marketplace and ethnically based nationalism. In both efforts, the ruling elites failed to enlist their respective subjects in the enterprise and were ultimately frustrated in their objective for their state's survival.

The Tanzimat era began in 1839 with the promulgation of what has become known as the *Hatt-ı Şerif* (the Noble Prescript) of Gülhane, after the park where it was first read.[9] This opening salvo of the Tanzimat was carefully crafted in its appeal to tradition; the document affirmed that the proposed reforms were simply a return to the good government of the halcyon days of Kanûnî Süleyman. Despite that comforting nod to tradition, it contained two important departures from established practice that would have a chilling effect on Muslims when they heard the proclamation read aloud in the provincial centers of the Ottoman Arab world. Individuals would henceforth be directly responsible to the state for taxation and military service. Non-Muslim adult males had, of course, always been required to register with the state's bureaucrats in order to pay the *jizya*, but Muslims had avoided any individual obligation for yearly taxes since the *tahrir* system was allowed to lapse at the end of the sixteenth century. The fact that they were now to be registered individually as taxpayers dismantled a fundamental difference between themselves and the *ahl al-dhimma*. That was, of course, precisely what the Tanzimat reformers had in mind. The sultan's order added almost as an afterthought: "These imperial concessions shall extend to all our subjects, of whatever religion or sect they may be." Cloaked in an appeal to an idealized past, the reigning social hierarchy had been dismantled in one terse sentence.

The innovations found in the document echoed the regime set into place in Syria by Ibrahim Paşa, Mehmed Ali's son who served as the military commander of the army of the Egyptian occupation.[10] He had also introduced general conscription and individual responsibility for taxation. As would be the case with the implementation of the later Ottoman experiments, many Muslim Syrians reacted with alarm to both military service and taxes.[11] Hundreds of young men were reported to have fled Syria for Ottoman-controlled Anatolia and northern Iraq,[12] and rebellions, initiated by Muslims and Druzes, occurred intermittently throughout the Egyptian occupation. Ibrahim Paşa also introduced a policy of political

[9] An English translation is found in Hurewitz, *Diplomacy*, pp. 113–16.
[10] Afaf Lutfi al-Sayyid Marsot, *Egypt in the Reign of Muhammad Ali* (Cambridge, 1984); Khaled Fahmy, *All the Pasha's Men: Mehmed Ali, his Army and the Making of Modern Egypt* (Cambridge, 1997).
[11] Dick Douwes, *The Ottomans in Syria: A History of Justice and Oppression* (London, 2000), pp. 188–210.
[12] Istanbul, BOA, HH 37190.

liberalization in regards to the political rights of Syria's non-Muslims. In Aleppo, a Suryani Catholic teacher, Na^cum Bakhkhash, began to jot down events of importance in weekly entries in 1835, halfway through the Egyptian occupation. Bakhkhash linked the fortunes of Ibrahim Paşa to those of his own community. In May of 1839, he noted that as the Ottoman army massed in an attempt to retake Syria, the Christians of Aleppo were afraid that the Muslims of the city would rise up to attack them. When word reached the city that the Egyptian army had defeated the Ottomans at Nezip, the Christians celebrated with the Egyptians, while the Muslims stayed off the city's streets in an explicit display of where their sympathies lay.[13]

The reactions in each community to the news of the outcome of the battle reflected their widely differing reception of the Egyptian regime. For Syria's Christians, it represented an improvement in their legal status. Besides eliminating the sartorial regulations of the shari^ca for non-Muslims, Ibrahim Paşa removed the ban on the building of new churches and allowed the various Catholic sects throughout Syria to practice their faith openly. Not all Christians were happy with this turn of events. The Orthodox Patriarch of Antioch fired off an appeal to the sultan, threatening that he might turn to Russia as the Catholics had to France, if the sultan did not intervene to preserve the prerogatives of the Orthodox *millet* that were under attack.[14] And even Syria's Catholics did not receive all innovations of the Egyptian occupation with equal enthusiasm. In 1837, Christians were rounded up, along with their Muslim neighbors, in a general sweep of Aleppo by Egyptian pressgangs. The Christians were eventually able to buy their way out of military service by hiring replacements from the more bellicose Armenians of Musa Dasğı, but they viewed the experiment in a non-sectarian military with distinct alarm.[15]

In 1841, the sultan's army returned to Aleppo and was met with approbation on the part of the Christian community and with general enthusiasm by the city's Muslims. The Christians in the city were, however, aware that Sultan Abdül-Mecid had issued his *Hatt-ı Şerif* in 1839. With that as his policy directive, the new Ottoman governor made a point of meeting with the leaders of the various Christian communities to assure them that his men would protect them from any Muslim mob action which might occur in the transition to Ottoman rule. He then made a public announcement to the city's population from the steps of the governor's *saray* that the sultan viewed the Christians as his loyal subjects. If anyone insulted them, he would be punished.[16] With that pronouncement, the Tanzimat made its debut in Aleppo. In an attempt to implement a more responsive local government, the Tanzimat reformers followed Ibrahim

[13]  Bakhkhash, *Akhbar*, vol. I, pp. 102, 104.
[14]  Istanbul, BOA, HH 33656.
[15]  Bakhkhash, *Akhbar*, vol. I, pp. 70–72.
[16]  *Ibid.*, p. 157.

Paşa's lead in Syria and instituted municipal advisory bodies (*meclis-i şura-ı belediye*) to advise the provincial governors in Aleppo and Damascus before similar reforms were introduced elsewhere in the empire. Plans were later laid in 1850 to establish commercial courts to handle contract disputes between members of different religious communities. Non-Muslims were eligible to sit on both these bodies, providing them for the first time in Ottoman history with an officially sanctioned, political voice in a non-sectarian governmental body.[17]

Christians demonstrated their approval of the new order, in turn, by their acceptance of that sartorial symbol of the Tanzimat era, the fez. Bakhkhash reported that when the order requiring the city's men to don the fez arrived in Aleppo in 1844, no one complied. In 1847, however, a group of young Christian men decided collectively to throw off their turbans in favor of the fez and make their support for Abdül-Mecid manifest.[18] Soon after, Christian males of the elite classes almost universally adopted it, as they also began to don European-style clothing. Imported vocabulary, such as *krifata* and *bantalun*, crept into Bakhkhash's diary. Other than the Ottoman officials and military, few Muslim men in the city followed their example. Rather, they retained their traditional turban, *qunbaz* (caftan), and *shirwal* (baggy trousers), thereby creating a new, and unintended, sartorial code by which the wearer's religion was obvious. In Baghdad, Jewish elite males made a similar fashion statement as they donned the fez and wore European-style clothing decades before their Muslim neighbors.[19] The non-Muslims were visibly enthusiastic about the modernity injected by the Tanzimat reformers; the Muslims were less sanguine, worried by what might come next.

If the *Hatt-ı Şerif* of 1839 had shaken the *status quo* while seeking to retain the language of tradition, the *Hatt-ı Hümayûn* of 1856 made no such attempt. Rather, it dismantled the legal hierarchy governing the relations between Muslims and non-Muslims established by the Pact of ᶜUmar with the blunt justification that such steps were necessary to save the empire. It, like the earlier document, had come at a time when European pressure, combined with the empire's need for European friends, was intense. But it would be wrong to think that either document simply represented political expediency on the part of its framers. Many in the generation of the Tanzimat reformers genuinely wanted to transform the political landscape of the empire in order to create Ottoman citizens who would hold the line against the empire's dissolution.[20] They might, at times, resent the pressure

[17] Bozkurt, *Gayrimüslim durumu*, p. 66.
[18] Bakhkhash, *Akhbar*, vol. I, p. 255; vol. II, pp. 47, 191.
[19] H. Cohen, *Jews of the Middle East*, p. 38.
[20] Istanbul, BOA, İ. Hariciye 462; Allan Cunningham, "Stratford Canning and the *Tanzimat*" in *Beginnings of Modernization in the Middle East: The Nineteenth Century*. Edited by W. Polk and R. Chambers (Chicago, 1968), pp. 245–66.

from the Europeans and what must have seemed to them constant meddling, but they still recognized the need for radical change to forestall further ethnic uprisings.

The *Hatt-ı Hümayûn* reiterated the principle that the sultan's subjects were equal, but went much further in outlining what that equality entailed. Freedom of the practice of religion was guaranteed. No distinction would be made on the basis of language, race, or religion among the sultan's subjects. Mixed tribunals, consisting of members of different religions, would replace shariᶜa courts for any commercial or criminal suits involving Muslims and non-Muslims. There would be no discrimination as to admission to government schools or service. A hint of the older tradition remained in the clause concerning the construction of new churches, however. They were to be allowed, but the *millet*s needed Istanbul's approval for construction of churches in areas where Muslims lived.[21] Symbolic of the radical transformation in the relationship between the state and its non-Muslim subjects, the framers refrained from employing either *ahl al-dhimma* or *reaya*[22] when referring to them in favor of a neutral neologism, *gayrimüslimler* ("other than Muslims").[23]

One sensitive area where the document was perhaps intentionally vague was military service. It proclaimed "Christian subjects, and those of other non-Mussulman sects, as well as Mussulmans, shall be subject to the obligations of the law of recruitment." It then went on to say that obtaining substitutes or purchasing exemptions were possible. The purchasing of exemption was institutionalized in the following year in a tax named the *bedel-i askeriye* ("substitute for military service"), which was levied on all adult non-Muslim males. This created discontent on all sides. Christians complained bitterly that it was simply the *jizya* with a new name. But significantly, they never asked to be drafted in lieu of payment of the tax. Muslims felt that their sons were unfairly carrying the defense of the empire, leaving the Christians to stay at home and prosper. It was not until 1909, that the Young Turk regime abolished the *bedel* and made military service compulsory for all males, regardless of religion.[24] The non-Muslim response to the promise of equality in the ranks was increased emigration.

The *Hatt-ı Hümayûn* of 1856 further decreed that the *millet* system was to be the model of self-government for all non-Muslim communities. Those smaller religious communities, which had not yet achieved official recognition, would henceforth be recognized with their own *millet*s. The internal rules of the *millet*s would be subject to periodic review by the central

---

[21] Hurewitz, *Diplomacy*, pp. 149–53.
[22] Originally meaning all the sultan's subjects, the term came to mean non-Muslims from the eighteenth century onward.
[23] Bozkurt, *Gayrimüslim durumu*, p. 70.
[24] *Ibid.*, pp. 120–29.

government and an assembly to be composed of the community's clerics and laity. This clause introduced the potential for future democratization of *millet* governance and was rightly interpreted by some clergy as undermining their authority.[25] Besides seeking a level playing pitch between Christians, Jews, and Muslims in the legal and political system, the document also addressed concerns of apparent Christian economic advantage over Muslims. Each non-Muslim community was instructed to conduct a review of its current immunities and privileges. This was to insure: "the powers conceded to the Christian patriarchs and bishops by Sultan Mahomet II and by his successors shall be made to harmonize with the new position which my generous and beneficent intentions insure to these communities." Foreigners, and by implication their protégés, would be allowed to purchase property only if they agreed to be subject to Ottoman law, thereby abdicating their extraterritorial status. These last two provisions were an attempt to erode the capitulatory regime. Cevdet Paşa, a key framer of the Tanzimat but one who was lukewarm to the new sectarian equality, wrote in his memoirs that the objective of reform was the implementation of a regime of complete equality for all the sultan's subjects. That meant there should be an end to the privileges and advantages enjoyed by the *beratlı*s, in return for the demise of Muslim political advantage.[26] The European powers would not yield on the question of extraterritoriality for their protégés, however, and it was not until after Mustafa Kemal Atatürk's successful War of Liberation (1920–23) that the capitulatory regime was repudiated by treaty.

A statement that all subjects were now equal in the sultan's eyes did not immediately transform relations between Christians and Muslims throughout the empire any more than the Civil Rights Act of 1964 ended psychological "Jim Crowism" in the United States. Not all government officials agreed with the notion of religious equality and these could not be counted on to act with equanimity toward all of the sultan's subjects. In Damascus, the Muslim chronicler Shaykh al-Ustuwani praised the city's governor, Said Paşa, for his standing up to the consuls, their *beratlı*s, and the patriarch in refusing to grant Christians what they wanted.[27] The *Hatt-ı Hümayûn* of 1856, as was the case of many of the reforms the Tanzimat administration introduced, sounded better on paper than was the reality of its implementation in the provinces. The fact was the state was cash-starved and ill equipped to brings its ambitions to fruition. This was true in

[25] Roderic Davison, "The *Millet*s as Agents of Change in the Nineteenth-Century Ottoman Empire" in *Jews and Christians in the Ottoman Empire*. Edited by B. Braude and B. Lewis (New York, 1982), vol. I, pp. 319–29.

[26] Cevdet Paşa, *Tezâkir* [Memoirs]. Edited by Cavid Baysun (Istanbul, 1953), vol. I, pp. 67–68.

[27] Shaykh Muhammad Saʿid al-Ustuwani. *Mashahid wa-ahdath fi muntasaf al-qarn al-tasiʿ ʿashar* [Witnessing the Events of the Middle of the Nineteenth Century] *1206–1277/ 1840–1861*. Edited by Asʿad al-Ustuwani (Damascus, 1994), pp. 153–54.

education, land reform, or for that matter the creation of a widely accepted notion of Ottoman citizenship.

The ultimate expression of the reformers' ambitions to create the Ottoman citizen was the Constitution of 1876. The sultanate was to be transformed into a constitutional monarchy and the sultan's subjects were to become properly Ottoman citizens, according to article 8, "everyone who is within the Ottoman state, whatever his religion or sect, is without exception to be labeled as an Ottoman." *Osmanlı* (Ottoman) had been reserved for the inner circle of the Ottoman governing elite before the period of the Tanzimat, but it would now define exactly who the sultan's subjects were. Just as the Tanzimat collapsed the difference between Muslim and *dhimmi*, it was now dismantling the long-standing social hierarchy of proper Ottomans and the "ruled" (*reaya*) into a new political category, that of Ottoman citizen. A refrain from a song sung by the Jews of Salonika in the Balkan Wars summed up the new ideal of civic equality with a simple rhyme, "*Somos judíos, cristianos y mussulmanos, todos ottomanos*" (We are Jews, Christians and Muslims, all of us Ottomans).[28]

Despite its affirmation of equality for all Ottoman citizens, the Constitution established Islam as the state religion and required those entering government service to know the "Turkish of the Ottomans." Otherwise, religious and cultural freedoms were guaranteed.[29] The Tanzimat elite was trying to broker a compromise that would grant cultural and political rights to the various minority religious communities in return for their loyalty to sultan and empire. In doing so, they sought an illusive nineteenth-century version of "multiculturalism" whereby the different communities would retain their languages, customs, and religions in social harmony, under the rubric of an Ottoman variation of "separate but equal." But by 1876, that ideal was already a battle lost. The Balkan Christian elites had attached their political ambitions to one or the other of the national monarchies jostling to claim what was left of the sultan's "protected domains" in Europe. The peasants and the urban poor were probably too busy eking out a living to think about their political identity. But the increasing availability of schools administered by the *millet*s opened the possibility that their children would be inculcated with newly minted nationalist sentiments.

Ottomanism, however liberally constructed, was simply not a political option that many Balkan Christians would seriously consider. There was perhaps still a chance the experiment might win the hearts and minds of the Christians of Anatolia over to the ideal of an Ottoman state where everyone was equal under a benevolent sultan. But the separatist pulls of the *megali idea* (the "big idea" or dream of a greater Kingdom of the Hellenes) or an

[28] Jak Esim and Cem Ikiz, cassette, "Türkiye aşkı için: Yahudi ezgiler ve Sefarad romanslar" [For the Love of Turkey: Jewish Melodies and Sephardic Romances] (Istanbul, 1993).
[29] Bozkurt, *Gayrimüslim durumu*, pp. 83–85.

*Azad Hayasdan* (Independent Armenia) subverted that possibility. The elites among groups which were clearly in the minority: Albanians, Jews, or Arab Christians, however, fervently embraced the new constitution and looked askance when it was suspended just two years later. For impoverished Muslims in both the Anatolian and Arab provinces, the promise of full equality must have seemed hollow as they witnessed their Christian neighbors continuing to make economic and educational advances, with little corresponding improvement in their own lot.

## Merchants, revisited

The secular trends that had transformed humble peddlers into a Christian mercantile elite in cities such as Aleppo, Sidon, and Damiette before 1800 intensified in the Tanzimat period. This was due in no small part to the increased political and economic leverage exercised by the European powers at the Porte. In 1838, Great Britain succeeded in winning a new commercial treaty that committed the empire to free trade with all but nominal tariffs. Britons were free to travel and to establish commercial operations in any part of the empire. In Lebanon, French commercial interests encouraged the growth of a silk industry that drew peasants from the mountains into the coastal cities. That, in turn, led to the burgeoning of Beirut's population. It was transformed, over the course of the nineteenth century, from an overgrown village with perhaps six to seven thousand inhabitants in 1800 to the most important commercial port of the Levant between Izmir and Egypt, with a population of over one hundred thousand in 1900.[30] Similarly, the cotton trade of Egypt reinvigorated Alexandria from a sleepy, backwater port into its being once again one of the great cities of the eastern Mediterranean, as polyglot and cosmopolitan as it had been in the Classical Age. Its population, within the crumbling city walls, was estimated at only 5,000 in 1806, but had reached 104,189 by 1848 and 231,396 in 1882.[31] The fortunes of both port cities were intimately linked to the dramatic increase of the Ottoman Arab world's trade with Europe. And Christians throughout the Levant, thanks to their knowledge of European tongues and willingness to deal with Europeans, were positioned to benefit more than their Muslim or Jewish neighbors.

It was not just the Levant that was affected by an accelerating globalization of trade. The sea-borne trade of Iraq increased thirty-seven times in the years between 1840 and 1914, while Syrian commerce increased twenty-fold in roughly the same period. Iraq had only been a minor player in the global trading world of the eighteenth century and its exports and imports still had

---

[30] Leila Fawaz, *Merchants and Migrants in Nineteenth Century Beirut* (Cambridge, MA, 1983), pp. 44–60.
[31] Michael Reimer, *Colonial Bridgehead: Government in Alexandria, 1807–1882* (Boulder, CO, 1997), pp. 90, 110.

not caught up to the volume of international trade handled through Syria's leading ports by the end of the Ottoman period. In 1907, the port of Beirut was handling eleven percent of the empire's total trade and Syria's other main port, Alexandretta (İskenderun), handled another five percent, as compared to six percent of the total for the trade passing through Baghdad.[32] The nature of the import–export trade everywhere was uneven; unprocessed agricultural products formed the bulk of the exports while manufactured consumer goods entered the country at steadily increasing rates. By the end of the century, even consumers of the middling economic level in the cities of the Levant had become reliant on European manufactured goods. The trade imbalance resulted in the bankruptcy of both Egypt and the Ottoman Empire with dire consequences for the continuing political independence of either regime. Egypt, which had been independent in all but name since the rise of Mehmed Ali, defaulted on its loans and was occupied by British forces in 1882. The Ottoman Empire retained its independence with its own default, but found its economic freedom severely limited by the Public Debt Administration established in 1881.[33]

The rising tide of imported European manufactured goods had a debilitating impact on the traditional craft industries of the Ottoman Arab provinces, as well as on the national balances of payment. The British consular report for Aleppo in 1890 stated that industry in the city had witnessed a steady decline in its output since mid-century. Similarly negative tales of declining output and increasing trade imbalances were posted from Damascus.[34] Recent scholarship has questioned the appropriateness of the gloom almost universally found in British consular reports on the decline of local industry due to foreign competition.[35] But even if Syrian artisans were not as hard hit as previously believed, there is little question that wages remained depressed in greater Syria for most of the nineteenth century, while prices rose due to imports and a number of very poor harvest years.[36] Such hardships affected the Jewish and Christian poor and working classes as well as Muslims. But the decline in living standards for some Muslims undoubtedly increased their growing sense of alienation as they witnessed

[32] Halil İnalcık and Donald Quataert (eds.), *An Economic and Social History of the Ottoman Empire, 1300–1914* (Cambridge, 1994), p. 831.
[33] Roger Owen, *The Middle East and the World Economy 1800–1914* (London, 1981), especially pp. 83–148.
[34] London, PRO, FO 861/22 "Detailed report of Halep vilayeti 1890," pp. 3–4; FO 78/3070, "Report on Syria," partially reproduced in Charles Issawi, *The Fertile Crescent 1800–1914: A Documentary Economic History* (New York, 1988), pp. 55–56; Abdul-Karim Rafeq, "The Impact of Europe on a Traditional Economy: The Case of Damascus, 1840–1870" in *Économie et sociétés dans l'Empire Ottoman (fin du XVIII^e – début du XX^e siècle)*. Edited by Jean-Louis Bacqué-Grammont and Paul Dumont (Paris, 1983), pp. 419–32.
[35] Donald Quataert, *Ottoman Manufacturing in the Age of the Industrial Revolution* (Cambridge, 1993), pp. 77–79; James Reilly, "From Workshops to Sweatshops: Damascus Textiles and the World-Economy in the Last Ottoman Century" *Review* 16 (1993): 199–213.
[36] Issawi, *Fertile Crescent*, pp. 9–12, 55–59.

an apparent increase in the wealth of Christians, manifested by the construction of new homes and churches.[37]

The question of the degree to which the living standards of non-Muslims actually surpassed those of the Muslims remains. When John Bowring surveyed Syrian trade in 1838, local merchants, including Christians, Jews, and Muslims, were all involved in the trade with Europe. He reported, however, that the wealthiest merchants in Aleppo were Christians, while those of Damascus were Jews.[38] Ottoman customs receipts from Aleppo in the 1840s show Sephardic Jews with European passports actually imported goods worth far in excess of those handled by the city's Catholic merchants. But the Christians were the leading merchants among the sultan's subjects, in partial justification of Bowring's assessment.[39] Elsewhere in Syria, Christians came to dominate the export trade of Beirut almost to the exclusion of either Muslims or Jews. Even in Damascus, Christian merchants were able to supplant eventually their Jewish rivals for second place in the trading hierarchy. But, by and large, the city's trade remained in Muslim hands. By way of contrast, Jewish merchants predominated in the all-important Indian trade with Iraq, although Christian and Muslim merchants were also active.[40]

The continuing presence of Muslim merchants almost everywhere in the Fertile Crescent is important to note. The European consular reports typically dismissed the role of Muslim merchants as insignificant or nonexistent, but we should treat such assertions with care.[41] Muslims were, in fact, often involved in the distribution of imports into the interior, or served as silent partners in investment schemes that were fronted by non-Muslims. An example of the latter can be found in the estate record of al-Hajj ʿAbd al-Qadir Çelebi Birizadah who died in 1836 in Aleppo. Previous to his death, he had dissolved a partnership with three other Muslims and a Christian, Yusuf Kabbaba, which had netted a profit of 128,306 *ghurush* off an investment of 364,375 *ghurush*. The Muslims had supplied most of the capital while Kabbaba had traveled to the "land of the Franks" and did the actual trading.[42] Similar examples of cross-communal partnerships were present in Beirut and Damascus.[43] Such evidence is anecdotal, but it serves to remind us that the Muslim and non-Muslim elites

[37] Letter of Joshua Ford, dated October 30, 1850, ABCFM reel 544, no. 15.
[38] Bowring, *Commercial Statistics*, pp. 80, 94.
[39] Istanbul, BOA, ML.VRD 399, 2179, 2244, 2258.
[40] Charles Issawi, "British Trade and the Rise of Beirut, 1830–1860" *International Journal of Middle East Studies* 8 (1977): 91–101. Fawaz, *Merchants and Migrants*, pp. 85–102; Issawi, *Fertile Crescent*, pp. 25–27.
[41] London, PRO, FO 861/22 "Detailed report of Halep Vilayeti 1890," p. 3.
[42] Damascus, Aleppo Court records, vol. CCXXXVI, no. 108.
[43] Fawaz, *Merchants and Migrants*, pp. 105–06. Abdul-Karim Rafeq, "New Light on the 1860 Riots in Ottoman Damascus" *Die Welt des Islam* 28 (1988): 412–30.

in the Fertile Crescent were not nearly as segregated as to their economic niches as were their counterparts in Anatolia.[44]

Despite the persistence of Muslims in Levantine commerce, the fortunes of a new class of non-Muslim merchants were undeniably on the rise in the Tanzimat period. A Christian commercial middle class emerged in every port on the eastern Mediterranean seaboard and in Mosul and Damascus as well, while a parallel Jewish bourgeoisie was present in Baghdad and Basra. The overwhelming majority of Christians and Jews living in the Ottoman Arab lands in the Tanzimat period were not merchants, however. In the cities of the region, most remained craftsmen or low-skilled workers. A British consular report from Baghdad at the end of the nineteenth century estimated that despite the obvious wealth held by the prominent Jewish families, only 5 percent of the Jewish population was actually well off. Another estimate put the percentage of poor and beggars in the community at a staggering 65 percent.[45] A *jizya* register, compiled in 1848–49 for Aleppo, uniformly characterized by foreign observers as being home to the wealthiest Christian community in Syria, listed 154 Christians and 22 Jews as owing the highest amount assessed, sixty *ghurush*. As these were listed by name, we can easily identify most as being from the leading non-Muslim commercial families in the city. A further 1,262 Christians and 211 Jews were listed as owing the middle category of the tax, but 2,259 Christians and 589 Jews paid the lowest amount.[46] By the government's reckoning, the majority of Aleppo's Christians and Jews were poor. American missionaries William Benton and Joshua Ford shared this perception: "A few (Christian) families are wealthy but multitudes are poor and necessitated to work from day to day for their daily bread for themselves and their families."[47]

There were also still Christian peasants as there had been in the sixteenth century. The migration of Christians out of their villages, so characteristic of the early centuries of Ottoman rule in the Arab lands, peaked by the late seventeenth century. But the flow of migrants picked up speed again in the nineteenth century as Christians fled the land at a much higher rate than did Muslims. In a *jizya* register from Aleppo in the year 1844, 748 men were listed as "foreigners" (*yabancı*). Of these, only 18 were identified as Jews. The rest were Christians but were undifferentiated by sect in the document. Even so, only 88 had distinctly Arab names or were identified as having come from towns in either Iraq or Syria. The remainder was composed of Armenians, as indicated by their Christian and family names, as well as

---

[44] Göçek, *Rise of the Bourgeoisie*, 87–116. Charles Issawi, *The Economic History of Turkey 1800–1914* (Chicago, IL, 1980), p. 14.

[45] Paul Dumont, "Jews, Muslims, and Cholera: Intercommunal Relations in Baghdad at the End of the Nineteenth Century" in *Jews of the Ottoman Empire*. Edited by A. Levy (Princeton, NJ, 1994), pp. 356, 371.

[46] Istanbul, BOA, ML.VRD.CMH 1177.

[47] ABCFM, Reel 542/16:8.1, "Annual Report for Aleppo," May 24, 1849.

their place of origin. More than a quarter of all those registered as "foreigners" had come from Arapgır in eastern Anatolia alone. The migrants' current occupations were also included; most were low-skilled workers, including porters (155), bakers (108), mule-drivers (102), and servants (88).[48]

Other migrants sought their fortunes farther away, drawn to the Syrian port cities, Egypt, and beyond. In the 1870s men from the Lebanese mountains began to leave for the New World. Between 1899 and 1914, a total of 86,111 Syrians entered the United States, 90 percent of whom are estimated to have been Christians.[49] Still others went to Latin America where communities of *"Turcos"* could be found in Sao Paulo, Caracas, Buenos Aires, and Mexico City by the start of the First World War. Syrian Jews also migrated both to the US and Mexico, as well as to Britain.[50] Between 1871 and 1909, 60,653 Syrians entered Argentina, the largest single destination for Syrian immigrants in Latin America. But unlike the pattern of emigration to the US and Mexico, the stream of migrants going to the New World's southern hemisphere was more evenly divided between Muslims and Christians and even included Druzes.[51] Most of the Christians and Jews who remained in the Arab Fertile Crescent were undeniably poor. But they found opportunities in the last decades of Ottoman rule, which had not been available to their forefathers or indeed to most of their Muslim contemporaries, in the form of education offered by a new wave of Christian missionaries and European Jewish reformers. It would transform many of their lives by providing them with the education and training to meet some form of the twentieth century.

## Missionaries and teachers: "a light unto the East"

With the dissolution of the Jesuit order in 1773, a century and a half of an activist Roman Catholic missionary presence in the Ottoman Arab lands came to an end. European religious of the Capuchin and Franciscan orders continued to serve the Uniate Catholic communities. But Arabs trained in Europe increasingly served alongside them in an ongoing process of a cultural Arabization of Catholicism in the region. That did not signal, however, that the struggle between Orthodoxy and Catholicism for the souls of the Christian Arabs was over. Religious tensions, in fact, intensified

[48] Istanbul, BOA, ML.VRD.CMH 401.
[49] Alixa Naff, *Becoming American: The Early Arab Immigrant Experience* (Carbondale, IL, 1985), p. 110.
[50] Walter Zenner, *A Global Community: The Jews from Aleppo, Syria* (Detroit, MI, 2000).
[51] Karpat, "Ottoman Emigration," pp. 198–99. Luz Maria Martinez Montiel, "The Lebanese Community in Mexico: Its Meaning, Importance and the History of its Communities" in *The Lebanese in the World: A Century of Emigration.* Edited by A. Hourani and N. Shehadi (London, 1992), pp. 379–92; and in the same volume, Ignacio Klich, "*Criollos* and Arabic Speakers in Argentina: An Uneasy *Pas de Deux*, 1888–1914," pp. 243–84.

in the 1820s as a burst of evangelical Anglo-Saxon religious fervor added yet another option into the religious mix of the Ottoman Levant. The arrival of Protestant missionaries from Britain and the US again focused attention on the status of non-Muslims in the Ottoman Empire and helped to generate a diplomatic scramble among the European powers for influence in the minority religious communities. Locally, the missionaries served to intensify questions of religious identity as the leaderships of the established religious communities – Catholic, Orthodox, Jewish, and for the first time Muslim – were put on guard lest their flock defect.[52]

The impact of the Western missions and educational projects, whether Protestant, Roman Catholic, or Jewish, is as controversial as any of the historical questions surrounding the religious minorities of the Ottoman Empire. Some Turkish historians have labeled the European missionaries, especially the French and Russians, as conscious agents of imperial designs on the empire. American missionaries, lacking an empire to promote, have been represented as ambassadors of a nascent American cultural imperialism that prefigured Walt Disney or McDonald's. If the accusation of cultural imperialism were not bad enough, the missionaries are also blamed for sowing the weeds of sectarian discord in a field where reputedly none had grown before.[53] But others recognizing the inherent altruism in the missionaries' ambitions, if not their results, have been more ambivalent.[54] Most Arab historians have expressed a similar equivocation. While decrying French involvement with the Maronites as being politically divisive, they have generally judged favorably the educational mission of the Jesuits and Protestants alike.[55]

The difference in perception between Turkish historians and their Arab counterparts as to the merits of the missionary enterprise is colored by their respective nationalist traditions. Turkish historians see the Protestant missions to the various Christian communities of the empire as encouraging separatist nationalisms; Arab historians, following in the tradition of George Antonius,[56] generally praise the mission schools for inculcating Arabism through their use of the Arabic language as a teaching medium. There is agreement in that both credit, or blame, the missionaries for helping to spread nationalist sentiments in their students through the medium of education in the local languages. But it is questionable whether the Protestant missionaries in the nineteenth century sought that outcome, any more than their Latin Catholic predecessors had envisioned that their

[52] Caesar Farah, "Protestantism and Politics: the 19th Century Dimension in Syria" in *Palestine in the Late Ottoman Period: Political, Social, and Economic Transformation*. Edited by D. Kushner (Jerusalem, 1986), pp. 320–40.
[53] Sonyel, *Minorities*, p. 194; Deringil, *Well-Protected Domains*, p. 112.
[54] Kocabaşoğlu, *Anadolu'daki Amerika*, p. 222.
[55] Kurd-ʿAli, *Khitat*, vol. VII, pp. 229–30, 232–39. George Antonius, *The Arab Awakening; The Story of the Arab National Movement* (New York, 1965), pp. 41–45.
[56] Antonius, *ibid.*, pp. 41–45, 93.

effort to evangelize the Syrian Christians would result in the emergence of a separate Arab Catholic Church.

The Protestant missionary impulse arose out of the second evangelical "great awakening" which spread across the English-speaking Atlantic world in the early nineteenth century. Unlike the Catholic missions of two centuries earlier, it sought not to influence established church hierarchies, but rather to bring the gospel to individuals so that they might find their "salvation in Christ." The various missionary societies that were formed in this period of optimism and self-confidence reflected a growing literacy in the Anglo-Saxon world and an increased determination among the laity to spread their faith to foreign realms. The movement was at its heart populist in that ordinary men and women felt the call to minister to the "heathen," or at the least, to support financially those who had received the "call." The enterprise was marked by an almost innocent enthusiasm to bear witness for the "light of Christ," as well as a casual arrogance that Anglo-Saxon culture was indeed superior to any the missionaries would encounter in the "field." In retrospect, it was that confidence, shared by Americans and Britons alike, in a modernity as defined in English, rather than their religious message, that would have the greatest impact on the inhabitants of the Ottoman Arab world.[57]

In 1792, the Baptist Missionary Society was founded in London, followed by the Church Missionary Society (1799) and the London Society for Promoting Christianity among the Jews (1809).[58] In the US, Congregationalist ministers from Massachusetts and Connecticut formed the Board of Commissioners for Foreign Missions – American was later added (ABCFM) – in Boston in 1810.[59] Both the American and British missions had as their initial goal the conversion of the Jews of the Holy Land. But Ottoman Jews proved just as resistant to the Protestant version of Christianity as had their forefathers to the earlier Catholic missions. Faced with indifference or open hostility in Jerusalem, the Americans moved their operations to Beirut in 1823 where they began to proselytize among the local Christians. They justified this targeting of their "brothers and sisters in Christ" by characterizing them as being "nominal Christians" in need of the "true Gospel." Accepted as Christians in name only, the missionaries were to instruct Christians of the Arab East as to what being Christian actually meant.

The Americans met immediate opposition from the local church hierarchies, especially the Maronites, who banned their flock from having any contact with them. Rome agreed with its protégés' alarm and on January 31, 1824, Cardinal Somaglia, Dean of the Sacred College of the *Propaganda*

[57] Ussama Makdisi, "Reclaiming the Land of the Bible: Missionaries, Secularism, and Evangelical Modernity" *The American Historical Review* 102 (1997): 680–713.
[58] A. L. Tibawi, *British Interests in Palestine, 1880–1901* (Oxford, 1961), pp. 5–6.
[59] Tibawi, *American Interests*, pp. 5–10.

*Fide*, urged the faithful to reject the Arabic-language bibles the missionaries were handing out. Catholic pressure led the Porte to ban the import of Bibles from Europe as almost exactly a century before Orthodox pressure had led to a similar banning of imported religious books by the Catholics.[60] An additional irony lay in the fact that the Bibles the Protestant missionaries were handing out were simply reprints of the Arabic translation of the Bible that Rome had produced in 1671, minus the Apocrypha. The Catholics had subverted the ban in their day by relying on the press at Aleppo, and later Shuwayr.[61] Whether the Americans were aware of that precedent or not, they moved their press from Malta to Beirut in 1834.

Although they shared a similar world-view and many of the same goals in their missionary endeavors, there were significant differences in the strategies employed by Anglican and American missionaries. The English continued to see proselytism among the Jews of the Holy Land as their principal immediate objective with their ultimate ambition, the conversion of the empire's Muslims. As such, they favored Jerusalem as their chief station and began construction of an Anglican cathedral there in 1839. But they also faced the reality that few Jews in the city were interested in their message. Rejected, they turned to the local Christians as a mission field. But many in the missionary movement in England, which was dominated by "high church" rather than chapel sentiments, felt unease at the prospect of ministering to already baptized Christians. This was especially true in the case of the Greek Orthodox Christians who were considered by some Anglicans to be the inheritors of the original, and therefore authentic, Church. Furthermore, the Church of Constantinople held the potential for solidarity with the Church of England against the universalistic claim of hegemony by Rome. As early as 1853, over a thousand Anglicans from throughout Britain signed a memorial decrying proselytism among the Greek Orthodox Christians.[62] Although the church hierarchy rejected the sentiment, Anglican missionary societies remained much more ambivalent about their relationship to the Eastern churches than did their American cousins, or for that matter the Irish and Scots Presbyterian churches who had established Syria as a mission field by the mid-nineteenth century.[63]

The American Congregationalists showed no such hesitation in confronting either the traditional churches or the Catholics. They were assisted in their polemic by one of their most controversial converts, Mikha'il Mishaqa. Originally a Melkite Catholic, he converted to Protestantism in 1848, as: "The Protestants were the only Christians who acted in accordance with the Gospel . . . and that the Papists were the farthest of all from the teaching of the Gospel – and this only if we can count them as Christians at

[60] *Ibid.*, pp. 27–28.
[61] Damascus, Aleppo Court records, vol. XXXIV, p. 39.
[62] Tibawi, *British Interests*, p. 112.
[63] Coakley, *The Church of the East*; Joseph, *Muslim–Christian Relations*, pp. 56–68.

all."[64] Mishaqa was not content to leave his old faith quietly and he entered into an extended debate in a series of letters with the Melkite Patriarch, Maksimus Mazlum.[65] The confrontational attitude the Americans and their protégés took toward the established churches helped to make life difficult for those who converted. The community they left often shunned the new Protestants, creating lingering, bitter recriminations on both sides. As a consequence and despite their enthusiasm, the Americans enjoyed only limited success in winning Christian Arab converts, beyond a few free-thinkers such as Mishaqa and the remarkable Butrus al-Bustani.

The fate of the ABCFM mission in Aleppo, the city where the Catholic missionaries had achieved their greatest triumph, is indicative of the general failure of the Congregationalists to win the souls of Syrian Christians to Protestantism. In 1847, the city was optimistically identified as an ideal location for a mission station.[66] Two missionaries and their families established the station in the following year. They proceeded to set up a school and to engage the local Christians in religious debate, but made few converts. They stayed on despite the death of several of their children, constant illness, and the riot of 1850. But by 1854, they were beginning to reassess their mission. The school for girls, which had been their pride, was reported to have a fluctuating student body of between six and sixteen pupils while the competing Melkite Catholic school for girls had over a hundred girls in daily attendance. Furthermore, Catholic women would routinely stand outside the Protestant school and hurl insults at those parents who brought their daughters to the school. Adding to their despondency, several of the girls they had "saved" were judged to have "doubtful moral character."[67]

Converts from the city's "nominal Christians" had come chiefly from the Armenian community and there had not been many of those. A British consular agent estimated that there were only forty local Protestants in Aleppo in 1860 after over a decade of missionary effort.[68] In 1854, the discouraged missionaries recommended that any new missionaries headed for the station should be instructed in Turkish and Armenian, rather than Arabic. That advice reflected that whatever minor successes they had had in winning converts was among recent Armenian migrants from Anatolia, and they were predominantly Turkish speakers. The ABCFM Aleppo station was, in fact, transferred in the following year from the responsibility of the Syrian Mission to that of the Armenian Mission and the last remaining

[64] Mishaqa, *Murder, Mayhem, Pillage, and Plunder*, p. 236.
[65] *Ibid.*, p. 237; Tibawi, *American Interests*, pp. 135–36; ABCFM, unit five, reel 544, letters 117 and 183, letters Eli Smith to Revd. Anderson.
[66] ABCFM, unit, reel 5, no. 17, letter to Rufus Anderson, dated January 28, 1847, signed Eli Smith, G. Whiting, William Thompson, Van Dyck, Henry Forest, and George Hunter.
[67] ABCFM, unit 5, reel 542, n. 159, Annual Report Aleppo Station, 1854.
[68] London, FO 226/148, dated November 13, 1860.

American missionary in the city was reassigned to Beirut. He summed up the reason for failure: "The Greek Catholics and Maronite sects were all rich and proud; immersed in business, fond of pleasure, they had no wants of mind and soul to be met by the Gospel."[69]

Congregationalist missionaries would return to Aleppo in the 1870s, as a part of their Central Anatolian mission station headquartered in Aintab (Gaziantep), but their primary objective remained the propagation of Protestant doctrine among the city's Armenians. Protestant missionaries would find a more receptive mission field among the Orthodox Arabs of Aleppo's satellite market towns, Antioch and Idlib, where Catholic missionaries had been unable to establish a presence in the 1700s. By and large, however, conversion to one form of Protestantism or another in northern Syria and southern Anatolia was a spiritual phenomenon experienced by the region's Armenian population. Protestant and Catholic missionary efforts, in their respective centuries, had appealed to Christians in Aleppo who were estranged from the hierarchies of their traditional churches and sought connections to a wider world. Aleppo's Melkite, Suryani, and Maronite Catholics already had achieved those goals by 1848 and were not swayed by the rhetoric of a new religious dispensation. The forces of the counter-reformation had, in large part, won the battle for the souls of Aleppo's Christian Arabs. The Armenian newcomers to the city in the nineteenth century, by contrast, saw in the Protestant missions many of the same advantages that had presented themselves to the Arabic-speaking Christians two centuries before – education, a responsive clergy, and connections to the West. As such, they responded more enthusiastically to the opportunity for "salvation." For Aleppo's Catholics and Protestants, conversion to an alternative form of Christianity indirectly spawned a "national" church, to be administered by locals in their own tongue. But in neither case had the missionaries sought, or even predicted, that outcome.

In the aftermath of Lebanon's civil war in 1860, the ABCFM began to shift its objective from conversion to education. The crowning achievement of the Board's endeavors was the establishment in 1866 of the Syrian Protestant College, later renamed the American University in Beirut. Missionaries from Great Britain also found the role of teacher attractive, with the hope that the men and women so engaged would serve as exemplars of proper Christian behavior for Syrians to emulate. Converts would be welcomed, but not actively recruited. In both the British and American schools, emphasis was placed on Arabic as the medium of expression in the classroom.[70] Significantly, Ottoman Turkish was not a part of the curriculum in the Protestant schools until it was mandated by the state.

After almost a century of activity, the British and American Protestants

[69] ABCFM, unit 5, reel 543, n. 421, William Eddy to R. Anderson, dated December 5, 1855.
[70] Abu-Ghazaleh, *American Missions in Syria*.

had achieved mixed success in the Ottoman Arab provinces on the eve of the First World War. The Ottoman census of 1906–07 returned 520 Protestants in the province of Jerusalem, 956 in Suriye (Damascus) province, 2,128 in Beirut, and 13,144 in Aleppo province. But the latter figure included the towns of Urfa, Maraş, and Aintab where Protestants comprised a significant minority of the Armenian population. The Christians of the city of Aleppo remained still largely resistant to the new dispensation, with only 191 Protestants counted in the city in 1908.[71] The Protestants succeeded more decisively in their educational mission. One indicator of this, 46.7 percent of the Syrian immigrants arriving in the US between 1899 and 1910 were literate and many of these had been educated in Protestant schools.[72] Throughout the empire, there were 12,800 students enrolled in British Protestant schools in 1912, and 34,317 in schools founded by American missionaries. Although this was still a tiny minority of the potential school-age population, it is significant when compared to other systems that were in operation at the same time. There were 81,226 pupils in government schools, 133,100 students in schools administered by the Armenian Patriarchate and 184,568 in schools under the Orthodox Patriarch of Constantinople. Additionally, 59,414 pupils were in schools run by the French and roughly 10,000 students were in Russian schools.[73]

As the latter statistics suggest, it was not only the Protestants who seized the opportunities present in an era of growing liberalization in the Ottoman Empire to establish influence through education. In 1831, the Jesuits returned to Syria. In the decades that followed, they opened a number of new schools to serve the various Uniate communities. In addition to their educational mission, Latin Catholic missionaries sought to proselytize "schismatic" – the Catholic equivalent of the Protestant "nominal" – Christians in regions for which the Latin Patriarch of Jerusalem was responsible or where there was no established Uniate church.[74] Whereas the Protestant endeavors were financed entirely by private subscriptions in the missionaries' home countries, the French government subsidized the Jesuits and the parallel mission to Syria's young women organized by the Sisters of Charity, giving an overtly political dimension to the renewed Catholic mission to the Levant. Symbolic of this new political direction, by the early 1830s French had replaced Italian, which had served as the principal foreign language taught in Catholic schools. It even served as the primary language

---

[71] Karpat, *Ottoman Population*, pp. 164–67; Frank Andrews Stone, "The Educational 'Awakening' among the Armenian Evangelicals of Aintab, Turkey, 1845–1915" *Armenian Review* 35 (1982): 30–52; *Salname-i Vilayet-i Haleb* [Yearbook for the Province of Aleppo] *1326* (Istanbul, 1909), p. 224.

[72] Naff, *Becoming American*, p. 115. Tibawi, *American Interests*, pp. 278–80.

[73] Kurt Grunwald, "Jewish Schools under Foreign Flags in Ottoman Palestine" in *Studies on Palestine During the Ottoman Period*. Edited by Moshe Ma'oz (Jerusalem, 1975), p. 165; Hopwood, *Russian Presence*, p. 150.

[74] Deringil, *Well-Protected Domains*, pp. 119–23; Rogan, *Frontiers of the State*, pp. 124–27.

of instruction in some schools, creating a cultural as well as political bond for many Arabic-speaking Catholics to France.

This not so subtle grab for influence reflected France's ambitions in its *mission civilitrice* to the Ottoman Empire's Christians. As they courted the Catholics of the region, French diplomats took the Catholics' side in disputes they had with local Muslims, Druzes, Orthodox Christians, or with the Porte. The Catholics, in turn, served often as convenient surrogates for French diplomats in forestalling the aspirations of other powers in the region, especially those of Russia and Great Britain.[75] This role was accelerated after France's military intervention in Lebanon in 1860 and the formulation of the *Réglement organique* establishing Mount Lebanon as an autonomous region with a Catholic, if not Maronite, governor.[76] This was not to say that the French educational activities in the region only had ulterior, political motives. As was the case of the Protestant missions, genuine altruism was involved, even if in both cases it were tinged with more than a hint of cultural superiority and smugness. The Jesuits, in particular, were praised by most contemporary observers for providing excellent educational facilities and the Jesuit university in Beirut, Université Saint Joseph, stands as a monument to their dedication to the cause of education in greater Syria.[77]

Unwittingly, the enthusiastic, if politically naïve, Protestant missionaries had set off a cultural war wherein European powers sought proxies in an escalation of the competition to influence the various religious communities of the empire. The local religious communities were well aware of their position in this "great game" and often played the European powers off against each other. This was especially true for Syria's various Catholic sects who found diplomats from Austria, Spain, and Italy, after its unification, to be convenient foils to French ambitions.[78] But even the Druzes held out the possibility of their conversion to Protestantism to gain Britain's support while the Yazidis of northern Iraq threatened to become Catholic to win that of France. Competition among the European powers for influence through the use of the missions had unquestionably furthered the politicization of religious identity in the region. It is telling of the blurring between one's religious and political self in nineteenth-century Syria that the Protestants were almost invariably referred to by Arabic-speakers as the "English sect" (*ta'ifat al-Ingiliz*) in a mirror image of the long-standing usage of *ta'ifat al-Afranj* for the Catholics. This despite the fact that Great

[75] Alfred Schlicht, *Frankreich und die syrischen Christen 1799–1861: Minoritäten und euro-päischer Imperialismus im Vorderen Orient* (Berlin, 1981), pp. 176–78, 181–89.
[76] William Shorrock, *French Imperialism in the Middle East: The Failure of Policy in Syria and Lebanon 1900–1914* (Madison, WI, 1976), pp. 14–17; Engin Akarlı, *The Long Peace: Ottoman Lebanon, 1861–1920* (Berkeley, CA, 1993).
[77] Tibawi, *American Interests*, pp. 118–19.
[78] Schlicht, *Frankreich und syrischen Christen*, pp. 171–79.

Britain, unlike France, made only half-hearted attempts to claim them as protégés.[79]

With the growing politicization of religious identity among Ottoman Christians, Russian officials felt compelled to enter the fray on the side of orthodoxy in Syria. They had long championed their fellow Orthodox Christians in the Balkans, but had previously left the affairs of the see of Antioch to the Greeks. But the community served by the see of Antioch still suffered from the dysfunctional linguistic relationship between a Greek hierarchy and Arab laity that had plagued it in the eighteenth century. Furthermore, Phanariote fortunes and influence had fallen precipitously in the aftermath of the establishment of the Kingdom of the Hellenes in 1832. In political disarray, the Orthodox faithful were the prime target for the Protestant missionaries, as well as an invigorated and emboldened Melkite Catholic clergy. In a memorial to the czar, dated September 1842, Methodios, the Orthodox Patriarch of Antioch, detailed the sorry state of the Orthodox Christians in Syria as contrasted to that of the Catholics. There were only two Orthodox schools, one in Damascus and the other in Beirut, while the Roman Catholics had thirteen schools throughout Syria and the Maronites had four. Everywhere the Catholics were winning converts and seizing Orthodox churches. He ended his woeful tale with an appeal for aid from the Orthodox Christians of Russia.[80]

In response to such forlorn appeals, Czar Nicholas I (1825–55) sent Porfiri Uspenski to investigate the status of the Orthodox Christians of the Holy Land in 1843–44. Uspenski's report to the czar confirmed the sad state of orthodoxy in the region. But he felt that the Melkite Catholics and the Protestants were making gains due in no small part to the respect that they showed to the Arabic language. The Orthodox hierarchy, in contrast, was seemingly contemptuous of its Arabic-speaking flock, he wrote, and it included too few Arabs among its ranks. Noting the attachment of the Uniates to the physical trappings of orthodoxy, i.e. vestments, icons, liturgy, Uspenski believed that the only reason that the Uniates existed at all was due to the resentment of the Arab laity to the dominant role of the Greek clergy. To preserve orthodoxy in Syria, Nicholas I named Uspenski to head a Russian mission to Palestine in 1847 to nudge the Greeks toward greater inclusiveness of the Arab laity and clergy.[81]

Russian ambitions were stalled, however, by the Crimean War (1853–56) which included among its causes the Catholic–Orthodox rivalry for control of the Church of the Holy Sepulcher in Jerusalem. In the war's aftermath, Czar Alexander II (1855–81) established the Palestine Committee in 1858 with a mandate to care for Russian pilgrims in the Holy Land and to

[79] Tibawi, *American Interests*, p. 36.
[80] Quoted in Neale, *History of the Holy Eastern Church*, pp. 199–212.
[81] Hopwood, *Russian Presence*, pp. 37–41.

educate the Orthodox children of the region.[82] Convinced only the Arabization of the church hierarchy would save orthodoxy in Syria, the Russians
began to work behind the scenes to restore the Patriarchate of Antioch to
Arabic speakers. This paralleled their strategy to encourage their Bulgarian
allies to press for a separate exarchate, free from the control of the
Ecumenical Patriarch of Constantinople. Russian aspirations in Syria
finally succeeded with the elevation of Meletius Dumani as patriarch in
1900, the first Arab to sit on the throne of the see of Antioch since 1725.[83]
Russian efforts helped to invigorate the sagging fortunes of orthodoxy in
greater Syria and to staunch the defection of the Orthodox faithful to either
the Uniates or the Protestants. But their intervention served, like that of the
French, to blur the loyalties of the sultan's subjects. When Russia waged
war on the empire as in 1853–56 and again in 1877–78, his Orthodox
subjects in Syria were, no doubt, in conflict as for whose victory, the sultan's
or the czar's, they should pray.

It was not only the Russians who worried over the possible success of
foreign missionaries in winning converts from among those who held to the
traditions of their forefathers. The "Damascus Affair" of 1840, as well as
the earlier French occupation of Algeria in 1831, had awakened concern
among the Jews of Western Europe for their coreligionists in the "Orient."
In 1860, a group of wealthy French Jews formed the *Alliance Israélite
Universelle* for the "regeneration" of the Jews of the East. Jews in other
European countries responded enthusiastically to their appeal and the
membership of the *Alliance* rose from eight hundred and fifty in 1861 to
over thirty thousand members in 1885.[84] Those figures indicate that the
modernist Jewish educational mission had striking parallels to the Protestant missionary enterprise in the Anglo-Saxon world. Like it, the *Alliance*
had captured the imagination of large numbers of middle-class people, as
well as the elites, and these were willing to make the voluntary contributions
that funded the *Alliance*'s mission. The *Alliance* was also every bit as
paternalistic toward the inhabitants of the Ottoman Empire as were the
Protestants. The difference was the Alliance sought to spread a French
vision of "modernity," rather than one articulated in English.

One of the problems facing the *Alliance*'s aspirations as a modernizing
force in the Arab lands was that the Jewish communities, outside of
Baghdad, had not benefited to the same extent as the Christians from the
empire's growing integration into a capitalist world economy. Many of the
Jews of the empire were still staunchly traditionalist in their outlook and
wary of contact with outsiders, even Jewish outsiders. As a result, the
success of the *Alliance* in convincing students to choose their modern Jewish

[82] *Ibid.*, p. 61.
[83] *Ibid.*, pp. 160–63, 166–72.
[84] Aron Rodrigue, *French Jews, Turkish Jews: The Alliance Israélite Universelle and the Politics of Jewish Schooling in Turkey, 1860–1925* (Bloomington, IN, 1990), pp. 22–23.

approach to education as opposed to that offered by either the Christian schools, which were seen as offering ties to the Western powers, or the traditional religious schools, *heders*, varied from city to city. An *Alliance* school was established in Baghdad in 1864. It initially offered four classes; only one hundred and fifty boys had completed all four between 1864 and 1886, as compared to the several thousand boys educated in the traditional Jewish schools in the same period. In 1890, the *Alliance* opened a vocational school for girls; an academic school for girls followed in 1893. Thereafter, the *Alliance* schools in Baghdad enjoyed steadily increasing enrollments, even attracting non-Jews, as parents grew to appreciate the benefits of the new education over the old.[85] But many Jews in Baghdad, while appreciating the education offered by the *Alliance*, resented the "modernist" secular message being taught in the schools. Not the least of which was that the psychological barriers between the religious communities should be torn down. They also resented the choice of French as a language of instruction over English, as they viewed the latter tongue as having greater practicality in commerce.[86]

In interior Syria, the traditional schools were even more successful in retaining their clientele than those of Baghdad. An *Alliance* school opened in Damascus in 1864, but closed in 1869 for lack of students. Midhat Paşa, in his capacity as the provincial governor, urged its reopening in 1880 and by 1910, it had 1,129 students.[87] The strength and diversity of the traditional Jewish schools in Aleppo, as well as the availability of education in the Catholic schools of the city, left the Jewish elite of Aleppo largely unimpressed with modernity as it was conveyed by the *Alliance*. Although a Damascene Jew established a "modern" school in 1869, it was still struggling to attract students by the end of the century.[88] Despite the pull of tradition and the prestige of the Catholic and Protestant alternatives, the Alliance could claim nevertheless substantial success in its mission "to bring light to the Jews of the East," especially in western Anatolia and the Balkans. There were 115 schools scattered throughout the Ottoman Empire at the start of the First World War when it was estimated that roughly 35 percent of school-age Jewish children in the empire were attending *Alliance* schools.[89]

French was the primary language of instruction in the *Alliance* schools in Anatolia, Beirut, Egypt, and North Africa; Arabic was used along with French in *Alliance* schools in Iraq and Damascus. Given that linguistic

[85] Ghanima, *Nuzhat al-mushtaq*, p. 187; H. Cohen, *Jews of the Middle East*, pp. 113–19.
[86] Zvi Yehuda, "Iraqi Jewry and Cultural Change in the Educational Activity of the Alliance Israélite Universelle" in *Sephardi and Middle Eastern Jewries: History and Culture in the Modern Era*. Edited by H. Goldberg (Bloomington, IN, 1996), pp. 134–45.
[87] H. Cohen, *Jews of the Middle East*, pp. 138–39.
[88] *Ibid.*, p. 139.
[89] Avigdor Levy "Introduction" to *Jews of the Ottoman Empire*, p. 114.

orientation, it has been suggested that while the schools helped to prepare the students to face the economic and social transformation of their societies, they did little to help integrate them politically into the wider Muslim community in which they lived.[90] Rather they served to create a cultural bond between the students and the West, which fostered emigration. The same critique is valid for most of the other missionary schools as well. While the children of the Jewish and Muslim elites might attend Christian schools, and Christian and Muslim students could on occasion be found in an *Alliance*-sponsored school, education remained largely sectarian in the Ottoman Arab lands. Non-Muslims generally avoided the government schools and Muslim clergy strenuously tried to prevent their flock from attending Christian schools.[91] By the start of the First World War, Jews and Christians enjoyed much higher rates of literacy than did their Muslim neighbors. But whether that education had served to prepare them adequately for their future in the region remained to be seen.

## Muslim reaction: a tale of two cities

Many Muslims in the Ottoman Arab world undoubtedly felt disquiet at the direction and increased pace of change in the nineteenth century. But their unease was fueled as much by fear of European military expansion as it was by anger at the Tanzimat reforms. Napoleon's occupation of Egypt intruded abruptly into the consciousness of Muslim Arabs in 1798. Ottoman intellectuals and bureaucrats in Istanbul had flirted in the eighteenth century with various Western imports and some had even come to recognize the necessity of learning European languages. Thanks to embassies sent to the European courts, they were also aware of changes occurring outside the boundaries of the "protected realms." Although most were certain of their own culture's moral superiority, some were ready to embrace elements of European culture, technology, and ever so tentatively its political ideology. Similarly, Christian Arab chroniclers with their connections to Catholic Europe could ponder the implications of the revolution in France in 1789.[92] But Arab Muslim elites, far from the battlefields in Europe and confronted only by the occasional Frankish merchant, did not have to think too often about the West, or the changes occurring there.

Napoleon's arrival in Cairo in 1798 shattered that complacency. In Cairo, the chronicler ʿAbd al-Rahman al-Jabarti noted both the flaws and

---

[90] Rodrigue, *French Jews, Turkish Jews*, pp. 85–90; Norman Stillman, *The Jews of Arab Lands in Modern Times* (Philadelphia, PA, 1991), pp. 27–35; H. Cohen, *Jews of the Middle East*, p. 106.

[91] Rashid Khalidi, *Palestinian Identity: The Construction of Modern Consciousness* (New York, 1997), p. 60; Deringil, *Well-Protected Domains*, pp. 116–17.

[92] ʿAbbud, *al-murtadd*, pp. 176–81.

strengths of his city's occupiers with apparent interest. Although he clearly detested the French, he recognized that their scientific curiosity about the world they encountered in Egypt was something Muslims should emulate.[93] Further afield, the Damascene chronicler Hasan Agha al-ʿAbd was less ambivalent. "In regards to Cairo, we were on edge until the news had been verified. The Christians had indeed taken it by force. There is no power and no strength save in God." The rhetoric of jihad again intruded into his narrative in the entry on the end of the French occupation. "The news spread that the Muslims had taken Cairo and killed all the Christians who were there. Celebrations went on in Damascus for three days and nights."[94]

Hasan Agha's choice of political categories helps us to comprehend the author's, and presumably his contemporaries', world-view. His world was starkly divided between Muslims and unbelievers. In that regard, his entry on the Greek War for Independence was typical.

> In this year was the rising of the infidel Greeks (*kafara al-Rum*) in Islambul [sic] and other provinces. People became very concerned. Their rising was among the most important of events. They took control of Morea and a number of places in the lands of Islam. We heard that they had killed many Muslims. Then God gave victory to Islam and the Muslims were able, after much violence and suffering, to take back much of what had been lost . . . Our lord Sultan Mahmud Khan ibn al-Sultan ʿAbd al-Hamid Khan – may God strengthen the pillars of his state until the end of time – sent his *mujahid* soldiers on both land and sea and instituted the jihad in the Morea until our present time in the year 1241 (1825–26).[95]

His political categories require little deconstruction. Muslims were under attack in the Peloponnese and only the sultan could save them. The author's rhetoric conflated Christians, whether foreign or domestic, into one mono-lithic and implacable foe. His myopia was not unique. Typically, selective and often garbled accounts of sectarian atrocities, invariably committed solely against their own kind, reached each religious community from afar. The Christian Naʿum Bakhkhash's entry for June 24–30, 1860 read in part: "We heard that the Druzes took Zahle and they killed and slaughtered a number of Christians. The Druzes are all-powerful. Upon hearing this news, Islam rejoiced."[96] Rumors helped to make every community feel uneasy and fearful, and this was no less true for the Muslim majority than it was for the Christians. The Muslims of greater Syria had hoped that the restoration of Ottoman authority would mean a return of the natural order of things, and all would become again as it had always been. But the pronouncements read

---

[93] Ibrahim Abu-Lughod, *Arab Rediscovery of Europe: A Study in Cultural Encounters* (Princeton, NJ, 1963), pp. 20–23.

[94] Hasan Agha al-ʿAbd, *Taʾrikh Hasan Agha al-ʿAbd: qitʿa minhu, hawadith sanat 1186 ila sanat 1241* [Chronicle of Hasan Agha al-ʿAbd: a portion of it on the events of the year 1186 until 1241]. Edited by Yusuf Jamil Nuʿaysa (Damascus, 1979), pp. 37, 54.

[95] *Ibid.*, pp. 166–67.

[96] Bakhkhash, *Akhbar*, vol. III, pp. 200, 202.

aloud to them by the Tanzimat's representatives shattered that hope. With European military intervention increasingly a reality, their former self-confidence could easily turn to panic.[97]

The mixture of anger, resentment, and fear with which many Muslims viewed the Tanzimat manifested itself violently first in Aleppo where the Catholics were, not coincidentally, reveling in their newly won freedom. When the Patriarch Mazlum returned from Istanbul to the city in 1849, having secured *millet* status for the Melkite Catholics, he led a triumphant procession through the city's streets, replete with large crosses and the discharging of firearms in celebration. The Catholics had arrived politically and they refused to be discrete any longer. The wealthy lay leadership of the various sects planned grand cathedrals to celebrate their new status. The prospect of new churches, in turn, became the emotional flash point of Muslim discontent with all that was wrong with the Tanzimat in Aleppo. Bakhkhash reported in January 1848 that an imperial *ferman* reached the city, stating that henceforth repairs and additions could be made to churches without application to the Porte.[98] The order did not provide a *carte blanche* to build new churches and, in fact, was in accordance with a liberal interpretation of the long-standing Pact of ʿUmar. But the Christians interpreted the order differently and pressed ahead with their construction plans. In protest, a group of Muslims occupied the building site of the Armenian Catholic Church and consecrated it as a mosque. Other Muslims brought suit in the shariʿa court to stop the construction of a Melkite Catholic cathedral. That site was also occupied briefly and was only vacated after the Melkites gave gifts to the qadi and the *naqib al-ashraf* (head of the *ashraf*).[99]

Muslim discontent erupted in October of 1850 with a spasm of violence directed at Christian churches, shops, and homes. The spark to the riot, which coincided with the Muslim celebration of ʿId al-Adha (Feast of the Sacrifice), was a rumor that conscription would be implemented in the city after the feast. There had been protests that had turned into riots in Aleppo's past but this was the first time that a riot had purely sectarian targets. Clearly something more than the prospect of the draft was troubling the city's Muslim population. An Ottoman account listed 20 Christians as killed by the rioters, with 6 churches, 36 shops, and 688 homes either totally destroyed or gutted.[100] Despite the wholesale sacking of the prosperous Christian quarters outside the city walls, Christian casualties were relatively light. Christian homes within predominantly Muslim quarters inside the city walls were not touched. Many of those from the afflicted quarters fled to the

---

[97] Göçek, *Rise of the Bourgeoisie*, pp. 112–13.
[98] Bakhkhash, *Akhbar*, vol. III, p. 114.
[99] *Ibid.*, vol. II, pp. 142, 146; Istanbul, BOA, İ. Dahiliye 13185/12 dated 6 Teşrin-i Sanî 1266/ November 18, 1850.
[100] Istanbul, BOA, İ. Dahiliye, 13493/7, dated 11 Dhu al-Hijja 1267/ October 7, 1851.

city's caravansaries where they found protection from the European consuls, or as was the case of Bakhkhash's family were saved through the intervention of Muslim neighbors or friends.

We know the rioters' grievances from a petition they sent to the sultan while they still ruled the city's streets.[101] They stated they would willingly turn in their arms, but they would not permit conscription. They further insisted that they were not rebels and pledged their loyalty, announcing their readiness to offer up their wealth, souls, and children for "our lord the sultan and the faith of Islam." As many of the rioters were from former janissary families, their offer of military service is not a contradiction to their opposition to conscription. Rather, it would restore them to their former status and income as the sultan's military in the city. That, of course, was precisely what the Tanzimat reformers did not want. Further demands included that the tax recently announced, the *vergü*, be assessed on property and not individuals. After these initial demands, the grievances became sectarian. Christians should not be allowed to ring church bells or to raise the cross above the heads of Muslims; neither the Christians nor the foreign consuls should be allowed to hold black slaves. The issue of non-Muslims holding African slaves, who were presumed by Muslims to be either already Muslim or potentially so as pagans, had arisen earlier as an imperial order in 1843 had directed Aleppo's priests and rabbis to be vigilant lest non-Muslims acquire Muslim slaves.[102] While not acknowledging their source, the rioters' demands would reinstate the former *status quo* of the Pact of ʿUmar. Finally, they insisted the Christians must treat all Muslims with respect. Their message was unambiguous. The Ottoman dynasty must return to its former place as the protector of Muslim privilege and end its flirtation with the Christians.

The rioters were not alone in their resentment of the Christians' recent behavior. Aleppo's leading Muslim clergy, including Sayyid Muhammad Sharayyifzadah, the *naqib al-ashraf*, and the city's mufti Taqi al-Din Mudarriszadah, dispatched their own report to the Porte on October 21, 1860. The Ottoman authorities would later exile both men on the suspicion of their complicity in the riot. Unlike the colloquial Arabic of the rioters' letter, their version of the events was written in formal Ottoman Turkish. The clergy blamed the Christians for having set off the riot with their provocative behavior. They cited the ringing of church bells and public displays of crosses as having infringed upon the public space of the Muslims. Their contempt for the Christians is best illustrated by their use of the Turkish colloquial slur for non-Muslims "*gâvur meydanı*" (Infidel Square) for the afflicted Christian quarters of Judayda.[103] Significantly,

---

[101] *Ibid.*, 13493/8.
[102] Damascus, Aleppo Awamir al-sultaniyya, vol. LII, p. 52.
[103] Istanbul, BOA, I. Dahiliye 13185/5.

there was no mention of conscription or the new taxes. A second memorial from the city's secular Muslim notables echoed the ʿulama's sentiments. The Christians had been attacked by the mob as they had exceeded the "limits" (*hudud*) placed upon them by the shariʿa.[104] The report on the crisis filed by the governor Mustafa Zarif Paşa simply summarized, without editorial comment, the testimony of the local Muslims. The rebels had given as the reasons for the rising that the Christians had rung their church bells, raised up crosses, held black slaves, ridden horses, and dressed like Muslims. He added that unless the rebels were punished, all of *Arabistan* would revert to its rebellious ways.[105] In these various accounts of the causes of the riot reaching Istanbul, taxes and conscription were fading fast into the background of the clamor of sectarian dissonance.

A Christian version of the causes of the riot, signed by all the chief clerics of the city save Mazlum who had escaped to Beirut in the melee, also emphasized the growing sectarian antagonism in the city.[106] As might be expected, they had a different set of villains. Since the Egyptian occupation of Syria, they complained that Muslims had been acting badly towards Christians in both words and deeds. Starting in the previous year, Muslims had begun to boast openly that they would soon take the Christians' homes and women away from them. The Christians wrote that Taqi al-Din Efendi had encouraged such talk rather than attempt to diffuse the situation. The clerics' letter highlighted the Muslim seizure of the two cathedral building sites as a crucial acceleration in the deterioration of communal relations, with the Porte having seemingly condoned the Muslim misbehavior by its inaction. This provided, they wrote, a clear signal to the Muslims that further outrages would be tolerated. The order for conscription had only served, in the Christians' view, to set off a social eruption that had been steadily building. At the time of the riot, it would seem that both Muslims and Christians could agree that the underlying causes of the violence were sectarian, rather than fear of conscription or taxes.

The central government, as the governor had suggested, could not allow the rioters a victory as that would undermine the legitimacy of the Tanzimat. The bureaucrats were also keenly aware, via Ottoman diplomats in Paris and London, that European newspapers were using the events in Aleppo as a test case to see if the sultan really cared about his Christian subjects.[107] The Ottoman army took Aleppo back for the sultan by storm between November 5 and November 9, 1850. The quarters of Bab al-Nayrab, Banqusa, and Qarliq, which reputedly served as the rebels' stronghold, were bombarded by artillery and then taken by fierce house-to-

---

104 *Ibid.*, 13493/8, no date.
105 *Ibid.*, 13358, dated 4 Muharram 1266/ November 9, 1850.
106 *Ibid.*, 13185/12, dated 6 Tişrin-i Sanî 1266/ November 18, 1850.
107 Istanbul, BOA, İ. Hariciye 3526 contains clippings and translations of various European newspapers forwarded to the Porte.

house fighting. It was a lopsided battle. Kerim Paşa, commander of the *Arabistan Ordusu* (Army of Arabia), reported 3,400 rebels were killed and 230 arrested, with Ottoman losses of only 27 dead and 92 wounded.[108] Of course, the Ottomans had the artillery. There were no estimates of Muslim civilian casualties. But they must have been considerable as contemporary sources reported that the targeted quarters were leveled.[109]

Sectarian tensions were on the rise elsewhere in greater Syria as well. In Lebanon, an ongoing competition for political dominance between Druze and Maronite emirs, which had emerged in the aftermath of the Egyptian occupation, provoked a simmering low level of communal violence with occasional sectarian murders, always answered in kind. Reports of that violence helped to keep communities elsewhere in Syria on edge. News of the Crimean War further acerbated tensions. Consul Werry described the difference with which the various inhabitants of Aleppo received the same news.

> The advice received here of the success of the sultan's troops on the passage of the Danube was received here by the whole Muslim population and the European with enthusiasm, but it was observed that this news was not so acceptable to the different rites of the Christian rayahs – this feeling may be partly explained as having its origins in the calamities they experienced during the insurrection which occurred here three years ago from which they obtained no indemnity but there is no mistake in placing the Orthodox Greeks and the majority of the Catholic Greeks in Syria, as the devoted allies of Russia.[110]

As a representative of Britain, an ally of the sultan in his war with Russia, Werry might be excused for seeing a Russian sympathizer in every Christian. He may have been correct in assessing the loyalties of the Orthodox Christians, but he was wrong in regards to the city's Catholics. The Catholic diarist Bakhkhash referred to the sultan's war against the Russians as a *jihad* and labeled the czar as an "enemy of peace" in one entry with news of the war, hardly the sentiments of a "devoted ally."[111] An American missionary in Aleppo also reported widescale support for the sultan in both Muslim and Christian communities.[112]

The same could not be said for the reaction of the various communities to the sultan's reform edict of 1856 that had come, in part, as repayment to the British for their support in the war with Russia. Even in the sultan's inner circle, Cevdet Paşa voiced the unease felt by some among the sultan's

---

[108] Istanbul, BOA, İ. Dahiliye 13495/3, dated 29 Muharram 1267/ December 4, 1850; *ibid.* 13304, no date.

[109] Report in the London *Standard*, forwarded from London to the Ottoman Embassy in Paris whence it was dispatched with an Ottoman translation, dated 27 Safar 1267/ January 1,1851. Istanbul, İ. Hariciye 3526.

[110] London, FO 861/4, Werry to Rose, November 26, 1853.

[111] Bakhkhash, *Akhbar*, vol. II, p. 385.

[112] ABCFM, unit 5, reel 542, no. 250, letter from William Benton to Revd. Anderson, dated November 25, 1983. See also Tibawi, *British Interests*, pp. 114–15.

leading bureaucrats at its reading.[113] Al-Shaykh al-Ustuwani, a Damascene qadi, recorded that his city's governor called the Muslim notables to hear the proclamation read aloud. He added, "All the Muslims became ashen faced and they asked God Most High that He glorify the faith and grant victory to the Muslims."[114] In sharp contrast, Bakhkhash's entry for March 2–8, 1856 described the Christians' enthusiastic reaction to the public reading of the sultan's order, at a reception held by the French consul to mark the occasion.[115]

Elsewhere, a British missionary urged the ringing of the church bells in the Palestinian market town of Nablus to announce the new era. When questioned by the town's governor if he had permission, he replied simply that the *Hatt-ı Hümayûn* gave him the right. Two days later, the honorary French consul in the town, a local Muslim, ran up the *tricolore* above his house to announce the birth of the son of Napoleon II. The combination of the two celebrations incensed the Muslim population. When another Protestant missionary returned from a hunting trip, replete with horse and rifle, he encountered a group of angry Muslims. He panicked, shot, and killed a beggar in the crowd. The missionary made his escape, but the crowd, enraged at his effrontery in violating two of the proscriptions of the Pact of ʿUmar as much as at the death he had caused, quickly turned into a mob. They attacked all symbols of the detested, new dispensation; they tore down the flags of the honorary consuls, dragged the bell off the Protestant mission house, and looted the homes of the newly converted Protestants. There was much material damage inflicted by the rioters, but only one elderly Christian was killed. Three years previously, there had been violence in Nablus between Protestants and Orthodox Christians and tensions were already running high among the town's Christian community. Significantly, Muslims had only targeted those with foreign protection, including several Muslims, and the hapless Protestants as symbols of the new order, while the larger Orthodox population in the town was spared.[116]

Sectarian relations had clearly deteriorated in Syria by mid-century. But it is difficult to know how relations between individual members of the communities were affected. In the aftermath of the riots, Bakhkhash was clearly traumatized. His diary entries reflect his fear that another rising was imminent. He recorded occasional incidents of violence or insults between members of the different communities throughout the 1850s as auguries of worse to come. The Syrian provinces with their large, prosperous, and self-confident Christian minority had become the battlefield where the forces of political centralization and modernization struggled against the resistance of tradition. Unfortunately, the Christians had come to represent in the

---

[113] Cevdet Paşa, *Tezâkir*, vol. I, p. 68.
[114] al-Ustuwani, *Mashahid*, p. 162.
[115] Bakhkhash, *Akhbar*, vol. III, p. 32.
[116] Tibawi, *British Interests*, pp. 115–16.

minds of many Muslims all that was wrong with innovation. It did not help that they were also perceived as prospering in this new environment while Muslims lagged behind. Perhaps nowhere was this perception more widely shared than in Syria's' unofficial capital, Damascus. Until the Egyptian occupation, it had been left largely untouched by the maelstrom of economic change. But in the Tanzimat era, its inhabitants began to experience most of the changes that had occurred in the coastal cities and Aleppo over the last two centuries, compressed into just three decades.[117] The spark to what would become the largest intercommunal conflagration in Syria, however, came from outside.

In the spring of 1860, the Druze leadership in Lebanon rallied their kinsmen and peasant retainers for a general offensive against the Maronites whom they felt had usurped their political privilege. The Maronite elite was in a weak position as an ongoing popular uprising in the Kisrawan region, beginning in 1858, had severely challenged its authority. The civil unrest generated by the rising spread into regions inhabited by both Maronites and Druzes and the Druze emirs concluded that it was now time to act. A series of strikes on Christian villages and towns followed, culminating in the sack of the Christian market towns of Zahle and Dayr al-Qamar in June 1860. Many hundreds of Christians were killed and most of the houses in the two formerly prosperous towns destroyed.[118] The "events" in Lebanon repeated an ugly pattern of sectarian violence, now termed "ethnic cleansing," which had first appeared in the Greek War for Independence with the massacre of Muslims in the Peloponnese and the responding Muslim attacks on Greeks elsewhere. Similar cycles of outrages followed by counter outrages in revenge, or as preemptive strikes before the other community had a chance to act, would erupt periodically elsewhere in the empire until its dissolution. In Lebanon, with the Christian men singled out for slaughter and Christian homes burned, the survivors fled for whatever safety they could find. Several thousand found their way to Damascus in the summer of 1860 further exacerbating tensions in that city. Adding to the general anxiety of the Muslim population, the victorious Druzes were reported to be converging on Damascus, joined by other Druzes and Bedouin from the Hawran who were rumored to be drawn in by the promise of loot. The Muslims of the city feared the Druzes about as much as did the Christians,[119] but sectarianism now so divided the communities that any common action was unimaginable.

ᶜId al-Adha, which was feared as an emotional flash point as it had been in Aleppo in 1850, passed without incident in early July. Shortly thereafter, a group of Muslim adolescents started painting crosses on the streets and

[117] Rafeq, "The Impact of Europe."

[118] Fawaz, *An Occasion for War*; Abraham, *Lebanon at Mid-Century*; Makdisi, *Culture of Sectarianism.*

[119] al-Ustuwani, *Mashahid*, pp. 172–73.

doorways of houses in the Christian quarter. Some of these were arrested by the Ottoman authorities on July 9, 1860 and were ordered to clean the streets under an armed guard. A Muslim crowd quickly gathered and demanded the boys be released. This led to a general melee in the city with various hotheads urging the Muslims to attack the Christians in revenge for all the imagined wrongs that the Muslims had suffered since the Egyptian occupation. Druzes and Muslim villagers poured into the city for loot, as feared, and an orgy of violence shook the city for eight days until order was finally restored. In the aftermath, the Christian Quarter of the city was a smoldering ruin and the estimates of the Christian dead ranged from a few hundred to ten thousand.[120]

As in Aleppo, the actual cause that served to set off the riot in Damascus had been unimportant. The destructiveness of the mob's fury and the target of their anger, however, serve to pinpoint where the true grievances lay. The Muslim elite of Damascus, in the aftermath of the riot, held remarkably similar opinions as their Aleppine counterparts as to where the blame for the destruction properly should be placed. The perpetrators had been the rabble of the city and, more importantly, outsiders. In Shaykh al-Ustuwani's view, the Ottoman army had also played a role as he claimed individual soldiers had led the way in seeking out Christian homes and shops to pillage. While not apportioning blame on the Christians for their own predicament, the Shaykh felt that they exaggerated their losses in the aftermath for illicit gain.[121] Muhammad Abu'l-Su'ud al-Hasibi, another Muslim notable who was arrested by the Ottomans for complicity in the riot, was less generous. He held the Christians' arrogance and greed responsible for their downfall.[122] In both Aleppo and Damascus, the Muslim elite felt that the punishment meted out to convicted rioters and the imposition of fines on the Muslim community collectively for compensation were excessive and unfair. The tragedy of the sectarian riots had widened the chasm between the communities as each community, in turn, could only see its own role as that of victim.

Elsewhere in the Ottoman Arab lands, the pace of change was much slower than had occurred in Syria. Conscription was not introduced in the provinces of Basra or Baghdad until 1870, following the appointment of the Tanzimat reformer Midhat Paşa as governor in Baghdad. He was also responsible for the introduction of various other manifestations of the new regime.[123] Trouble did break out between Jews and Muslims in Baghdad in 1889 after the burial of a prominent member of the Jewish community in a

[120] Fawaz, *Occasion for War*, pp. 78–100. For the estimates of the casualties, see Linda Schatkowski Schilcher, *Families in Politics: Damascene Factions and Estates of the 18th and 19th Centuries* (Stuttgart, 1985), pp. 89–90.
[121] al-Ustuwani, *Mashahid*, pp. 184–85, 199.
[122] Salibi, "The 1860 Upheaval," pp. 190–91.
[123] Longrigg, *Four Centuries*, pp. 281, 298–300.

shrine venerated by believers in both religious traditions. But quick action by the Ottoman authorities and members of the local Muslim elite prevented any deaths and quieted the city.[124] Kurdish tribes in the north unleashed a number of raids against Christian villagers in Mosul province and southeastern Anatolia, beginning in the 1840s and these would intensify towards the end of the century. But the nineteenth century ended in the southern Iraqi provinces without any further major outbreaks of sectarian violence.

Further afield, a riot occurred in Jeddah in Arabia in 1858. It could be more accurately described as a reaction to the privilege of foreign protégés rather than an outburst of sectarianism as some of those attacked, as had been the case in Nablus two years earlier, were Muslims who held foreign passports. Its origins, however, were fueled by the resentment held by local elites at the attempts by Istanbul to assert its control in the region as well as their anger over the injustice of the capitulatory regime. Otherwise, the massacre of twenty-two foreigners and their protégés could not be said to have grown out of grievances over the Tanzimat's promise of equality between the religious sects *per se*.[125] Nonetheless, in far off Aleppo, Bakhkhash recorded the event: "We heard that in Jeddah, they killed all the Franks even though the son of the emir, the son of the ruler saved (some?) from the massacre. On Crete, Christians and Islam are fighting. The Christians rose, were victorious, and they killed Islam."[126] The linkage of the two events in one brief entry is telling. Bakhkhash's world-view reduced all political news into one simple question, "What did it mean for the Christians?" In that regard, his was not so different from the world-view held by the Damascene chronicler, Hasan al-Agha in that all reports were refracted through the prism of religious identity.

## Conclusion

The Aleppo riot curiously prefigured the riot in New York City in July 1863, in regards to its immediate cause and the ultimate human targets of the rioters' outrage.[127] The latter was also fueled by conscription anxieties, but quickly turned both anti-establishment and anti-African-American. The African-American victims of the New York mob were targeted because of their race in the same way that Aleppo's Christians had been targeted due to their religious identity. Both groups had historically been viewed as subordinate in terms of the politically dominant group and both were now

---

[124] Dumont, "Jews, Muslims, and Cholera," pp. 353–72; Ghanima, *Nuzhat al-mushtaq*, p. 179.
[125] William Ochsenwald, *Religion, Society, and the State in Arabia: The Hijaz under Ottoman Control, 1840–1908* (Columbus, OH, 1984), pp. 137–51.
[126] Bakhkhash, *Akhbar*, vol. III, p. 126.
[127] Iver Bernstein, *The New York Draft Riots: Their Significance for American Society and Politics in the Age of the Civil War* (New York, 1990).

enjoying, or about to enjoy, emancipation of sorts. Both sets of riots mobilized the marginalized underclass of what might be seen as the majority populations of either city – whites in New York, Muslims in Aleppo. The largely Irish-born mob in New York included many recent arrivals who viewed the African-Americans as economic competitors and a barrier to their own advancement, as well as symbols of a war they did not want to fight. The rioters in Aleppo came from neighborhoods that were also on the periphery of the city – both physically and socially – and they felt displaced by the changes that reintegration into the empire entailed.[128] The rioters in New York acted out of fear that their economic and social upward mobility was blocked; Aleppo's rioters were no doubt plagued by the sense that everything was getting worse for them in a spiral of downward mobility. But once a spark had ignited their anger, diverse grievances in both sets of rioters collapsed into rage at a segment of the population they perceived to be "outsiders."

There were parallels to the two cases in the causes of the riot in Damascus as well. There, of course, had been no threat of conscription in Damascus. That innovation was already in place providing the unruly conscripts representing the sultan's writ in the city. But there were fears rampant in the Muslim community of attack by either the Druzes or Christians and there was lingering Muslim resentment at the public processions mounted by the triumphalist Melkite Catholics through the city on various occasions. Furthermore the poor of the city, who would ultimately be charged with the responsibility for the damage, must have felt akin to the New York mob in that a new set of rules had been put in place that would leave them at the bottom of the social heap. Muslims perceived their Christian, and especially Melkite Catholic, neighbors as "uppity," arrogant in their wealth and privilege. In this regard the ʿulama of Damascus and Aleppo were partially correct in assessing the causes of discontent. In Aleppo, the mob had tellingly targeted Mazlum, his new cathedral, and wealthy *Avrupa tüccarıs* with particular wrath and vengeance; in Damascus, the first targets were locals who worked for foreign consulates and held protégé status. The targets in either city were not just random Christians, but those whose wealth and political advantage provided the evidence, if any were needed, that the traditional social hierarchy which held that any Muslim was superior to any non-Muslim had been overturned.[129]

It was a complex set of circumstances that led the mob to target Christians as the focus of their anger. Fear, more than loathing, was perhaps the crucial emotion in the mix. In the case of Damascus, there was

---

[128] Bruce Masters, "The 1850 'Events' in Aleppo: An Aftershock of Syria's Incorporation in the Capitalist World System" *International Journal of Middle Eastern Studies* 22 (1990): 3–20.

[129] For a discussion of the causes of the Mosul riot of 1854, see Sarah Shields, *Mosul Before Iraq: Like Bees making Five-Sided Cells* (Albany, NY, 2000), pp. 86–89.

fear of the violence in Lebanon spreading to the city; in Aleppo there was the fear of the draft. In both cities, there was fear of the new order the Tanzimat regime was imposing upon people who were ill prepared to adapt to it. Greed was clearly another element at play as in both Aleppo and Damascus the quarters where poor Christians lived survived unharmed. But it was also in the poorer quarters that Christians and Muslims lived together as neighbors and in both Damascus and Aleppo, Muslims in mixed quarters protected their Christian neighbors from harm. Those eventually named or punished for either riot were almost entirely from the poor Muslim quarters of both cities – some ironically coming from those same mixed quarters – or were outsiders. Nevertheless, the fact that the Muslim elites sat by without intervention in both cities tells us it was more than greed and fear alone that fueled the outrages. Aleppo had seen many civil disturbances in the century preceding 1850, and rioters had often sought to loot the Christian quarters as an easy mark. In the earlier troubles, Muslim notables had intervened quickly before the situation became too destructive or deadly. In 1850, they hid with the governor in a barracks outside the city. Similarly, with the exception of the lionized ᶜAbd al-Qadir al-Jaza'iri, most Muslim notables in Damascus sat out the troubles at home.

Their inaction represented their reception of the Tanzimat reforms, rather than arising out of long-standing bigotry against Christians. The Muslim elites of Syria resented the speed of change and the diminution of their authority that the Tanzimat had set in motion. Throughout the long eighteenth century, the Muslim notables of Syria's great inland cities had developed a political *modus vivendi* that existed largely outside the direct control of Istanbul. They had done things the way that they had wanted and had got away with doing so, with only the minimum of intervention from Istanbul. Now the state was intruding into their lives and livelihoods in an unprecedented way. The apparent rise of the Christians was simply emblematic of all that had gone wrong. In Aleppo, the Christians had been content to have clientage relationships with the Muslim elites in the long eighteenth century, but now they were acting as equals or worse. In Damascus, the change of economic and political status for Christians had occurred much more quickly and seemed to be propelling Christians to unprecedented wealth and influence at a time when local Muslims felt their traditional privilege threatened.

The Ottoman authorities and European observers blamed the ᶜulama in Damascus and Aleppo for having incited anti-Christian feeling. Although we have no direct evidence of that, it is reasonable to assume that individual members of that class might have invoked the Pact of ᶜUmar in their sermons leading up to the violence when inveighing against the Tanzimat reforms. Nonetheless, their sins of omission seem greater than any sins of commission that they might have committed. In the aftermath of the riots, they might console themselves that the Christians had received their well-deserved chastisement, while they themselves were personally innocent of involvement. But that satisfaction must have been bitter–sweet. The humiliation of the Christians by a mob made up of men, whom they detested almost as much as they resented the Christians, must have evoked mixed emotions for the Muslim elites of Aleppo and Damascus as they surveyed the damage wrought by that mob's fury to their respective cities.

# CHAPTER 6

# After the "events": the search for community in the twilight of empire

Inhabitants of the British Isles came to identify themselves as Britons during their own "long" eighteenth century, 1707–1837. "Britishness" as constructed by the elites of the three historically separate peoples was a supranational political identity, which united diverse traditions under one crown, even as those elites continued to revel in their own separate cultural identities. Once articulated, the notion that there was a political community comprised of Britons trickled down to the less-fortunate subjects of the king and they too, in time, largely adopted that identity as their own. Remaining loyal sons and daughters of Scotland, England, and Wales, they could agree that ultimately they were also Britons. Linda Colley posits that this political cohesion was fostered by four distinct cultural and institutional strands shared by those who would come to imagine themselves as Britons – Protestantism, pride in and ambitions for empire, a "cult of commerce," and loyalty to the Hanoverian monarchy over Jacobite claimants.[1] The prominent place of religion in defining who was properly British effectively kept the majority of the inhabitants of the second isle in the kingdom, Ireland, from acknowledging that they too were Britons.[2]

A similar transformation in the boundaries of political community would be necessary for the subjects of the Ottoman sultans, and for those of the Hapsburg emperors and Romanoff czars as well, if their multi-ethnic empires were to survive the rising tide of ethnically based nationalisms in the late nineteenth century. The political situation for the elites of all three empires, however, could not have been more different from that blessing the would-be Briton elites in the previous century who were able to weather all challenges to their hegemony both at home and abroad. Even so, Abdül-Hamid, the last effective sultan in the line of Osman (1876–1909), tried to introduce religion and the institution of the sultanate as a transnational glue to hold his empire together – whether consciously following a foreign model

---

[1] Linda Colley, *Britons: Forging the Nation 1707–1837* (New Haven, CT, 1992).
[2] David Hempton, *Religion and Political Culture in Britain and Ireland: From the Glorious Revolution to the Decline of Empire* (Cambridge, 1996).

or not. But without viable economic incentives for his myriad subjects to remain Ottoman and lacking an inculcated pride in empire, his was a Sisyphean task, doomed with historical hindsight to failure.

Sultan Abdül-Hamid ascended the throne of the House of Osman surrounded by murky circumstances. Insurrection had broken out in Bosnia in 1875 and quickly spread to Bulgaria. The Tanzimat reformers seized the developing crisis as an opportunity. They convinced Istanbul's chief mufti on May 30, 1876 to issue a deposition order for Sultan Abdül-Aziz, whom they saw as an impediment to reform. They then installed Murad, his nephew and more importantly the son of Abdül-Mecid who remained every reformer's favorite sultan, on the throne. The new sultan proved incapable of coping with the burdens of office and was himself deposed within four months in favor of his brother, Abdül-Hamid. Abdül-Hamid became sultan with the troubles in Bulgaria threatening to escalate into war with Russia and the European powers pressing for debt repayment. Nonetheless, he appointed Midhat Paşa, the darling of the reformers, as his prime minister and allowed for the promulgation of the new constitution in a bow to the Tanzimat bureaucrats to whom he owed his throne. The empire's experiment in democracy was short-lived. Russia invaded the Ottoman lands in 1877, ostensibly to help the Bulgarian rebels, and the sultan, facing a losing war, dismissed the parliament in 1878.

The European media of his day reviled Abdül-Hamid as a tyrant and despot. Armenian historians regard him as the instigator of pogroms that pitted Turks and Kurds against Armenians, initiating a spiral of communal violence that would culminate in the tragedy of the First World War and the extirpation of the ancient Armenian communities from Anatolia.[3] Recently, however, there has been some revisionism of Abdül-Hamid's place in history.[4] This scholarly recasting of the period is still ongoing, but it has already provided a more sophisticated interpretation of the sultan beyond the long-standing Western stereotype of "Abdul the Damned" so popular in the Victorian press. But even with this revisionism, it must be noted that Abdül-Hamid employed the rallying cry of a politicized Islam to try to save his empire and that could only be repellent to the empire's diverse Christian minorities. His playing of the "Islamic card," coupled with ongoing nationalist agitation against the empire, resulted in increasingly bitter ethnic/religious polarization in Anatolia where Greek and Armenian nationalist ambitions, when added to Muslim fears, produced a volatile tinderbox. Ironically given the outcome in neighboring Anatolia, Abdül-Hamid's use of religion had a calming effect in the Ottoman Arab provinces. There the sultan's rhetoric comforted the Muslim elites to fear no

[3] Christopher Walker, *Armenia: The Survival of a Nation* (London, 1980), pp. 121–73.
[4] Deringil, *Well-Protected Domains*. Also, Stanford Shaw and Ezel Kural Shaw, *Ottoman Empire and Modern Turkey*, vol. II, *The Rise of Modern Turkey* (Cambridge, 1977), pp. 211–21.

longer that Christian upstarts would usurp their formerly dominant political and economic positions. With that threat removed, the Muslim elites could return to their former attitude of *noblesse oblige* toward the non-Muslims. As the rest of the empire descended into communal warfare, the waning decades of the nineteenth century witnessed a political reconciliation of sorts among the elites of the various religious communities in the Ottoman Arab world.

## Ottomanism and Arabism

The "events" of 1850 in Aleppo and 1860 in Lebanon and Damascus had a sobering impact on the Muslim elites throughout Syria. Despite the terror among some in Aleppo's Christian population that the Muslim common people would rise up again to become a mob and repeat their actions of 1850, the worst did not happen. William Benton, an American Congregationalist missionary in the city, wrote on January 20, 1854 that while the ordinary Muslims on the street were insolent toward Christians, there had been no further outbreaks of violence. He credited this turn of events to the leading Muslims in the city, who having given written guarantees to the governor that they would protect the Christians, remained true to their pledge to keep the city quiet.[5] J. H. Skene, the British consul in the city echoed Benton's observation, noting that religious tolerance was provincial government policy; the city's ᶜulama had rebuked Muslims who had accosted Christians on the street and preached sermons highlighting the equality of all humankind before God.[6] In the summer of 1860 as rumors of the fighting in Lebanon reached Aleppo, the city's Muslim poor began to agitate against perceived Christian privilege once again. The governor met the threat with a firm show of force, apparently having learnt from the fatal mistake of his predecessor in 1850 not to let things get out of hand. The Christians had also absorbed a valuable lesson from the past and they offered "protection" money to potential rioters. Further dampening the tensions, the Muslim notables organized patrols in the Christian quarters in a demonstration of civic responsibility. When Damascus erupted in July, Aleppo stayed calm through the combined efforts of the foreign consuls, the Ottoman officials, and not least the Muslim notables.[7]

There is less evidence of the Damascene ᶜulama having taken a similarly positive role in defusing potentially disruptive situations after 1860. But it

[5] ABCFM, Reel 542, no. 251.
[6] Consul Skene to Sir H. Bulwer, Aleppo, August 20, 1860 contained in *British Documents on Foreign Affairs: Reports and Papers from the Foreign Office Confidential Print*, Part I, Series B (*The Near and Middle East, 1856–1914*). Edited by David Gillard. University Publications of America, 1984, vol. VI, pp. 1–3.
[7] Letter Consul Skene to Sir H. Bulwer, August 18, 1860 in *ibid.*, vol. VI, pp. 37–38; London, PRO, FO, 406, no. 8, p. 378. Letter Consul Skene to Lord J. Russell.

should be noted that ʿAbd al-Razzaq al-Bitar took the risk of delivering a sermon condemning the rioters while the unrest in his city was still under way.[8] Anti-Christian incidents did not become deadly when sectarian tensions flared up again in Damascus during the economic depression in the 1870s and we must assume that the city's Muslim notables had become more vigilant to prevent a repetition of the "events" of 1860.[9] Elsewhere, Muslim notables in Beirut, which had escaped sectarian violence in 1860, often acted in conjunction with their Christian counterparts to keep simmering sectarian tensions from breaking out into full-scale warfare. Similarly Muslim notables in Baghdad worked with Jewish community leaders to diffuse potential flash points.[10] Sectarianism continued to pervade the political atmosphere of the Ottoman Arab lands through the end of the nineteenth century and resentment of perceived Christian privilege still haunted the Muslim poorer classes. But these did not lead to any further major communal outbursts and we are left with the question, "why not?"

The Arab nationalist explanation, advanced most eloquently by George Antonius, suggests an ideological convergence of Muslim and Christian elites occurred in the second half of the nineteenth century.[11] Together they promoted the articulation of an Arab national identity to supercede former communal religious identities and which they hoped would lead to a political reconciliation among Syria's diverse religious communities. The nationalist historians contend that Christian intellectuals began to immerse themselves in the classical Arabic culture in the aftermath of the troubles of mid-century. They were encouraged in this pursuit, in no small part, by the education in classical Arabic that they had received in the Protestant mission schools. Over time, Christian intellectuals in Beirut, and later Cairo, Paris, and New York, established links with like-minded Muslims. Together, they promulgated variations on a spectrum of political ideals that scholars have labeled "Arabism," whether their ultimate aspirations lay with cultural autonomy within the empire or actual independence outside it.[12] Pride in the Arab past, and the hope of creating an equally proud Arab future, lay at the heart of what was initially a literary movement. None-theless, the cultural awakening had political implications as it redrew the boundaries of the politically imagined community. With the defining element of inclusion transferred from religion to language, the sectarianism

[8] David Dean Commins, *Islamic Reform: Politics and Social Change in Late Ottoman Syria* (New York, 1990), p. 39.
[9] Philip Khoury, *Urban Notables and Arab Nationalism: The Politics of Damascus, 1860–1920* (Cambridge, 1983), p. 45.
[10] Fawaz, *Merchants and Migrants*, pp. 113–20; Ghanima, *Nuzhat al-mushtaq*, pp. 179–81.
[11] Antonius, *Arab Awakening*, pp. 93–100.
[12] C. Ernest Dawn, *From Ottomanism to Arabism: Essays on the Origins of Arab Nationalism* (Urbana, IL, 1973).

of the mid-nineteenth century was subverted by the nationalist ambitions of the early twentieth century.

As in the case of most linear, causal historical explanations, the Arab nationalist version of the past, while compelling in its simplicity, has come under very effective revisionist fire.[13] Language-based nationalism no longer seems to be the inevitable outcome of political "modernity," as was once taken for granted in historical narratives. The reemergence of Islam as a political ideology has had a sobering effect on the formerly optimistic, and now seemingly premature, assessment of the death of sectarianism in the Arab world advanced by the nationalists. The consensus of the historical revisionists is that while the cultural renaissance was important in helping Christian Arabs to imagine themselves as being primarily Arab in terms of their cultural identity, it had little, if any, impact on Muslim Arabs. Before the nineteenth century, Arab Christians, with a few notable exceptions, had been lax in their interest, and subsequent knowledge, of classical Arabic grammar and syntax as is demonstrated by the loose colloquial style of their chronicles and petitions. The often nearly incomprehensible dialect in which Na'um Bakhkhash, who frighteningly tutored Ottoman officers in Arabic, jotted down his journal entries, provides further evidence that even supposedly educated Christians were blithely unconcerned about the grammatical rules or vocabulary of *fusha* (the classical literary language). By mid-century, however, individual Christians had begun to study and learnt to appreciate the classics of Arabic literature. In the process, they began to incorporate its literary standards as their own. Their discovery and glorification of what were largely secular classics, is known in Arabic as the *nahda* (renaissance). With that newly acquired appreciation, many in the Arab Christian elite started to define themselves culturally as Arabs with an acquired pride in a brilliant literary past that they acknowledged as shared with, and produced by, the ancestors of their Muslim neighbors.

They were, no doubt, aided in this construction by the tendency established among Christian Arab historians in Syria to identify themselves as "Syrians" as early as the eighteenth century.[14] As previously noted, this identification grew out of the struggle between Catholics and Orthodox over the definition of what constituted the "traditional" church in the see of Antioch. Once having established an identity based on residence in a

[13] Besides Dawn, Rashid Khalidi, "Ottomanism and Arabism in Syria before 1914: A Reassessment" in *The Origins of Arab Nationalism*. Edited by R. Khalidi, L. Anderson, M. Muslih, and R. Simon (New York, 1991), pp. 50–69; see also C. Ernest Dawn's "The Origins of Arab Nationalism" in *ibid.*, pp. 3–30. Hasan Kayalı, *Arabs and Young Turks: Ottomanism, Arabism, and Islamism in the Ottoman Empire, 1908–1918* (Berkeley, CA, 1997). James Gelvin, *Divided Loyalties: Nationalism and Mass Politics in Syria at the Close of Empire* (Berkeley, CA, 1998).
[14] Abu Husayn. "Duwayhi as a historian," pp. 1–13; Thomas Philipp, "Class, Community, and Arab Historiography in the Early Nineteenth Century: The Dawn of a New Era" *International Journal of Middle Eastern Studies* 16 (1984): 161–75.

defined geographical space that included an implicit acceptance that Muslims could also be fellow "Syrians," the shift to an identity based on the language spoken by those who shared that geographically defined territory was relatively easy. But it is questionable how deeply such sentiments permeated into the self-understanding of ordinary Christian Arab men and women. Syrian immigrants to the US before the First World War routinely identified themselves by their religious community when asked their nationality by immigration officials.[15]

In contrast to this tentative progression toward Arabism embarked upon by some Christian intellectuals in Egypt and the Fertile Crescent, very few Arabic-speaking Jews participated in the secular Arab literary revival before the First World War. There were, of course, the notable exceptions of the Egyptian satirist, Yaᶜqub Sanuᶜ (nom de plume, Abu Naddara in the Egyptian colloquial Arabic in which he wrote), the Jewish literary society of Damascus, and Murad Faraj's work in helping to define Egyptian music in the early twentieth century.[16] But as was noted earlier, the majority of the Jews of the Ottoman Arab provinces were slow to embrace an ideological modernity that included an imagining of a political community that transcended religious difference. The exceptions seem to highlight the generalization that most of the Jews who did embrace a European imagined "modernity" found it in the schools of the Alliance, and those, unlike the Protestant schools, did not foster any identification with an imagined Arab past. It also should be noted that the Jews' major experience with sectarianism in the nineteenth century had come at the hands of Christian and not Muslim antagonists. Jews had continued to live circumspectly in the Tanzimat period and unlike the Christians did not attract the fury of Muslim mobs. Having weathered the storm of Muslim sectarianism anonymously, Arabic-speaking Jews may not have felt the need to establish themselves as Arabs politically or culturally and they remained content within their community as established by "tradition."

Zionism was still a relatively novel ideology among the empire's Jews at the outbreak of the First World War. And when it did find a local resonance, it was more often messianic in its inspiration than nationalist. But the continued psychological isolation of Jews from their Christian and Muslim neighbors would mean that the restoration of Zion would become an increasingly attractive political option for many in the aftermath of the war.[17] The aspirations of other Jews in the post-war Arab lands led them to

[15] Philip M. Kayal, "Arab Christians in the United States" in *Arabs in the New World: Studies on Arab-American Communities*. Edited by Sameer Abraham and Nabeel Abraham (Detroit, MI, 1983), pp. 45–61.

[16] Cohen, *Jews of the Middle East*, p. 44. Sasson Somekh, "Participation of Egyptian Jews in Modern Arabic Culture, and the Case of Murad Faraj" in *The Jews of Egypt: A Mediterranean Society in Modern Times*. Edited by Shimon Shamir (Boulder, CO, 1987) pp. 130–40.

[17] Esther Benbassa, "Associated Strategies of Ottoman Jewish Society in the Nineteenth and

seek foreign protection, as was the case of the Jews of Baghdad in 1919,[18] or continued emigration to Europe or the Americas. Among Arabic-speaking Jewish intellectuals, however, there was a growing interest in cultivating an Arab identity in the mandate period,[19] even if most Jews in the region preferred to cling to the older definition of community that kept the religions separate. It was, after all, a strategy that had help them weather so much unrest in the past. The sectarian turmoil of the nineteenth century had left their communities untouched. By maintaining a low profile, the region's Jews had avoided conflict and collectively they saw no need to rethink intercommunal relations. That choice while understandable would produce tragic consequences for the continued survival of the ancient Jewish communities of the Arab east in the twentieth century when the creation of the State of Israel brought into question their loyalty to avowedly nationalist Arab regimes. In much the same way, external events had led Muslims to question the loyalties of their Christian neighbors in the nineteenth century.

The *nahda* undoubtedly encouraged some Christian Arabs to recast themselves as Arabs. But scholars have suggested that it was the Islamic reformist movement, known as the *salafiyya* (literally, "the way of the ancestors"), which promoted a revived Arab identity among Muslims in the second half of the nineteenth century.[20] With luminaries such as Muhammad ʿAbduh in Egypt and Rashid Rida in Syria, the *salafiyya* existed as an intellectual movement that was autonomous from, and often oblivious to, the *nahda* of the Christians. But each, in its turn, helped to accomplish the same goal, i.e. the emergence of an Arab cultural consciousness among Arabic-speaking elites, whether Christian or Muslim. The proponents of the *salafiyya* sought to invigorate Islam by identifying its fundamental truths and values and then to apply them to fashion a society that would be both Muslim and modernist at once. As such, the movement was even less overtly nationalist in its inspiration than the *nahda*. Rather its proponents declared their goal to be the restitution of the Islamic truths and values of the first generation of Muslims that had been hidden beneath the accretion of obscurantist legal scholarship for centuries. Although the reformers proclaimed they were simply returning to the "tradition" of their ancestors, the modernity the movement sought and the values it promoted were very much defined by the West. That was perhaps unavoidable as the *salafiyya*, unlike the reformist message of Muhammad ibn ʿAbd al-Wahhab in the eighteenth century to which it bore more than a passing resemblance,

Twentieth Centuries" in *The Jews of the Ottoman Empire*. Edited by A. Levy (Princeton, NJ, 1994), pp. 457–84.

[18] Stillman, *Jews of Arab Lands in Modern Times*, pp. 256–58.

[19] Amial Alcalay, *After Jews and Arabs: Remaking Levantine Culture* (Minneapolis, MN, 1993), pp. 233–47.

[20] Dawn, "The Origins of Arab Nationalism."

arose out of a measured response to the polemics against Islam so freely proffered by its late nineteenth-century European critics.[21]

In seeking the spiritual revival of Islam, the intellectual vanguard of a Muslim modernity could not ignore the fraught political environment of the late nineteenth-century Middle East. An essential component of political modernism, as defined in the West, was the nation-state and by necessity the scholars of the *salafiyya* had to address the concepts of nationality and citizenship in their scheme of reform. Although a few such as Jamal al-Din al-Afghani sought to create a fully fashioned pan-Muslim nationalism, most accepted that a building block to that idealized *umma* had to be either an Arab nation or the continuation of the Ottoman regime, albeit in a more democratically fashioned incarnation. Before the First World War, most would still hold that the Ottoman sultanate remained the last best hope of an independent Islamic polity. Such a conclusion was fairly obvious for ᶜAbduh in Egypt, with a British occupation force stationed in his country. But even in more remote Baghdad, fears of European colonialism contributed to pro-Ottoman sentiments among local Muslim elites.[22] The empire, for most Muslims and even some Christians, was simply seen as the only remaining political force capable of forestalling European imperial ambitions. On the other hand, fears that the Ottoman state might not survive left some to contemplate what might stand in its place to prevent a European land-grab. For Aleppo's native son, ᶜAbd al-Rahman al-Kawakibi, the apparent inability of the Ottomans to save Muslims from imminent disaster suggested the need to revive a properly Arab caliphate whose very authenticity rooted in history would serve as a rallying point for Muslim resistance. His was an appeal to which very few responded before the First World War. The majority among the Muslim Arab elites seemed content to imagine an Islamic modernity under the protection of a liberal sultanate rather than to contemplate a new state constructed on the foundations of Arabism, however defined.[23]

In their discussion of a reinvigorated Islam, few of the would-be Islamic modernists addressed the question of the role of non-Muslims in a reformed Muslim polity directly. But their contention that the inherited, calcified shariᶜa tradition did not reflect the true spirit of the *Qur'an* and the Prophet's *Sunna*, opened the possibility of discarding the centuries old legal baggage derived from the Pact of ᶜUmar. Furthermore when looking to the *Qur'an* for inspiration, the reformers chose to emphasize the positive verses concerning the *ahl al-dhimma* in place of the negative ones. Similarly, rather

---

[21] Aziz al-Azmeh, *Islams and Modernities* (London, 1996), pp. 88–100. Fazlur Rahman, *Islam and Modernity: Transformation of an Intellectual Tradition* (Chicago, IL, 1982), pp. 43–83.

[22] Mahmoud Haddad, "Iraq before World War I: A Case of Anti-European Arab Ottomanism" in *The Origins of Arab Nationalism*. Edited by. R. Khalidi, L. Anderson, M. Muslih, R. Simon (New York, 1991), pp. 120–50.

[23] Kayalı, *Arabs and Young Turks*, pp. 207–12.

than dwell on the Prophet's later misadventures with the Jewish clans of Medina, they cited the "Constitution of Medina" as a model of good sectarian relations. If the Prophet could extend political rights to non-Muslims then so too could a modernist Islamic polity, without endangering its Islamic character. Indeed, the reformers pointed to the traditions of political tolerance for the *ahl al-dhimma* in the early Islamic period as a sharp contrast to the intolerance they claimed was rampant in premodern Europe. In this analysis, they paralleled their contemporaries in the European Jewish scholarly community who were advancing a depiction of an idealized Islamic golden age of religious tolerance with which to chastise their Christian fellow citizens.

Beyond the Qur'an, the *Salafi* movement looked to the history of Islam in its early centuries as an inspiration, having been in their view an age of intellectual liberalism, philosophical debate, and scientific exploration, the equal of which Europe could only boast in the late nineteenth century. As such, the *Salafi*s were also drawn to the classics of Arabo-Muslim culture but for different reasons than attracted their Christian Arab contemporaries. They saw the works as primarily *Islamic*, rather than Arab, classics. The end result was, however, an increasing pride in that civilization as Arab, and a concomitant disregard of Islamic classics written in languages other than Arabic. For them, the glories of Islamic civilization were all Arab and the centuries of non-Arab rule were consigned to an Islamic "Dark Ages," with history written invariably as decline after 1258 and the end of the Abbasid caliphate. In their recasting of early Islamic history, the reformers cited the cooperation between the Christian Arab tribes and the Muslim armies in spreading the rule of Islam. However they sought to justify it, many Muslim intellectuals seemed to agree that society at the dawning of the twentieth century should be one in which Muslims, Christians, and Jews would enjoy equal citizenship, even if the law of the land were based in the principles of Islam. Theirs was a liberal Islam at ease with the political categories advanced by the West, even as they remained supremely confident of the spiritual superiority of their own tradition. Unlike the political Islamists of a century later, they saw no contradiction in blending the two. In short, their vision was not at odds with the Ottoman constitution of 1876, in being both modernist and Islamic at once.

Further encouraging an imagining of their future as Ottomans, the increasing inclusion of Arab Muslim elites into the Ottoman regime strengthened the ties between the sultan and his subjects in the Fertile Crescent. The anti-Christian outbursts in the mid-nineteenth century had come, in part, as a reaction to the displacement of those elites by the Tanzimat regime. Not surprisingly, anti-Christian sentiments diminished as the state recruited the children of the formerly alienated notables into its ruling class and extended to them new opportunities for acquiring wealth.

After 1860, scions of most of the leading Muslim families of Jerusalem, Damascus, Aleppo, and Baghdad, as well as newly arrived upstarts, found places in the ranks of the Ottoman provincial bureaucracies, having received education in the new government schools, at home or in Istanbul. This trend greatly accelerated in the reign Abdül-Hamid as a part of his attempts to broaden the ruling class to include non-Turkish Muslims.[24] The established Muslim elites prospered materially as well. The Ottoman Land Code of 1858 permitted the acquisition of formerly state-held lands (*miri*) by private individuals. Although the intent had been to provide ownership to peasant proprietors, in reality the Muslim Arab elites quickly moved to take possession of newly available agricultural resources.[25] With a boom in the export trade of commodities such as wheat, cotton, and tobacco after the depression of the early 1870s, Muslim landowners could rightly feel that they too were profiting from the new imperial order.

Muslim elites throughout the Ottoman Arab provinces during the reign of Abdül-Hamid could harbor both Arabist and Ottomanist sentiments at the same time.[26] Pride in an Arab identity did not necessarily preclude loyalty to the Ottoman sultan, any more than pride in being a Scot prevented identification with Britain for a late eighteenth-century resident of Edinburgh. Increased opportunities for schooling and the proliferation of newspapers and books in Arabic led to an increased awareness of the Arabs' past among those of the elite who could read. The glory of the medieval period, which even European scholars were assessing as brilliant, seemed to indicate to many that another cultural renaissance was not only possible but inevitable. In the recasting of the past, the ancestors, whether Christian or Muslim, had been given a thoroughly Arab pedigree by proponents of both the *nahda* and the *salafiyya*, although it is highly doubtful that those same ancestors would have identified themselves as such. But that did not matter for those Christians and Muslims who were willing to face the new century together as Arabs.

Beyond a cultural convergence that led some Muslims and Christians to imagine a common future based on a newly constructed common past, political and economic expediencies also encouraged a confluence of political interests among Muslim and Christian elites that linked their destinies to a reinvigorated empire. While some Christians, most notably the Maronites, still yearned for European protection, others of the educated elite, including Butrus al-Bustani, had become wary of European and/or

[24] Philip Khoury, *Urban Notables*, pp. 26–52; Khalidi, *Palestinian Identity*, pp. 63–84; Kayalı, *ibid.*, pp. 17–51.
[25] Khoury, *ibid.*, pp. 26–28; James Reilly "Urban Hegemony in the Hinterland of Ottoman Damascus: Villages, Estates and Farms in the Nineteenth Century" in *Histoire économique et sociale de l'Empire ottoman et de la Turquie (1326–1960)*. Edited by Daniel Panzac (Paris, 1995), pp. 455–70.
[26] Khalidi, *Palestinian Identity*, pp. 63–69.

North American cultural and political imperialism.[27] Most simply understood that their political futures lay within a society where Islam was the
dominant cultural paradigm. Their newly acquired Arab identity encouraged cooperation with their Muslim neighbors, who no longer seemed quite
the outsiders they had once been perceived to be. The gradual reduction of
official discrimination by the state also fostered a new confidence among the
Christian Arab commercial classes in the sultan's ability to provide them
with a secure environment for their continued economic prosperity.

## Becoming Ottoman in Aleppo

> As she raised him up from childhood fearful of her responsibilities
> So must he now guide the nations with the reins of kingship.[28]

Maryana Marrash, perhaps the best-known woman poet in nineteenth-
century Syria, dedicated those lines to Abdül-Hamid's mother upon his
accession to the throne. She was not alone in her native city of Aleppo in
welcoming the accession of Abdül-Hamid. Based on the written record they
have left us, it seems that many of the Christians of Aleppo tentatively
began to conceive of themselves as belonging within the Ottoman Empire in
the second half of the nineteenth century. From their example, we may
assume that similar transformations of identity were occurring among other
Christians and Jews elsewhere in the Fertile Crescent as well. This newly
configured Ottoman identity explicitly acknowledged definitions of political
community wider than those the non-Muslims had previously entertained –
city or *millet*. This "imagining" of a more broadly defined community did
not constitute an intellectual embrace of a fully articulated Ottoman
nationalism, however. Rather, it was a psychological drift away from a
collective identity circumscribed by religious allegiances to one located
within the boundaries and institutions of the empire. Indices of a nascent
Ottoman identity among Aleppo's Christians included a sense of personal
connection to events in the wider empire, an affection for the Ottoman
royal house, and a confidence that the Ottoman state provided the best
protection for their survival. Faced with the perceived continuing hostility
from their Muslim neighbors, many Christians in the city saw the Ottoman
army as their protectors.

Evidence of this transformation can be found in the diary of Naʿum
Bakhkhash, recorded between 1835 and 1875 and which provides one of the
very few surviving, non-elite voices from the period. Over time, Bakhkhash
came to appreciate the Ottoman state as the best insurance that the
sectarian violence, which had devastated his community in 1850 and had

---

[27] Butrus Abu-Manneh, "The Christians between Ottomanism and Syrian Nationalism: The
Ideas of Butrus al-Bustani" *International Journal of Middle East Studies* 11 (1979): 287–304.
[28] al-Tabbakh. *Iʿlam al-nubala*, vol. VII, p. 568.

threatened it again in 1860, would not recur. As a member of a self-conscious minority, a non-national empire whose sultan viewed all his subjects equally worthy of protection undoubtedly seemed the best political option to forestall rule by the "mob" of his nightmares. It was an ideological transition that did not come easily to the diarist, however. Bakhkhash initially saw the world divided into stark sectarian camps. One of the most striking features of his diary is the virtual absence of Muslims in his entries before 1860, other than the undifferentiated collective "Islam" of his fears. With his silence, Bakhkhash is perhaps a fitting representative of the insularity bred by the voluntary sectarian segregation that marked most of his city's residential quarters at the beginning of the Tanzimat period. Living as he did in the almost exclusively Christian neighborhoods of Judayda, he saw no need to mention individual Muslims at all. There were a few exceptions. Bakhkhash sheltered the son of Sayyid Ahmad Nayyal for four days in 1835 from an Egyptian sweep of the city for conscripts. He and his family were, in turn, taken in during the riots of 1850 by Mustafa Sakif, who also sent the Bakhkhash family *baqlawa* on the feast marking the end of Ramadan.[29] We know from other entries that Bakhkhash taught the elder Nayyal to read, but nowhere does he explain his relationship to Mustafa Sakif.

The silence underlies what was an almost impermeable social divide among the various religious communities that existed for Bakhkhash. But his insularity was seemingly more a product of his class than his religious faith. The elites of all communities continued the patterns of mutual reciprocation and contacts, that were already established in the eighteenth century and reestablished in the aftermath of 1850. Such relationships are only vaguely alluded to in the rare accounts of social gatherings of prominent Muslims, Christians, and Jews, to which the diarist noted that he was not invited. Bakhkhash's parochialism is indicative of the deep psychological divisions that existed among those who were not numbered among the city's notables, whether Muslims, Christians, or Jews. For the lower classes of every sect, social, and even more so political, life remained intimately linked to one's own religious community. With little to connect him with the lives of his ordinary Muslim neighbors, Bakhkhash viewed them as an enigma at best, the source of his greatest fears at worst.

Nonetheless, Bakhkhash's entries in the aftermath of the "events" of 1850 represented a personal evolution toward a political Ottomanism that would have pleased the Tanzimat reformers. An unabashed supporter of Ibrahim Paşa, he was initially unconvinced of the Ottomans' stated intentions to extend the same freedoms to his community that the Egyptian administration had. But with the Tanzimat reforms, Bakhkhash became a partisan of the Ottoman royal house. In 1854, he recorded with approbation

---

[29] Bakhkhash, *Akhbar Halab*, vol. I, pp. 36, 316; vol. II, p. 208.

that Abdül-Mecid had issued a decree putting an end to bribery in the courts and at the governor's saray in a vow to return justice to the empire.[30] As events heated up in Lebanon in 1860, Bakhkhash's old fears resurfaced. They quickly evaporated when the city's governor mobilized his troops to patrol the Christian quarter as rumors of the rising in Damascus reached the city. The governor read a public proclamation that he would not allow any attacks, either verbal or physical, against Christians. It seemed to work, as by the third week of July calm returned to the city. Putting aside his earlier reservations about the Ottoman state's willingness to protect his community, Bakhkhash was well on his way to becoming an Ottoman enthusiast. He frequently reported the governor's walking tours in the Christian quarter with genuine admiration, noting that once the governor had even greeted him personally.

A year later, the Christians of Aleppo felt confident enough of the state's protection that they held parties to celebrate the accession of Abdül-Aziz as their new "king" (malakuna).[31] The choice of words Bakhkhash used was significant. "King" rather than "sultan" had Biblical associations for Arabic-speaking Christians. Its presence in the entry suggests Bakhkhash's acceptance of the new sultan as his personal sovereign rather than simply being a distant alien ruler. In sharp contrast to the enthusiasm displayed by Aleppo's Christians for their new sultan, Shaykh al-Ustuwani in Damascus noted that the event had passed in his city without celebration, except for the decorations hung on official buildings by the Ottoman officials.[32] Further hints of Bakhkhash's personal odyssey toward Ottomanism occur in his characterizations of the courtly manners of the Ottoman officers whom he tutored in Arabic, the grandeur of official ceremonies he attended, his prayers for Ottoman victories over Christian enemies, and the enthusiasm bordering on patriotism that he experienced at military band concerts. In short, it seems that Bakhkhash was willing to embrace the Ottoman state and its public ceremonies as long as it continued to protect his community from what he perceived as the continuing potential for physical harm emanating from the Muslim common people of his native city. While that compact was maintained, he was perfectly content to be loyal to the sultanate, to rejoice in its celebrations, and to worry over its defeats.

Although Bakhkhash's Ottomanist leanings are unfortunately anecdotal, there are indications that others in his native city shared his sympathies. The diary of the Armenian Catholic lay sodality of the Holy Spirit recorded many of the same reactions to Osmanlılık in Aleppo as described by Bakhkhash. The recording secretaries noted that Sultan Abdül-Mecid had contributed 25,000 ghurush for the construction of the Shaybani Armenian

[30] Ibid., vol. II, p. 392.
[31] Ibid., vol. III, pp. 203, 258.
[32] al-Ustuwani, Mashahid, pp. 223–24.

Catholic Church, the largest single donation received, dwarfing the gift proffered by the French consul; a plaque thanking him was proudly displayed inside the church.[33] The diary also noted the festivities in the city surrounding the accession of Abdül-Hamid to the throne in 1876, as well as the telegrams of congratulations sent by all the Catholic Metropolitans in the city to him on that occasion.[34] As was the case with Bakhkhash, the Arabic-speaking recorders of the Armenian Catholic diary referred to the new monarch as "our king." They further recorded in 1877 that the Ottoman army had provided the pomp and ceremony for the arrival of the papal nuncio in the city. As an index of their willingness to promote an Ottoman identity, the Catholic schools in Aleppo voluntarily added Turkish as a part of their established curriculum by 1878, before Istanbul made it mandatory. The city's governors frequently attended Catholic school graduation ceremonies and star pupils delivered speeches in Ottoman Turkish for their benefit, followed by shouts of *"Padişahımız çok yaşa"* (Long live our sultan) from the audience.[35]

The recorders' complacency with the sultanate was shattered by the events of the summer of 1908 when a military revolution ushered in the regime of the Committee of Union and Progress. The new regime was nationalist in its outlook and although its initial proclamations contained affirmations of religious tolerance, ethnic lines were being hastily redrawn everywhere in the empire. The next year after an attempted counter-coup to restore Abdül-Hamid, widescale violence directed against Armenians erupted throughout southeastern Anatolia. It is unclear from the historical record to what extent the anti-Armenian pogroms spread to Aleppo. The diary of the sodality records only that Armenians were arrested in Aleppo and is silent as to any deaths. It did, however, record murders of Armenians in both Antioch and the nearby hill town of Kasab.[36] Significantly, unlike the case of 1850 when Muslim anger had been indiscriminate and targeted all Christians, this outburst was clearly ethnic, rather than sectarian in nature, as Christian Arabs were untouched by the violence. The CUP regime in Aleppo called on the headmasters of the city's schools to organize their students in a parade as part of victory celebrations over the forces of the counter-revolution. The city's Arab Catholics agreed to participate, while the Armenians kept their children home for fear of what might happen.[37] Although the military government eventually restored order in Anatolia, it did not restore confidence among Aleppo's Armenians and the

[33] Such plaques were sometimes of concern to Ottoman officials who felt they might incense the sultan's Muslim subjects. Deringil, *Well-Protected Domains*, pp. 33–34.
[34] Taoutel, "Watha'iq akhidhan," vol. 43, pp. 541–42.
[35] *Ibid.*, vol. 43, pp. 552–53, 571.
[36] Sanjian, *Armenian Communities in Syria*, p. 280. Taoutel, *ibid.*, vol. 43, pp. 576–77.
[37] Taoutel, *ibid.*, vol. 43, p. 578.

diary reported that by 1912, between thirty and forty Armenians were leaving the city every week for the New World.[38]

With the end of the First World War, there were fears in Aleppo that the Muslim–Armenian violence convulsing southeastern Anatolia would spread to the city. A large number of the Armenians who had survived the deportations from Anatolia in 1915 had ended up in the city as refugees. As food stores were scarce in the city and famine stalked the Syrian country-side, the Muslim poor increasingly resented their presence. In February 1919, Muslim rioters attacked Armenian refugee camps in and around the city. At least forty-eight Armenians were killed and many more injured.[39] As in 1909, none of this anger was directed at Arabic-speaking Christians, although there were attacks by Muslim bands on Christian Arab villagers elsewhere in northern Syria. Providing an indication that categories of identity were changing, the local newspaper, *al-Halab*, eschewed sectarian identities in its articles in 1919 in favor of national ones.[40] The readers were implored to remember the horrors committed against their Armenian brethren by the Turks and to be generous toward them, as was the Arab tradition. Nationalist rhetoric had drowned out the voice of sectarianism, at least in the public record. Further seeking to diffuse sectarian tensions, the Amir Faysal visited the city and delivered a speech on the unity of the Arabs, regardless of religion. Some of the city's prominent Muslims established a Committee of Arab Brotherhood, modeled after one already established in Damascus to promote Faysal's claim to Syria, through which they sought to inculcate the city's commoners with the ideals of a non-sectarian Arabism.[41]

In the winter of 1919–20, violence erupted between Armenians and Turks in the nearby Anatolian towns of Maraş, Kilis, and Aintab, which had formed part of the former Ottoman province of Aleppo. There were fears that communal warfare would soon spread to Aleppo as well. These were fueled by the harrowing accounts of missionaries who had narrowly escaped tragedy in Anatolia. They reported a wave of religious warfare fanning out from Turkey that would surely soon engulf Aleppo. J. B. Jackson, the American consul, wrote to Admiral Mark Bristol, his superior in Istanbul, that the city had seemed primed to explode. The Muslim population was encouraged by the military victories of the Turkish Nationalists in French-occupied Cilicia while British and French agents were trying to stir up Christian fears of Muslim "fanaticism." But a heavy snowfall during the week of February 14th kept the potential rioters indoors and the anticipated rising failed to materialize. Consul Jackson credited himself with the "non-event" as he had gone with the Italian consul to see the governor, Naji Bey

[38] *Ibid.*, vol. 43, p. 588.
[39] Gelvin, *Divided Loyalties*, p. 45.
[40] Articles reproduced in Taoutel, "Watha'iq akhidhan," vol. 43, pp. 592–96.
[41] Gelvin, *Divided Loyalties*, pp. 82–83.

al-Suwaydi, to seek an increase in the presence of the Arab Army on the city's streets. His visit had an effect, he wrote, as both police and army patrols were intensified and "the hordes of Bedouin Arabs, Kurds, Turks, and Circassians at present temporarily taking refuge in the city was held in check for the day."[42] Some seventy years after the "Events" of 1850 in the city, the "usual suspects" – tribals and outsiders – had remained constant.

In the wake of the non-event, Amir Faysal again visited the city to calm tensions. Probably at his urging, handbills appeared on March 8, 1920 with messages, designed to heal potential communal fractures in a broad appeal to Arabism. Consul Jackson recorded these as: "The Arabs are Arabs before Moses, Christ, and Muhammad." "In spite of himself, the Moslem is the brother of Christian and Jew" "Religion is God's and the Fatherland belongs to His children."[43] That such propaganda was deemed necessary seems to indicate that despite the aspirations of Arabism, sectarian tensions remained buried in the psyche of Aleppo's population. Not long after Faysal's visit, an Arab Club was formed and unlike the earlier Committee included members of prominent Christian and Jewish families, as well as the prominent Muslims who had already shown their commitment to Faysal, in a show of solidarity with the anti-French front.[44] The old alliance between Muslim and Christian elites in Aleppo had reinvented itself as Arab nationalism. Some Muslims in the city might still conceive of an anti-imperialist crusade, inchoate in the religious rhetoric of a *jihad* that would unite the Arabs of Aleppo with the Milli Kurds and Mustafa Kemal Paşa's now triumphant army in Cilicia. Some Catholics in the city would alternatively welcome the coming of the French. But for most Christians and Muslims, the Amir Faysal had become their choice as monarch. The Christians undoubtedly shared with some of their Muslim neighbors a deep ambivalence at what an Arab kingdom, with a Hashimite on its throne, might mean. But in 1920, it was the only viable political option left besides French occupation.

Aleppo's Catholics had come a long way from their origins as a newly configured, sectarian community in the eighteenth century. They had been among the first peoples in the Middle East to embrace the new ideologies and technologies of the West. By doing so, they advanced collectively from being an economically deprived community to one that was both prosperous and self-confident. In the struggle to assert their own stamp on the parameters of their community, they had to contend with both the Ottoman state and Rome, each with its own differing ideas as to the chain of

[42] Washington, "Records of the Department of State Relating to Internal Affairs of Asia 1910–1929," series 722, roll 8, letter dated February 24, 1919.
[43] Gelvin, *Divided Loyalties*, pp. 181–88.
[44] Washington, "Records of the Department of State Relating to Internal Affairs of Asia 1910–1929," series 722, roll 8, letter from Consul Jackson to the US Secretary of State, dated 13 March, 1920.

command the community should respect. By 1900, Aleppo's Catholics could be reasonably smug about the fact that they had won both battles and their church now reflected their interests, rather than those of some distant potentate, be he pope or sultan. Their story was a triumph of localism, at the same time their economic and ideological positions reflected a newly imagined cosmopolitanism.

This is not to say that Aleppo's Catholics were unprepared to accommodate a nationalist restructuring of their identity as Arabs. Their ties to their city's Muslim elites were key to making such an "imagined community" possible. The history of their struggle within the politics of the *millets* could be evoked to establish their identity as Arabs or, at the least, Syrians. Nonetheless, it was an identity that sparked little initial enthusiasm among them. While Christians in Damascus and Palestine were often in the vanguard of Arab nationalism, Aleppo's early nationalists were almost exclusively Muslim. The latest evolution of their identity into citizens of Syria and of the wider Arab homeland (*watan*) was one the city's Christians had not participated in articulating. Aleppo's Christians had fought to establish themselves as Catholics and they had moved tentatively toward defining themselves as Ottomans. But Arabism had largely been imposed on them from outside their community. Their struggle to create a Syrian "national church" in the guise of the Melkite *millet*, which was articulated in Arabic as an Arab church meant, however, that the psychological leap to reconfigure themselves politically as either Syrians or Arabs was not insurmountable.

## Conclusion

The end of the First World War caught most of the inhabitants of the Ottoman Arab province off-guard politically. In that regard, the Catholics of Aleppo were not alone. Those who were now to be configured as Arabs suffered little of the war's destruction as was wrought on the inhabitants of eastern Anatolia during the war, or experienced by those of western and southeastern Anatolia in its aftermath. But disease and famine had decimated the inhabitants of the Arab provinces during the war years and the region was economically devastated at its end. Adding to the physical and emotional trauma endured by the region's inhabitants, there was confusion over the ends for which the war had been fought. Wilson's fourteen points seemingly promised that the Allies would promote political self-determination among the peoples of the former Ottoman Empire. But it was also clear that the British and French armies in Iraq, Palestine, and Syria were not there simply to drive the Ottomans out as the Bolsheviks had published the Allies' plan to partition the post-war Middle East.

With the demise of Ottomanism, a nation-state seemed the only political option to many. But which nation remained a problem for Arabic-speaking elites who, unlike their contemporaries in the Balkans, had not yet fashioned in their political imaginations the physical boundaries of their nation, or nations, to be. Some Christian intellectuals had envisioned Syria as a nation with a history and culture unique unto itself to which Muslims, Christians, and Jews were equally the heirs. But others argued for the separation from it of an equally distinct Lebanon, which would be both "Phoenician" and Christian. Muslims in the region were slower to find comfort in a geographic identity that was devoid of religious sentiment. Identification as Arabs with an evocation of a glorious, and unambiguously Muslim, past undoubtedly seemed more comforting to them than an appeal to Syria's myriad preIslamic civilizations. Elsewhere in the predominantly Muslim regions of the empire, others found the translation of loyalties from *umma* to nation equally problematic.

Perhaps it was only in Egypt that the political elites could easily gravitate to the idea of "nation" in the aftermath of the Great War. The experience of the British occupation in Egypt, added to the growing economic chasm between the country's indigenous poor and its non-Egyptian industrial and commercial bourgeoisie, helped to sow the seeds of a populist and nativist nationalism. A simple slogan, "Egypt for the Egyptians" could give voice to both political and economic aspirations. Anti-foreign sentiments had erupted in Egypt in 1882 and remained ever present in the country, providing a social cohesion to the discontented.[45] But even in Egypt, which has had a distinct geographic and cultural identity for millennia, Copts could revel in the glories of Egypt's Pharaonic past but few Muslims took comfort in it. Islam held out for them a political, as well as a spiritual message, and urban ennui was channeled away from the nationalist Wafd party to the Muslim Brotherhood of Hasan al-Banna in the 1930s. The Brotherhood, unlike the Wafdists, made no attempt to mollify the Copts, sparking fears among them that a regime controlled by the Brothers might mean a return to the Pact of ʿUmar.

Turkish intellectuals had been grappling with the definition of Turkism that would define the speakers of Turkish as a nation in the decades preceding the war. Nevertheless, Muslim peasants in Anatolia still did not easily conceive themselves as being Turks any more than their counterparts to the south of the new international boundary thought of themselves as Arabs. The advocates of Arabism dreamed of creating a future by remembering the glories of the past. Turkism would abolish the past for some glorious vision of the future. But both movements were little more than intellectual exercises taken on by each nation's would-be elites and their currents had barely touched the imagination of the ordinary putative Turks and Arabs at the war's end. Mustafa Kemal would win his war against the

---

[45] Juan Cole, *Colonialism and Revolution in the Middle East: Social and Cultural Origins of Egypt's ʿUrabi Movement* (Princeton, NJ, 1993).

post-war world order – imposed by Christian armies in the imagination of ordinary Turks – cloaked in the rhetoric of *gaza* (holy war). The Amir Faysal, fighting in the name of Arabism, would lose. Mustafa Kemal's victory gave him the legitimacy, and the military force, to impose his own secular vision on his countrymen and -women. Faysal's defeat by the French and subsequent rescue by the British could only serve to delegitimate both his regime and his legacy.

For the Arabs of what would become the mandates of Lebanon, Syria, Palestine, Trans-Jordan, and Iraq, the parameters of political identity and the definition of Anderson's "imagined community" were much more complex. In Egypt, almost everyone could at least agree that they were Egyptian, even if the thornier issues of whether or not they were also Arabs and should their state be Islamic remained. The Turkish state simply mandated that all its Muslim citizens were Turks whether they spoke Turkish or not, postulating a new identity for the nation's Kurds as "Mountain Turks." One Nationalist publication making the claim for Turkey's right to annex the sanjak of Alexandretta (Hatay) from French-occupied Syria stated that the proof of the district's "Turkishnes," was the dialect of Arabic spoken as the mother tongue of its ʿAlawi inhabitants. Who but a Turk, its author asked rhetorically, could speak Arabic so badly?[46]

The inhabitants of the Fertile Crescent, now artificially carved into five mandated nations-to-be, lacked either the history or the political cohesion of a victorious elite to foster a smooth transfer from communal to national identities. Most of the elites of the region had come to imagine themselves as "Ottomans" by 1914. They, as was the case for the Catholics of Aleppo, recognized that, whatever their competing definitions of individual identity, i.e. Sunni Muslims, Orthodox Christians, Syrians, Palestinians, Baghdadis, Jerusalemites, or Arabs, they were subsumed under a broader political rubric as being the subjects of the Ottoman sultan. That loyalty was created largely by default in that it allowed them to retain whatever identity they held as primary to be included in a broader coalition of Ottoman citizens. Whether they would have remained content to identify themselves as such had the war not occurred and given the increasingly Turkish nationalist ideology of the CUP regime in Istanbul, remains a question of intense speculation.

With the end of the war, and despite the hopes of some Muslims in the Aleppo region, reconstituting the empire was not an option. Faced with that understanding, Muslim elites and not a few Christians across Syria scrambled to express their allegiance to Faysal's Arab Kingdom as their only alternative to French or British occupation. The definition of what an Arab was had not yet been fully articulated and the parameters for inclusion

[46] A. Faik Türkmen, *Mufassal Hatay* [Hatay in Detail] (Istanbul, 1937), p. 227.

into that political community were, and still are not for that matter, entirely clear. That some could construct their political selves primarily as Arabs, with their religious identity subordinate to a national one, represented a real revolution in the "imagining" of political community in the region. The hopes of that nascent identity would be challenged, however, by the new mandatory regime that the Europeans had put into place in newly drawn political entities whose borders had been drawn reflecting European, and not Arab, political and economic aspirations.

# The changing boundaries of political community in the Ottoman Arab world

Political identity for the sultan's Arab subjects was initially vested in the town or village they inhabited or by their tribal affiliation if they were not sedentary. Any sense of social or political loyalty beyond those narrowly defined limits was invariably vested in religious faith. Language differences were undoubtedly noted, but a shared language did not create endogamy. This was most apparent among the Muslim elites where Turkish-speaking Ottomans posted to the Arab lands often sought out brides from local *Ashraf* families. Among the Christians, Greek-speakers from Cyprus or beyond were absorbed over time into the Arabic-speaking Rum of Syria but the Armenians in Aleppo, who by the eighteenth century were largely Arabic-speakers, remained Armenians in their communal identification whether adherents of the Gregorian or Catholic rite. If asked to which community they belonged, we must assume that the ancestors of those who call themselves Arabs today would have responded, as many still do in the Middle East, by stating their religion. It was perhaps only the Bedouin who entertained the possibility of actually being Arabs but that identity would have been at best secondary to their tribal affiliation. These time-honored parameters of "imagined community" did not change when the Ottomans added the Arabic-speaking regions to their empire. The stability the new regime provided in the first centuries of its rule, however, opened the door to an increased European commercial presence in the region. That, in turn, had a dramatic impact on some of the region's Christian and Jewish inhabitants, first economically and then ever so slowly on their sense of political community. Change affected only a very few, yet the articulations of identity by those commercial elites who emerged in the period of transition were crucial in the evolution of the "imagined" boundaries of community, first from *ta'ifa* to *millet* and then from empire to nation for the region's non-Muslims.

The rise of the nation-states in Western Europe and the concomitant expansion of European commercial and political power in the early modern period affected every part of the globe in the centuries following the voyages of Columbus and da Gama. Contact with the Europeans proved devastating for the indigenous peoples of the Americas and parts of sub-Saharan Africa. But everywhere, economic, social, and political hierarchies were challenged, if not overturned. No place was ever quite the same as it had been before, although not everyone suffered from the transition to what Wallerstein has termed the "capitalist world economy." Those indigenous elites who were complicit in the European expansion prospered in the age of transition. Included in that category were those kingdoms in West Africa that enriched themselves off the slave trade, the Chinese merchants who expanded their operations into South-East Asia following the Europeans, and an emerging non-Muslim commercial class in the Ottoman Empire.

Europeans had traded in the Middle East since the Middle Ages. As such, there was no dramatic entrance as so often marked their arrival elsewhere, or any accompanying "culture shock" for the indigenes. Europeans had merely been one of the many groups of strangers who had found their way to the caravan cities of the Arab world before the arrival of the Ottomans, jostling in the region's markets with myriad other outsiders – Indians, Africans, Byzantines, and Central Asians. Due to that familiarity, the Europeans faced few of the restrictions that sometimes greeted their arrival elsewhere in Asia. But over time the relationship, which once had been more or less that of equals, changed as the balance of military power shifted in Europe's direction. With that shift, the Europeans, armed with a new assertiveness, were able to win concessions for themselves and their protégés, who were almost exclusively non-Muslims. That they were from the minority religious communities would eventually create significant shifts in the social hierarchy governing Muslim relations with non-Muslims. But that role was not established by European design. Rather, the non-Muslims, and especially Syria's Christians, were simply more willing to learn the prerequisite languages and skills for dealing with the Franks than were local Muslims. And the Europeans themselves for reasons of religious prejudice or simple political expediency preferred to employ them over Muslims who might better them in the local Muslim courts.

Using that connection to the wider world, individual Christians in Syria became wealthy through trade in the eighteenth century. This is not to say that the vast majority of Christians were still either peasants or in the ranks of the urban poor. Rather, a Christian Arab commercial elite emerged where none had existed before. While it is tempting to link this transformation to the explosion in the numbers of *berat*s issued by European consuls to local Christians, many of the prominent Christian merchants in Lebanon and Syria never held the post of dragoman, honorary or otherwise. Most were, however, Uniate Catholics. I do not mean to suggest that their Catholicism was somehow causal to their commercial interests, providing a "Catholic mercantilist ethic" to stand in opposition to Weber's Protestant capitalist one. Nor had the missionaries anticipated that outcome. Rather than seeking to create a class of incipient entrepreneurs, they held out the possibility of education as an inducement to apostasy, confident that only ignorance and "fanaticism" kept the Eastern-rite Christians from acknowledging the Holy Father in Rome as their true spiritual guide. But those educated by the missionaries were better equipped to take advantage of change. Alternatively, those who had already emerged as members of the mercantile elite in Syria increasingly saw the Catholic option as furthering their own political ambitions, whether they had received a Catholic education or not.

The political options the local Christians had for most of the Ottoman centuries were vested in control of the local hierarchies of the various Eastern-rite churches. The see of the Patriarch of Antioch, under whose authority most Arabic-speaking Christians in Syria were subsumed, enjoyed a centuries-old tradition of autonomy. The clergy and the laity of Damascus had for most of that period chosen the men who would occupy the ecclesiastical throne. While that might still be acceptable in the main, resentment began to grow among the Christian commercial bourgeoisie elsewhere over Damascus' control over the appointment of the men who would occupy the metropolitan sees in their own cities. The antagonism between the various urban centers was further fueled by the fact that Damascene Christians, relatively untouched by a European presence, had not experienced the same degree of economic transformation as had their coreligionists in either Aleppo or the coastal port cities. Instead, preexisting trading hierarchies prevailed in Damascus, with Arabic-speaking Jews and Muslims dominating the commercial sectors and Christians largely confined to the artisan or laboring classes.

Damascene Christian sources suggest that the Orthodox of the city viewed their coreligionists in Aleppo as crass commercial upstarts, without the centuries of refinement and clerical traditions that they assigned to their own community. Damascus' sons disproportionately filled Syria's seminaries and typically controlled the high offices of the church in Syria. The contest for control of the see of Antioch between pro-Catholic and Orthodox factions could be interpreted as a clash between a newly emerging commercial class and an established ecclesiastic elite. There were nonetheless many in Damascus who supported the Catholic cause and geography alone does not explain why certain individuals would choose one faction over the other. Rather, on the one side stood those who had profited, or hoped to profit, from change and on the other were those who clung to "tradition" as it had served them well. As theological discussions played only a minuscule part in the polemic and counter-polemic, the divide seemingly lay between those who welcomed contact with the Franks and those who were wary of them – a European imagined "modernity" versus a secure Middle Eastern "tradition."

The political dynamics of the conflict heated up dramatically in the eighteenth century as the *millet*s were articulated in Istanbul as an instrument of state policy. The increasing interference of the Patriarch of Constantinople in the politics of the patriarchate of Antioch in the seventeenth century gave way to outright intervention in the eighteenth century. This intrusion was not necessarily interpreted by those involved as having an ethnic subtext, however. Fr. Burayk was willing to cast his lot with a Cypriot-born Patriarch rather than an Arab pretender. The Western world-view that many of the Catholics had absorbed from their Latin mentors undoubtedly helped them to "imagine" the conflict in "national" categories.[1] In their correspondence to the Vatican, they characterized their enemies as "Greeks" and themselves as "Arabs" even if they remained simply the "loyal Rum" in their letters to the sultan. The use of ethnic categories was not simply a construction designed to appeal to the Latin West as the men who controlled the *patrikhane* in Istanbul increasingly envisioned their church as properly the political preserve of Hellenes. What had been initially a regional or perhaps even a class contest, as well as incidentally a theological one, was now transformed by the rhetoric of ethnic struggle. That identification was aided both by the adoption of Arabic by the Catholic faction as their liturgical language and by their appeal to newly reconfigured history as the "authentic Church" in the see of Antioch, i.e. Syria, in the petitions forwarded to the Porte in their defense.

The Porte had by the mid-eighteenth century firmly moved to support Orthodoxy. To win their autonomy, Syria's Catholics had to establish that their desired autonomy from the church of Constantinople was justified by the weight of "tradition." By necessity, they invoked a history that posited that there had always been a separate "Syrian" church. That understanding was finally given official approval with the establishment of the Melkite *millet* in 1848. Although the majority of the community of the Rum in Syria remained loyal to Orthodoxy throughout the Ottoman period, the emergence of a Syrian-based church, articulated in Arabic, had repercussions for them as well. As prosperity and education became more widely distributed among Syria's Rum in the nineteenth century, the issue of the linguistic dysfunction between laity and clergy reemerged. Throughout the Arab provinces, the question of which language one spoke was injected into questions of religious identity, a development encouraged as the Melkite Catholics and Protestants began to make inroads into the ranks of the faithful by offering education in Arabic. As was the case elsewhere in the Ottoman Empire, an identity vested in language and religious community proved difficult to ignore. Ironically, given their ancestors' initial passivity to the issue of their Arabness, the Orthodox Christians of Syria could be counted, more than any other Christian community, firmly in the ranks of the nationalists by 1918. In contrast, many of the Uniates opted for the French, reflecting the revived Latin Catholic educational mission of the

---

[1] Haddad, *Syrian Christians in Muslim Society*, pp. 53–54.

second half of the nineteenth century and the use of religion by France to create a political bridgehead in the region.

The embrace of Arabism by Christian Syrians contrasts markedly to the stubborn allegiance of Baghdad's Jewish community to an identity defined solely by faith. The Syrian Christian and Iraqi Jewish commercial elites had emerged as a result of a growing European commercial presence in their homelands and were products of an evolving world-system dominated by the West. Both groups responded creatively to the challenges of the new order. By the start of the twentieth century, both had embraced various aspects of a European-defined "modernity," outwardly symbolized by their adoption of Western dress and their openness to Western education for their children. Both had developed trade networks far beyond their home-lands and had become committed to a political Ottomanism by 1914 as the best practical option to maintain their prosperity and protect their commu-nity. But when that was no longer a viable political option, most Christians in Syria, with the notable exception of the Maronites, were willing to adapt to the politics of nationalism, albeit even if not always enthusiastically. In contrast, the Jewish leadership in Baghdad sought British protection, as the Maronite leadership in Lebanon cast their lot with the French.

The Jews of Iraq and the Maronites of Lebanon stand as counter-examples to the various factions of Syria's Rum who had tentatively moved beyond Ottomanism to Arabism. Neither of the former two communities had suffered the internal political dissension that had so plagued the Rum in Syria for most of the Ottoman centuries. As a result, communal identity for them remained as it had been at the start of the Ottoman period, vested in their religious identity. True in a nod to the rhetoric of nationalism, Maronites could dream of an independent Lebanon, but it was envisioned, for all practical purposes, as a Maronite condominium. Some Iraqi Jews began to flirt with Arab nationalism in the 1920s. But concurrent with their experiment with Arabism, was a growing interest among others in their community in political Zionism, another religious communal identity reconfigured as nationalism. These two examples indicate that the dawn of the twentieth century did not necessarily mean the end of sectarian identities as primary in the Middle East. Rather, older definitions of community, based on religious faith, could simply be repackaged as nationality in an overlay through which the Middle Eastern traditions of communalism were visible as palimpsest in newly minted nationalisms.

In historical retrospect, Christian Syrians were undoubtedly nudged to imagine themselves as Arabs in the early twentieth century by their disastrous experience with their Muslim neighbors in the mid-nineteenth century. The same economic trends that had served to benefit Syria's Christians materially and politically had created a growing chasm between them and Syria's Muslims. The surviving historical record does not support a thesis that non-Muslims were subject to debilitating discrimination during the early centuries of Ottoman rule. Yet, there can also be no question that they enjoyed complete equality with the Muslims either. Even more critical than the discrimination they faced under certain circumstances in the Muslim courts, however, was the psychological hierarchy that governed relations between the communities, imposed by custom, law, and tradition. Muslims rightly felt that the shari$^c$a established their precedence over non-Muslims, and non-Muslims must have sensed that in regards to the majority's political consciousness, they were marginalized at best.

All that began to change with the rise of a non-Muslim commercial bourgeoisie. More important than their wealth, as there had always been individual non-Muslims who were rich, was the growing political assertiveness that some Christians began to display. In part, this was due to their links to the West and the support they could increasingly expect from the European ambassadors and consuls. That assertiveness was ironically also a product of the frequent squabbles between the religious factions played out in the Muslim courts. Alexander Russell noted in the mid-eighteenth century that the monetary extortion to which the Christians were frequently subjected by the Ottoman authorities in Aleppo was due to the attention they had called to themselves by their protracted bickering in the Muslim courts. In this regard, they again provide a telling contrast with the region's Jews, many of whom also enjoyed European protection and were wealthy, but who were rarely subjected to Muslim anger in the Ottoman period. The circumspect anonymity the latter community exercised in avoiding the Muslims' public gaze proved to be an effective strategy. But by frequently taking their troubles to the local Muslim courts and beyond to the Porte, Syria's Christians gained political confidence and experience that would serve them in pressing their concerns on other matters as well. Their growing confidence and political acumen also contributed to a Muslim perception that the Christians were openly challenging the established social hierarchy, which in fact they were. It was that sense of political confidence, more than their wealth or religious faith, which served to distance them from their Muslim neighbors. In addition to all these factors, the Christians suffered another disability that served to distinguish them from their Jewish rivals in that they shared a religious faith with the European powers and were frequently identified with them in the minds of the Muslim majority. A similar association, whether deserved or not, had helped to bring about a period of genuine historical persecution by the state in the early Mamluk period. A revived rhetoric of crusade and *jihad*, articulated by both Europeans and Muslims, in the nineteenth century similarly served to deepen the psychological chasm between Muslims and Christians.

Putting aside the question of whether the House of Osman was more tolerant than other Muslim regimes in its early centuries, the Ottoman state did take the lead in proclaiming the equality of all the sultan's subjects in the nineteenth century. While that positive intervention served to alienate

Muslim Arabs from the Ottoman ruling elite, it created bonds of appreciation for the sultan, if not actual loyalty, among the Christians of the Arab
provinces. He was no longer an alien and capricious ruler but had been
transformed into a benign "king" in their collective imagination. For the
first time, Christians could look beyond their *millets* and began to imagine
themselves as Ottomans, in a newly found patriotism that they incidentally
shared with Jews throughout the empire. Fear of the bigotry of the Muslim
mob pushed Christians in Syria toward an embrace of Ottomanism just as
fear of the Christian mob moved Jews in the Balkans to do the same.

As the Ottoman state moved to proclaim the equality of all, Muslims,
and especially those in the urban underclass, must have felt that the
Christians had lost their right to protection by violating the long-standing
hierarchy established by the Pact of ʿUmar. Feelings of fear, loathing,
jealousy, anger, and a deep sense of betrayal combined to set off the
intercommunal violence of mid-nineteenth century Syria. In no other part
of the Ottoman Arab world was a non-Muslim community so visible in its
embrace of the new world-order, or for that matter, more vigorous in
pushing for enlargement of its rights. The extent of the violence and the
anger expressed by Muslims against Christians in Syria led Europeans to
posit that Muslims had always been deeply bigoted against non-Muslims.
They found further proof of this in the anti-Christian violence that broke
out in the Balkans and Anatolia in the waning decades of the century.

There was, however, an important difference in the two cases. The latter
violence was interethnic as well as being inter-communal as it contained a
subtext of newly inculcated nationalisms. Muslims in the Arabic-speaking
lands might lash out at the local Christians out of some visceral fear of the
"Franks." But their coreligionists in the Balkans and Anatolia faced the
very real possibility of being physically displaced should their Christian
neighbors triumph. That had happened to Muslims previously in Greece,
Serbia, and the Caucasus. Muslim refugees from those areas contributed to
the growing religious/ethnic polarization in regions that were still ethnically
mixed. From the perspective of late twentieth-century nationalist violence,
the anti-Christian violence in Syria at mid-nineteenth century seems
somehow more "medieval" and less explicable than the ethnically based
outbursts that would haunt the empire from 1875 onward. But the lack of
an ethnic dimension to the conflagration in an age when all identities were
being recast along ethnic lines helps to explain why there were no further
major sectarian outbursts in Syria after 1860.

There is little doubt that on the surface, the intercommunal rupture
between Muslims and Christians had been partially restored by 1914. In
part, the chasm was never probably as deep as the levels of destruction at
mid-century would suggest. Elite Muslims and Christians had much in
common before the "events" and those common interests, while damaged,
did not vanish in the aftermath of the riots. Both groups undoubtedly

became more sensitive to potential sectarianism than before, due to the violence unleashed by the Muslim "mob" – a collective which each detested for differing reasons. Common interests again helped to produce common action and elites on both sides of the religious divide worked to diffuse any further potentially explosive incidents. Religious hatred did not disappear entirely, but as in earlier centuries the Muslim urban elite had learnt that it must be controlled. For Christians, the "events" came as a sobering wake-up call. Some reacted to the sectarian outbursts as the final push to send them fleeing to safety in Beirut, Egypt, or the Americas, but many more realized that their futures continued to lie in the cities where they were born. For elite Muslims, the chastisement of the Christians had come at great cost and it is doubtful many would have welcomed a return to violence. For both groups, the breathing spell provided between 1860 and 1914 permitted a reassessment of both the past and the future. The result was a tentative reformulation of identity that, while not eliminating religion as a key component of any individual's sense of self-identity, provided a broader notion of political community that might accommodate religious differences.

Disparate intellectual trends also helped to bring about reconciliation. For the Syrian Christians, their long struggle with the Greeks in the *millet-i Rum* had led them first to conceive of themselves as Syrians and then as Arabs. Once that identity was established, they were able to perceive the secular classics of the Muslim Middle Ages as their own. Other Christians reached the same conclusion, thanks to the education they received in classical Arabic in missionary schools. Muslims could share in the appreciation of the same tradition, while positing that its greatness was primarily the result of its having been Muslim and only secondarily as being Arab. In the Muslims' interpretation of the past, the Arabs had found greatness as Muslims. Islam had provided the inspiration for Arab civilization and without it, the Arabs would have remained marginalized on the world stage. Christian Arab intellectuals, by contrast, often pointed to the genius of Arabic culture *before* Islam. The differing emphases were subtle and could be ignored in a general rush to embrace Arabism, but they were nonetheless significant.

This newly transfigured conception of identity was at odds with what had prevailed for most of the history of the Ottoman period when religion had stood as the primary signifier of political community. But that orderly universe began to crumble in the second half of the nineteenth century with the reconfiguring of religious identity as nationality and with the counter attempts by Ottoman intellectuals and bureaucrats to fashion an Ottoman political identity that might transcend ethnically based nationalisms. For people such as Na‘um Bakhkhash, it remained inconceivable that a collective identity could embrace both his people and "Islam" painlessly. The Ottoman state had, on the other hand, effected a tentative policy of non-sectarian equality. Muslims were still dominant politically, but the state was becoming less Muslim in its law and orientation. Adding to their susceptibility to a newly articulated identity as Ottomans, the Jewish and Christian elites in the Arab lands had become cosmopolitan in their economic and cultural interests. The possible division of the empire into hostile states based on ethnicity could only harm those interests. Loyalty to the sultan in a non-national empire was self-evidently in their best economic and political interests.

In their tentative embrace of *Osmanlılık*, however, non-Muslims had stepped outside the more narrowly defined boundaries of their communities as *millets*. Ottomanism served as an ideological transition from an identity configured solely by religious faith to nationalism being advanced by the intellectual elites among Arabic-speaking Muslims and Christians. That is not to say that religious community had lost its primacy for most of the inhabitants of the empire, Muslim and non-Muslim alike. But the "events" had proven to many in all religious communities that more widely constructed political identities were also possible and indeed perhaps necessary. It remained to be seen if that realization would produce a construction of political community defined by culture rather than religion. More importantly, the question of whether a political community, which was imagined by and conformed to the interests and values of elites of whatever religion, would percolate down to those who did not enjoy the same economic and social status. The violence of the mid-century had represented the response of ordinary Muslims to change and it is not at all clear that they were yet ready to imagine themselves within a community defined solely as Arab without the modifier Muslim.[2]

In the heady days of Arab nationalism following the First World War, Kamil al-Ghazzi wrote the history of Aleppo in the tradition of the Muslim chroniclers of his native city. His account was heavily weighted toward the Ottoman period, as befit a lawyer trained in Ottoman academies. Significantly, Christians appear only twice in his narrative, firstly in a pro-Catholic version of the events of 1818 and then as victims of the riot of 1850. Both accounts reflect the elite Muslim sensibilities prevalent in his native city. The first was an affirmation that the ongoing alliance between Catholic and Muslim elites in the city, forged in the "long" eighteenth century, was still intact. Al-Ghazzi's version of the "events" of 1850 posits lawless outsiders as the perpetrators of the anarchy, thereby invoking the Muslim elite's attempt to distance themselves from the rioters after the fact. Al-Ghazzi went further, however, as he used the outbreak of sectarianism in his native city as an object lesson for the ideology of nationalism. Immediately following his account of the riots, he inserted a homily on the Arab

---

[2] On the dysfunction between elites and non-elites in Syria as to the reception of the Arab nationalist message, see Gelvin, *Divided Loyalties*.

traditions of hospitality and love for those with whom they share the same tongue.[3] Although it is telling that he seemingly conflates "Arabs" with "Muslim Arabs," his parameters of good citizenship were far from subtle. Good Syrians do not kill their neighbors even if they practice a different religion. In Damascus, Muhammad Kurd-ᶜAli's history of Syria carried much the same message without al-Ghazzi's ambiguity over the authenticity of the Christian Syrians' "Arabness." That such calls for sectarian reconciliation were written so soon after intercommunal violence had wracked neighboring Anatolia tells us much about the lessons learned by Syria's Muslim elites in the second half of the nineteenth century.

This recasting of the history of the Ottoman period grew out of a sense of optimism. It now seemed possible to reimagine political community in the Arab world without sectarianism. The communal rupture signaled by the sectarian violence of the mid-nineteenth century was not completely healed, however. Representatives of the old Muslim elites in the newly configured mandates of Syria and Iraq could find common ground with their more recently arrived Jewish and Christian counterparts under the banner of Arabism. In Egypt, nationalists protesting the continued British occupation in 1919, whether Muslims or Copts, marched under a flag that linked cross and crescent as a national symbol. But in the newly created mandates of Lebanon and Palestine, sectarianism was enshrined as law. Furthermore, the only two independent Arab states to emerge out of the Ottoman debacle, Yemen and Saudi Arabia, proclaimed themselves to be governed solely by Muslim law, even if it were the Zaydi Shiᶜa version in the former and the Hanbali in the latter.

National identity, based on language, has not eliminated sectarian identities in the lands of the former Ottoman Empire. Even in places where the rhetoric of nationalism is particularly strong, it is often conflated with religion. Turkey's ruling elite stubbornly clings to Atatürk's secular vision, but does not find that at odds with the fact that the liberator is given the honorific title of *Gazi* (warrior of the faith). In Serbia, former Communists wrapped themselves in the trappings of Orthodoxy and vowed to save "Holy Kossovo." Events of the late twentieth century have also shown that sectarianism as political ideology could reemerge in the former Arab provinces of the empire and in the State of Israel. But religion has remained potentially a political rallying symbol for some in the United States as well and it is not just in the lands of the former Ottoman Empire that religious identity has survived modernity into the age of postmodernism. The history of the non-Muslim communities in the Ottoman Arab world suggests, as many postmodernist scholars now hold, that any identity, whether political or otherwise, is indeed vested in an intellectual construction. But as long as

---

[3] Kamil al-Ghazzi, *Nahr al-dhahab fi ta'rikh Halab* [The River of Gold in the History of Aleppo] 3 vols. (Aleppo, 1923–26), vol. III, pp. 382–88.

that construction holds validity for those who embrace it, it is for them as solid and unchanging as if it were primordial. Unlike a presumably primordial identity, however, it can shift as the alternatives are articulated and accepted by the individual as being equally valid. Such a process occurred among the non-Muslims of the Ottoman Empire with many making the conscious choice at various times throughout the four centuries of Ottoman rule to embrace a political community beyond that which they had inherited as "tradition."

# Glossary

*ahl al-dhimma*   Christians, Jews, and Zoroastrians who have accepted the political sovereignty of Muslims over their lives in return for freedom of worship, life and property

*Arabistan*   commonly used in Ottoman Turkish for geographical Syria; in Modern Turkish, Arabia

*ashraf*   those descended from the Prophet's family; singular, *sharif*

*Avrupa tüccarı*   a non-Muslim merchant who held a patent from the sultan conferring most of the privileges enjoyed by the protégés of the Europeans

*berat*   a patent of office issued by the sultan

*beratlı*   one holding a *berat*, but more commonly a protégé of the Europeans under the terms of a capitulatory treaty

*bid'a*   innovation, deemed a sin by Muslim scholars

**Capitulations**   treaties allowing Europeans to reside and trade in the sultan's domains

**Catholicos**   spiritual head of the Armenian and Nestorian churches

*dhimmi*   non-Muslim subject of a Muslim ruler

**dragoman**   translator

**Ecumenical Patriarch**   the Patriarch of Constantinople, title connotes that he was the supreme head of all the Orthodox faithful

*Eretz Israel*   the Land of Israel, the word Jews used to name the geographical space that was for Christians, Palestine

*fatwa*   judicial ruling by a Muslim legal authority

**Frank**   Western European Christian to the inhabitants of the Ottoman Empire, later more specifically a European Roman Catholic

*ghurush*   Arabic name for one of two silver coins, the Netherlands *leeuwenthaler* and the Spanish *réal*, which were roughly equivalent and which served as the monetary standard in the Ottoman Arab Levant before the Ottoman currency reforms of the Tanzimat

*hizmetkâr*   literally "servant" but in Ottoman patents it designated a commercial agent

**Jacobite**  A Christian who follow in the monophysite tradition established by Ya'qub Barda'i. Known in Arabic as *Suryani*

*jizya*  head-tax levied on all adult male non-Muslim subjects of a Muslim ruler

*kafir*  an infidel who does not believe in the one indivisible God of the Qur'an

**mamluk**  a male slave; also the name of the dynasty that dominated Egypt and Syria from 1260 until 1517

**Maronite**  A Christian following in the tradition established by St. Marun in the sixth century.

**Melkite**  an Arabic-speaking Greek Orthodox Christian, later those of the community who became Uniates

*millet*  the political body governing non-Muslim religious communities in the Ottoman Empire in the eighteenth and nineteenth centuries

*millet başı*  the head of a *millet*, either patriarch or chief rabbi

**Monophysite**  Christian dogma holding that Christ had only one nature, divine

**Mufti**  Muslim legal scholar recognized by the government to issue judicial rulings

*Osmanlılık*  embodying "Ottoman-ness"; ideology of patriotism to the Ottoman state and sultan

**Pact of 'Umar**  the legal contract governing the rights and limitations of non-Muslims in a Muslim state

*patrikhane*  the patriarchate. Literally meaning the residence of the patriarch, it was used in the Ottoman period as a synecdoche for the office itself

**Porte**  the Ottoman government in Istanbul. Europeans came to call the Foreign Ministry the "Sublime Porte" after its remarkable gateway but natives of the Ottoman Arab lands called the Ottoman government the "gate" long before that

*Rum*  Greek Orthodox Christians.

*Salafiyya*  Muslim reformist legal school that developed in the late nineteenth century

*saray*  palace; seraglio

*Sephardim*  Jews originally from the Iberian peninsula

*şeyhülislam*  chief jurist in the Ottoman state

*shari'a*  body of Muslim law

**Tanzimat**  period of Ottoman reform, 1839–78.

*Türkçülük*  embodying "Turkishness"; ideology of Turkish nationalism

# Bibliography

**Primary sources**

*Archives*

Boston, Harvard University
    Papers of American Board of Comissioners for Foreign Missions (ABCFM) (microfilm series)
Damascus, Dar al-Watha'iq (National Archives)
    Aleppo Court records
    Awamir al-sultaniyya series, Aleppo
    Awamir al-sultaniyya series, Damascus
Istanbul, Başbakanlık Osmanlı Arşivi (Prime-Minister's Ottoman Archive) BOA
    Ahkâm-ı Halep series
    Ahkâm-ı Şam-ı Şerif series
    Cevdet Adliye series
    Cevdet Dahiliye series
    Cevdet Hariciye series
    Ecnebi series: Firansa, İngiltere
    Gayri Müslim Cemaat series: Melkit Katolikler
    Hatt-ı Hümayûn series (HH)
    İrade Dahiliye series (İ. Dahiliye)
    İrade Hariciye series (İ. Hariciye)
    Maliye Nezareti Cizye series (ML.VRD.CMH)
    Maliye Nezarati Varidat (M.VRD)
    Maliye'den Müdevver series (MM)
    Mühimme Defterleri (MD)
London, Public Record Office (PRO)
    State Papers (SP)
    Foreign Office (FO)
Washington, National Archives (microfilm)
Records of the Department of State Relating to Internal Affairs of Asia 1910–1929 series 722, roll 8

**Published**

al-ʿAbd, Hasan Agha. *Ta'rikh Hasan Agha al-ʿAbd: qitʿa minhu, hawadith sanat 1186 ila sanat 1241* [Chronicle of Hasan Agha al-ʿAbd: a selection from it, the events of the year 1186 until the year 1241]. Edited by Yusuf Jamil Naʿisa. Damascus, 1979.

Arutin, Bulus. *Ahamm hawadith Halab fi nifs al-awwal min al-qarn al-tasiʿ ʿashar* [The Most Important Events in Aleppo in the First Half of the Nineteenth Century]. Cairo, 1933.

Bakhkhash, Naʿum. *Akhbar Halab* [The Events of Aleppo]. Edited by Fr. Yusuf Qushaqji, 3 vols. Aleppo, 1987–1992.

Beydilli, Kemal. *Recognition of the Armenian Catholic Community and the Church in the Reign of Mahmud II. (1830)*. Cambridge, MA, 1995.

Binark, İsmet (ed.). *Musul-Kerkük ile ilgili arşiv belgeleri* [Archival Documents concerning Mosul and Kirkuk] *(1525–1919)*. Ankara, 1993.

Bowring, John. *Report of the Commercial Statistics of Syria*. Reprinted New York, 1973.

Burayk, Mikha'il al-Dimashqi. *Ta'rikh al-Sham* [A Chronicle of Damascus], *1720–1782*. Edited by Qustantin al-Basha. Harrisa, 1930.

Cevdet Paşa. *Tezâkir* [Memoirs]. Edited by Cavid Baysun. 4 vols. Istanbul, 1953–63.

Düzdağ, M. Ertuğrul. *Şeyhülislam Ebussuud Efendi fetvaları ışığında 16. asır Türk hayatı* [Turkish Life in the Sixteenth Century in Light of the Fatwas of Şeyhülislam Ebussuud Efendi]. Istanbul, 1983.

Evliya Çelebi. *Evliya Çelebi Seyahatnamesi* [The Travelogue of Evliya Çelebi], vol. 9. Edited by Mehmed Zillîoğlu. Istanbul, 1984.

al-Hasibi, Muhammad Abu Suʿud al-Dimashqi. "Mudhakkirat" [Memoirs] in *Bilad al-Sham fi al-qarn al-tasiʿ ʿashar* [Syria in the Nineteenth Century]. Edited by Suhayl Zakkar. Damascus, 1982.

Hillel, David d'Beth. *Unknown Jews in Unknown Lands: The Travels of Rabbi David d'Beth Hillel*. Edited by Walter Fischel. New York, 1973.

al-Jabarti, ʿAbd al-Rahman. *ʿAja'ib al-athar fi al-tarajim wa al-akhbar* [Curious Impressions from Biographies and Events], 7 vols. Cairo, 1958–67. For a partial English translation see, *Napoleon in Egypt: al-Jabarti's Chronicle of the French Occupation*. Translated by Shmuel Moreh. Princeton, NJ, 1993.

bin Kannan, Muhammad al-Salihi. *Yawmiyyat shamiyya* [Damascus Diary] *min 1111 h. hatta 1153 h.–1699 m. hatta 1740 m.* Edited by Akram Hasan al-ʿUlabi. Damascus, 1994.

Kayat, Assaad (Asʿad al-Khayyat). *A Voice from Lebanon*. London, 1847.

Kurdakul, Necdet. *Osmanlı devleti'nde ticaret antlaşmaları ve kapitülasyonlar* [Commercial Treaties and Capitulations in the Ottoman State]. Istanbul, 1981.

Lane, Edward. *Manners and Customs of the Modern Egyptians*. London, 1908.

Mazlum, Maksimus. *Nabdha ta'rikhiyya fi ma jara li-ta'ifat al-Rum al kathulik mundhu sanat 1837 fi ma baʿduha* [An Historical Tract on What Occurred to the Melkite Catholics from 1837 onward]. No place of publication, 1907.

Mishaqa, Mikha'il. "Mashhad al-aʿyan bi-hawadith Suriyya wa Lubnan" [An Eyewitness to the Events in Syria and Lebanon], in *Bilad al-Sham fi al-qarn al- tasiʿ ʿashar*. Edited by Suhayl Zakkar. Damascus, 1982. An English translation of the manuscript was published with the title, *Murder, Mayhem, Pillage, and*

*Plunder: The History of Lebanon in the 18th and 19th Centuries.* Translated by Wheeler Thackston. Albany, NY, 1988.

al-Nabulusi, ʿAbd al-Ghani. *al-Haqiqa wa al-majaz fi rihlat bilad al-Sham wa Misr wa al-Hijaz* [The Truth and the Crossing of a Journey to Syria, Egypt, and the Hejaz]. Damascus, 1989.

Papadopoullos, Theodore. *Studies and Documents Relating to the History of the Greek Church and People under Turkish Domination.* Brussels, 1952.

Polonyalı Simeon. *Polonyalı Simeon'un seyahatnamesi* [The Travelogue of Polonyalı Simeon] *1608–1619.* Translated by Hrand Andreasyan. Istanbul, 1964.

Purchas, Samuel (ed.). *Purchas His Pilgrimes.* Vol. VIII. Glasgow, 1905.

Rabbath, Antoine (ed.). *Documents inédits pour servir à l'histoire du Christianisme en Orient.* 2 vols. (Paris, 1905–11). Reprinted (New York, 1973).

Russell, Alexander. *A Natural History of Aleppo.* London, 1794.

Taoutel, Ferdinand. "Wathaʾiq taʾrikhiyyaʿan Halab akhidhan ʿan dafatir al-akhawiyyat wa ghayriha" [Historical Documents on Aleppo, taken from the Diaries of the Religious Orders and Elsewhere] *al-Mashriq* 42 (1948): 215–41, 371–412; vol. 43 (1949): 140–60, 297–320, 537–603.

"Wathaʾiq taʾrikhiyya ʿan Halab fi al-qarn al-thamin ʿashar" [Documents on Aleppo in the Eighteenth Century] *al-Mashriq* 41 (1947): 249–270.

Teixeira, Pedro, *Travels of Pedro Teixeira.* London, 1902.

Salname-i Vilayet-i Haleb [Yearbook for the Province of Aleppo] *1326.* Istanbul, 1909.

ʿUjaymi, Hindiyya. *Aqwal al-rahiba Hindiyya ʿUjaymi al-halabiyya wa tarjamat hayatiha* [Sayings of Sr. Hindiyya ʿUjaymi, the Aleppine, and her Biography]. Edited by Butrus Fahd. Jounieh, Lebanon, 1972.

al-Ustawani, al-Shaykh Muhammad Saʿid. *Mashahid wa-ahdath fi muntasaf al-qarn al-tasiʿ ʿashar* [Witnessing and Events of the Middle of the Nineteenth Century] *1206–1277/ 1840–1861.* Edited by Asʿad al-Ustawani. Damascus, 1994.

### Unpublished

ʿAbbud, Yusuf Dimitri al-Halabi, *al-murtadd fi taʾrikh Halab wa Baghdad [A Revisiting of the History of Aleppo and Baghdad].* Edited by Fawwaz Mahmud al-Fawwaz, M.A. thesis, University of Damascus, 1978.

### Secondary soruces

### Published

Abd-Allah, Umar. *The Islamic Struggle in Syria.* Berkeley, CA, 1983.

Abdel-Nour, Antoine. *Introduction à l'histoire urbaine de la Syrie ottomane (XVIᵉ–XVIIIᵉ siècle).* Beirut, 1982.

Abou-Bakr, Omaima. "The Religious Other: Christian Images in Sufi poetry" in *Images of the Other: Europe and the Muslim World before 1700.* Edited by David Blanks. Cairo, 1997, pp. 96–108.

Abou-el-Haj, Rifaʾat Ali. "Power and Social Order: the Uses of the *Kanun*" in *The Ottoman City and its Parts.* Edited by Irene Bierman, Rifaʾat Abou-El-Haj and Donald Preziosi. New Rochelle, NY, 1991, pp. 77–99.

"The Social Uses of the Past: Recent Arab Historiography of Ottoman Rule" *International Journal of Middle Eastern Studies* 14 (1982): 185–201.

Abou Manneh, Butrus. "The Christians between Ottomanism and Syrian Nationalism: The Ideas of Butrus al-Bustani" *International Journal of Middle East Studies* 11 (1979): 287–304.

Abou Nohra, Joseph. "L'évolution du système politique libanais dans le contexte des conflits régionaux et locaux (1840–1864)" in *Lebanon: A History of Conflict and Consensus*. Edited by Nedim Shehadi and Dana Haffar Mills. London, 1988, pp. 31–48.

Abraham, A. J. *Lebanon at Mid-Century: Maronite–Druze Relations in Lebanon 1840–1860*. Lanham, MD, 1981.

Abu-Ghazaleh, Adnan. *American Missions in Syria: A Study of American Missionary Contribution to Arab Nationalism in 19th Century Syria*. Brattleboro, VT, 1990.

Abu Husayn, Abdul-Rahim. "Duwayhi as a Historian of Ottoman Syria" *Bulletin of the Royal Institute for Inter-Faith Studies* (Amman) 1/1 (1999): 1–13.

Abu-Lughod, Ibrahim. *Arab Rediscovery of Europe: A Study in Cultural Encounters*. Princeton, NJ, 1963.

Ahmed, Leila. *Women and Gender in Islam: Historical Roots of a Modern Debate*. New Haven, CT, 1992.

Akarlı, Engin. *The Long Peace: Ottoman Lebanon, 1861–1920*. Berkeley, CA, 1993.

Aladdin, Bakri. "Deux fatwa-s du Şayh ʿAbd al-Ḡani al-Nabulsi (1143/1731): présentation et édition critique" *Bulletin d'Études Orientales* 39–40 (1987–88): 9–37.

Alcalay, Amiel. *After Jews and Arabs: Remaking Levantine Culture*. Minneapolis, MN, 1993.

Anderson, Benedict. *Imagined Communities: Reflections on the Origin and Spread of Nationalism*. New York, 1991.

Angel, Marc. "The Responsa Literature in the Ottoman Empire for the Study of Ottoman Jewry" in *The Jews of the Ottoman Empire*. Edited by A. Levy. Princeton, NJ, 1994, pp. 669–85.

Antonius, George. *The Arab Awakening: The Story of the Arab National Movement*. New York, 1965.

Ashtor, Eliyahu. *Levant Trade in the Later Middle Ages*. Princeton, NJ, 1983.

Atiya, Aziz. *A History of Eastern Christianity*. Notre Dame, IN, 1968.

ʿAwad, ʿAbd al-ʿAziz Muhammad. *Al-Idara al-ʿUthmaniyya fi Wilayat Suriyya* [Ottoman Administration in the Province of Syria] *1864–1914*. Cairo, 1969.

al-Azmeh, Aziz. *Islams and Modernities*. London, 1996.

Bağış, Ali İhsan. *Osmanlı ticaretinde gayri Müslimler* [Non-Muslims in Ottoman Commerce]. Ankara, 1983.

Bakhit, Muhammad Adnan. "The Christian Population of the Province of Damascus in the Sixteenth Century" in *Christians and Jews in the Ottoman Empire*. Edited by B. Braude and B. Lewis. Princeton, NJ, vol. II, pp. 19–66.

Barbir, Karl. "Memory, Heritage, and History: the Ottoman Legacy in the Arab World" in *Imperial Legacy: The Ottoman Imprint on the Balkans and the Middle East*. Edited by L. Carl Brown. New York, 1996, pp. 100–14.

Bardakjian, Kevork. "The Rise of the Armenian Patriarchate of Constantinople" in *Christians and Jews in the Ottoman Empire*. Edited by B. Braude and B. Lewis. New York, 1982, vol. I, pp. 89–100.

Barkan, Ömer Lutfi. "Essai sur les données statistiques des registres de recensement dans l'empire ottoman aux XVe et XVIe siècles" *Journal of the Economic and Social History of the Orient* 1 (1957): 9–36.

"Research on the Ottoman Fiscal Surveys" in *Studies in the Economic History of the Middle East*. Edited by M. A. Cook. London, 1970, pp. 163–71.

Barnai, Jacob. *The Jews in Palestine in the Eighteenth Century: Under the Patronage of the Istanbul Committee of Officials for Palestine.* Translated by Naomi Goldblum. Tuscaloosa, AL, 1992.

Batatu, Hanna. *Syria's Peasantry, the Descendants of its Lesser Rural Notables, and their Politics.* Princeton, NJ, 1999.

Bat Ye'or. *The Dhimmi: Jews and Christians under Islam.* Translated from the French by David Maisel, Paul Fenton and David Littman. Rutherford, NJ, 1985.

Bayly, Christopher A. *The Imperial Meridian: The British Empire and the World 1780–1830.* London, 1989.

"The Pre-history of 'Communalism'? Religious Conflict in India, 1700–1860" *Modern Asian Studies* 19 (1985): 177–203.

Benbassa, Esther. "Associated Strategies of Ottoman Jewish Society in the Nineteenth and Twentieth Centuries" in *The Jews of the Ottoman Empire.* Edited by A. Levy. Princeton, NJ, 1994, pp. 457–84.

"Zionism in the Ottoman Empire at the End of the 19th and the Beginning of the 20th Century" *Studies in Zionism* 11 (1990): 127–40.

Bernstein, Iver. *The New York Draft Riots: Their Significance for American Society and Politics in the Age of the Civil War.* New York, 1990.

Betts, Robert Brenton. *Christians in the Arab East.* Atlanta, GA, 1978.

Bosscha Erdbrink, G. R. *At the Threshold of Felicity: Ottoman–Dutch Relations during the Embassy of Cornelis Calkoen at the Sublime Porte, 1726–1744.* Ankara, 1975.

Bosworth, C. E. "The Concept of *Dhimma* in Early Islam" in *Christians and Jews in the Ottoman Empire.* Edited by B. Braude and B. Lewis. New York, 1982, vol. I, pp. 37–51.

Bozkurt, Gülnihâl. *Gayrimüslim Osmanlı vatandaşlarının hukukî durumu* [The Legal Status of Non-Muslim Ottoman Citizens] *(1839–1914).* Ankara, 1989.

Braude, Benjamin and Bernard Lewis (eds.). *Christians and Jews in the Ottoman Empire.* 2 vols. New York, 1982.

Brauer, Erich. *The Jews of Kurdistan.* Completed and edited by Raphael Patai. Detroit, MI, 1993.

Brummett, Palmira. *Ottoman Seapower and Levantine Diplomacy in the Age of Discovery.* Albany, NY, 1994.

Bruinessen, Martin van. *Agha, Shaikh, and State: The Social and Political Structures of Kurdistan.* London, 1992.

Charon (Korolevsky), Cyril. *History of the Melkite Patriarchates, Vol. I, Pre-modern Period (869–1833).* Translated by John Collorafi. Edited by Bishop Nicholas Samra. Fairfax, VA, 1998.

Chevallier, Dominique. "Non-Muslim Communities in Arab Cities" in *Christian and Jews in the Ottoman Empire.* Edited by B. Braude and B. Lewis. New York, 1982, vol. II, pp. 159–65.

Clogg, Richard. *Anatolica: Studies in the Greek East in the 18th and 19th Centuries.* Aldershot, UK, 1996.

Coakley, J. F. *The Church of the East and the Church of England: A History of the Archbishop of Canterbury's Assyrian Mission.* Oxford, 1992.

Cohen, Amnon. *Jewish Life under Islam: Jerusalem in the Sixteenth Century.* Cambridge, MA, 1984.

"On the Realities of the Millet System: Jerusalem in the Sixteenth Century" in *Christians and Jews in the Ottoman Empire.* Edited by B. Braude and B. Lewis. New York, 1982, vol. II, pp. 7–18.

"The Ottoman Approach to Christians and Christianity in Sixteenth-century Jerusalem" *Islam & Christian Muslim Relations* 7 (1996): 205–12.

"The Receding of the Christian Presence in the Holy Land: A 19th Century Sijill in the Light of 16th Century Tahrirs" in *The Syrian Land in the 18th and 19th Century.* Edited by T. Philipp. Stuttgart, 1992, pp. 333–40.

*Palestine in the 18th Century.* Jerusalem, 1973.

Cohen, Amnon and Bernard Lewis (eds.). *Population and Revenue in the Towns of Palestine in the Sixteenth Century.* Princeton, NJ, 1978.

Cohen, Hayyim. *The Jews of the Middle East, 1860–1972.* New York, 1973.

Cohen, Mark. *Under Crescent and Cross: The Jews in the Middle Ages.* Princeton, NJ, 1994.

Cole, Juan. *Colonialism and Revolution in the Middle East: Social and Cultural Origins of Egypt's ʿUrabi Movement.* Princeton, NJ, 1993.

Colley, Linda. *Britons: Forging the Nation 1707–1837.* New Haven, CT, 1992.

Commins, David Dean. *Islamic Reform: Politics and Social Change in Late Ottoman Syria.* New York, 1990.

Courbage, Youssef and Philippe Fargues. *Christians and Jews under Islam.* Translated by Judy Mabro. London, 1996.

Cunningham, Allan. "Stratford Canning and the *Tanzimat*" in *Beginnings of Modernization in the Middle East.* Edited by William Polk and Richard Chambers. Chicago, IL, 1968, pp. 245–64.

Dalrymple, William. *From the Holy Mountain: A Journey among the Christians of the Middle East.* New York, 1998.

David, Abraham. *To Come to the Land: Immigration and Settlement in Sixteenth-Century Eretz-Israel.* Translated by Dena Ordan. Tuscaloosa, AL, 1999.

David, Jean-Claude. "L'espace des chrétiens á Alep: ségrégation et mixité, stratégies communautaires (1750–1850)" *Revue du Monde Musulman et de la Méditerranée* 55–56 (1990): 152–70.

Davison, Roderic. *Essays in Ottoman and Turkish History: The Impact of the West.* Austin, TX, 1990.

"The *Millet*s as Agents of Change in the Nineteenth Century" in *Christians and Jews in the Ottoman Empire.* Edited by B. Braude and B. Lewis. New York, 1982, vol. I, pp. 319–37.

Dawn, C. Ernest. "The Origins of Arab Nationalism" in *The Origins of Arab Nationalism.* Edited by. R. Khalidi, L. Anderson, M. Muslih, R. Simon. New York, 1991, pp. 3–30.

*From Ottomanism to Arabism: Essays on the Origins of Arab Nationalism.* Urbana, IL, 1973.

Deringil, Selim. *The Well-Protected Domains: Ideology and the Legitimation of Power in the Ottoman Empire 1876–1909.* London, 1998.

Deshen, Shlomo and Walter Zenner (eds.). *Jews among Muslims: Communities in the Precolonial Middle East*. London, 1996.

"Baghdad Jewry in Late Ottoman Times: The Emergence of Social Classes and Secularization" in *Jews among Muslims: Communities in the Precolonial Middle East*. Edited by Shlomo Deshen and Walter Zenner. London, 1996, pp. 187–96.

Djordjevic, Dimitrije and Stephen Fischer-Galati. *The Balkan Revolutionary Tradition*. New York, 1981.

Douwes, Dick. *The Ottomans in Syria: A History of Justice and Oppression*. London, 2000.

Dumont, Paul. "Jews, Muslims, and Cholera: Intercommunal Relations in Baghdad at the End of the Nineteenth Century" in *The Jews of the Ottoman Empire*. Edited by Avigdor Levy. Princeton, NJ, 1994, pp. 353–72.

Eldem, Edhem, Daniel Goffman, and Bruce Masters. *The Ottoman City between East and West: Aleppo, Izmir, and Istanbul*. Cambridge, 1999.

El-Sheikh, Nadia Maria. "Arab Christian Contributions to Muslim Historiography on Byzantium" *Bulletin of the Royal Institute for Inter-Faith Studies*, 1/2 (1999): 45–60.

Emmett, Chad. *Beyond the Basilica: Christians and Muslims in Nazareth*. Chicago, IL, 1995.

*Encyclopedia of Islam*, 2nd edition. Leiden, 1960 .

Esim, Cak and Cem Ikiz. Cassette recording, "Türkiye aşkı için: Yahudi ezgiler ve Sefarad romanslar" ['For the Love of Turkey': Jewish Melodies and Sephardic Romances]. Istanbul, 1993.

Establet, Colette and Jean-Paul Pascual. *Familles et fortunes à Damas: 450 foyers damascains en 1700*. Damascus, 1994.

Fahmy, Khaled. *All the Pasha's Men: Mehmed Ali, his Army and the Making of Modern Egypt*. Cambridge, 1997.

Farah, Caesar. "Protestantism and Politics: The 19th Century Dimension in Syria" in *Palestine in the Late Ottoman Period*. Edited by D. Kushner. Jerusalem, 1986, pp. 320–40.

Faroqhi, Suraiya. *Towns and Townsmen of Ottoman Anatolia: Trade, Crafts and Food Production in an Urban Setting*. Cambridge, 1984.

Fawaz, Leila Tarazi. *Merchants and Migrants in Nineteenth Century Beirut*. Cambridge, MA, 1983.

*An Occasion for War: Civil Conflict in Lebanon and Damascus, 1860*. Berkeley, CA, 1995.

"Zahle and Dayr al-Qamar: Two Market Towns of Mount Lebanon during the Civil War of 1860" in *Lebanon: A History of Conflict and Consensus*. Edited by Nadim Shehadi and Dana Haffar Mills. London, 1988, pp. 49–63.

Findley, Carter. *Bureaucratic Reform in the Ottoman Empire: The Sublime Porte, 1789–1922*. Princeton, NJ, 1980.

Fleischer, Cornell. *Bureaucrat and Intellectual in the Ottoman Empire: The Historian Mustafa Âli (1541–1600)*. Princeton, NJ, 1986.

Frankel, Jonathan. *The Damascus Affair: "Ritual Murder," Politics, and the Jews in 1840*. Cambridge, 1997.

Frazee, Charles. *Catholics and Sultans: The Church and the Ottoman Empire, 1453–1923*. London, 1983.

Geertz, Clifford. "The Integrative Revolution: Primordial Sentiments and Civil

Politics in the New States" in *Old Societies and New States*. Edited by Clifford Geertz. New York, 1963, pp. 105–57.

Gelvin, James. *Divided Loyalties: Nationalism and Mass Politics in Syria at the Close of Empire*. Berkeley, CA, 1998.

Gerber, Haim. *State, Society, and Law in Islam: Ottoman Law in Comparative Perspective*. Albany, NY, 1994.

Gervers, Michael and Ramzi Jibran Bikhazi (eds.). *Conversion and Continuity: Indigenous Christian Communities in Islamic Lands, Eighth to Eighteenth centuries*. Toronto, 1990.

Ghanima, Yusuf Rizq-Allah. *Nuzhat al-mushtaq fi ta'rikh Yahud al-ᶜIraq* [A Nostalgic Ramble through the History of the Jews of Iraq]. Baghdad, 1924.

al-Ghazzi, Kamil. *Nahr al-dhahab fi ta'rikh Halab al-shahba* [The River of Gold in the History of Aleppo, the Milky-White]. 3 vols. Aleppo, 1922–26.

Gibb, Sir Hamilton and Harold Bowen. *Islamic Society and the West: A Study of the Impact of Western Civilization on Muslim Culture in the Near East*. 2 vols. London, 1950–57.

Gillard, David (ed.). *British Documents on Foreign Affairs: Reports and Papers from the Foreign Office Confidential Print*, Part I, Series B (The Near and Middle East, 1856–1914) 20 vols. University Publications of America, 1984.

Göçek, Fatma Müge. *Rise of the Bourgeoisie, Demise of Empire: Ottoman Westernization and Social Change*. New York, 1996.

Goffman, Daniel. *Britons in the Ottoman Empire 1642–1660*. Seattle, WA, 1998.

*Izmir and the Levantine World, 1550–1650*. Seattle, WA, 1990.

"Ottoman Millets in the Early Seventeenth Century" *New Perspectives on Turkey* 11 (1994): 135–58.

Goitein, S. D. *Jews and Arabs: Their Contact through the Ages*. New York, 1955.

Goldberg, Harvey (ed.). *Sephardi and Middle Eastern Jewries: History and Culture in the Modern Era*. Bloomington, IN, 1996.

Gondicas, Dimitri and Charles Issawi (eds.). *Ottoman Greeks in the Age of Nationalism: Politics, Economy, and Society in the Nineteenth Century*. Princeton, NJ, 1999.

Goodwin, Jason. *Lords of the Horizons: A History of the Ottoman Empire*. New York, 1998.

Goyau, Georges. "Le rôle religieux du consul François Picquet dans Alep (1652–1662)" *Revue d'Histoire des Missions* 12 (1935): 160–98.

Greene, Molly. *A Shared World: Christians and Muslims in the Early Modern Mediterranean*. Princeton, NJ, 2000.

Grunwald, Kurt. "Jewish Schools under Foreign Flags in Ottoman Palestine" in *Studies on Palestine during the Ottoman Period*. Edited by Moshe Ma'oz. Jerusalem, 1975, pp. 164–74.

Hacker, Joseph. "Jewish Autonomy in the Ottoman Empire: Its Scope and Limits. Jewish Courts from the Sixteenth to the Eighteenth centuries" in *The Jews of the Ottoman Empire*. Edited by A. Levy. Princeton, NJ, 1994, pp. 153–202.

Haddad, Mahmoud. "Iraq before World War I: A Case of Anti-European Arab Ottomanism" in *The Origins of Arab Nationalism*. Edited by R. Khalidi, L. Anderson, M. Muslih, R. Simon. New York, 1991, pp. 120–50.

Haddad, Robert. "Constantinople over Antioch, 1516–1724: Patriarchal Politics in the Ottoman Era" *Journal of Ecclesiastical History* 41 (1990): 217–38.

"Conversion of Eastern Orthodox Christians to the Unia in the Seventeenth and Eighteenth Centuries" in *Conversion and Continuity*. Edited by M. Gervers and J. Bikhazi. Toronto, 1990, pp. 447–59.

*Syrian Christians in a Muslim Society: An Interpretation*. Westport, CT, 1970.

Hajjar, Joseph. *Les chrétiens uniates du proche orient*. Damascus, 1995.

Hanna, Nelly. *Making Big Money in 1600: The Life and Times of Isma'il Abu Taqiyya, Egyptian Merchant*. Syracuse, NY, 1998.

Harel, Yaron. "Jewish–Christian Relations in Aleppo as Background for the Jewish Response to the Events of October 1850" *International Journal of Middle Eastern Studies* 30 (1998): 77–96.

Hempton, David. *Religion and Political Culture in Britain and Ireland: From the Glorious Revolution to the Decline of Empire*. Cambridge, 1996.

Heyberger, Bernard. "Le Catholicisme tridentin au Levant (XVII$^e$–XVIII$^e$ siècles)" *Mélanges de l'École Française de Rome* 101 (1989): 897–909.

"Les chrétiens d'Alep (Syrie) à travers les récits des conversions des missionaires Carmes Déchaux (1657–1681)" *Mélanges de l'École Française de Rome* 100 (1988): 461–99.

*Les chrétiens du proche-orient au temps de la réforme catholique*. Rome, 1994.

Hitti, Philip. *History of the Arabs*. New York, 1970.

Hobsbawm, Eric J. *Nations and Nationalism since 1780*. Cambridge, 1990.

Hobsbawm, Eric and Terence Ranger (eds.). *The Invention of Tradition*. Cambridge, 1985.

Holt, P. M. *Egypt and the Fertile Crescent, 1516–1922: A Political History*. London, 1966.

Hopwood, Derek. *The Russian Presence in Syria and Palestine, 1843–1914: Church and Politics in the Near East*. Oxford, 1969.

Hourani, Albert. *Arabic Thought in the Liberal Age 1798–1939*. London, 1962.

"The Changing Face of the Fertile Crescent in the XVIIIth Century" *Studia Islamica* 8 (1957): 89–122.

Hourani, Albert and Nadim Shehadi (eds.). *The Lebanese in the World: A Century of Emigration*. London, 1992.

Humphreys, R. Stephen. *Islamic History: A Framework for Inquiry*. Princeton, NJ, 1991.

Hurewitz, J. C. *Diplomacy in the Near and Middle East: A Documentary Record: 1553–1914*. Princeton, NJ, 1956.

İnalcık, Halil. *The Ottoman Empire: The Classical Age 1300–1600*. London, 1973.

"The Status of the Greek Orthodox Patriarch under the Ottomans" *Turcica* 21–23 (1991): 407–36.

İnalcık, Halil and Donald Quataert (eds.). *An Economic and Social History of the Ottoman Empire, 1300–1914*. Cambridge, 1994.

İslamoğlu-İnan, Huri (ed.). *The Ottoman Empire and the World Economy*. Cambridge, 1987.

Israel, Jonathan. *European Jewry in the Age of Mercantilism 1550–1750*. Oxford, 1985.

Issawi, Charles. "British Trade and the Rise of Beirut" *International Journal of Middle East Studies* 8 (1977): 91–101.

"Comment on Professor Barkan's Estimate of the Population of the Ottoman Empire, 1521–1530" *Journal of the Economic and Social History of the Orient* 1 (1957): 329–31.

*The Economic History of Turkey 1800–1914.* Chicago, IL, 1980.

*The Fertile Crescent 1800–1914: A Documentary Economic History.* New York, 1988.

"The Transformation of the Economic Position of the *Millet*s in the Nineteenth Century" in *Christians and Jews in the Ottoman Empire.* Edited by B. Braude and B. Lewis. New York, 1982, vol. I, pp. 261–85.

Jennings, Ronald. *Christians and Muslims in Ottoman Cyprus and the Mediterranean World, 1571–1640.* New York, 1993.

Joseph, John. *Muslim–Christian Relations and Inter-Christian Rivalries in the Middle East: The Case of the Jacobites in an Age of Transition.* Albany, NY, 1983.

Kafadar, Cemal. *Between Two Worlds: The Construction of the Ottoman State.* Berkeley, CA, 1994.

Kakar, Sudhir. *The Colors of Violence: Cultural Identities, Religion, and Conflict.* Chicago, IL, 1996.

Karpat, Kemal. "*Millet*s and Nationality: The Roots of the Incongruity of Nation and State in the Post-Ottoman Era" in *Christians and Jews in the Ottoman Empire.* Edited by B. Braude and B. Lewis. New York, 1982, vol. I, pp. 141–69.

"The Ottoman Emigration to America, 1860–1914" *International Journal of Middle Eastern Studies* 17 (1985): 175–209.

*Ottoman Population, 1830–1914: Demographic and Social Characteristics.* Madison, WI, 1985.

Kasaba, Reşat. Çağlar Keyder, and Faruk Tabak. "Eastern Mediterranean Port Cities and their Bourgeoisie: Merchants, Political Projects, and Nation States" *Review* 10 (1986): 121–35.

Kayal, Philip M. "Arab Christians in the United States" in *Arabs in the New World: Studies on Arab American Communities.* Edited by Sameer Abraham and Nabeel Abraham. Detroit, MI, 1983, pp. 45–61.

Kayalı, Hasan. *Arabs and Young Turks: Ottomanism, Arabism, and Islamism in the Ottoman Empire, 1908–1918.* Berkeley, CA, 1997.

Kedourie, Elie. "The Jews of Baghdad in 1910" *Middle East Studies* 7 (1971): 355–61.

Keyrouz, Sr. Marie. *Chant traditionnel maronite,* compact disc. Arles, France, 1991.

Khalaf, Samir. "Communal Conflict in Nineteenth-Century Lebanon" in *Christians and Jews in the Ottoman Empire.* Edited by B. Braude and B. Lewis. New York, 1982, vol. II, pp. 107–34.

*Persistence and Change in 19th Century Lebanon.* Beirut, 1979.

Khalidi, Rashid, Lisa Anderson, Muhammad Muslih, and Reeva Simon (eds.). *The Origins of Arab Nationalism.* New York, 1991.

Khalidi, Rashid. "Ottomanism and Arabism in Syria before 1914: A Reassessment" in *The Origins of Arab Nationalism.* Edited by R. Khalidi, L, Anderson, M. Muslih, and R. Simon New York, 1991, pp. 50–69.

*Palestinian Identity: The Construction of Modern Consciousness.* New York, 1997.

Khoury, Dina Rizq. *State and Provincial Society in the Ottoman Empire: Mosul, 1540–1834.* Cambridge, 1997.

Khoury, Philip. *Urban Notables and Arab Nationalism: The Politics of Damascus, 1860–1920.* Cambridge, 1983.

Khoury, Philip and Joseph Kostiner (eds.). *State Formation in the Middle East.* Berkeley, CA, 1990.

Kitroeff, Alexander. *The Greeks in Egypt, 1919–1937: Ethnicity and Class*. London, 1989.

Kitromilides, Paschalis. *The Enlightenment as Social Criticism: Iosipos Moisiodax and Greek Culture in the Eighteenth Century*. Princeton, NJ, 1992.

" 'Imagined Communities' and the Origins of the National Question in the Balkans" *European History Quarterly* 19 (1989): 149–94.

Klich, Ignacio. "*Criollos* and Arabic Speakers in Argentina: An Uneasy *Pas de Deux*, 1888–1914" in *The Lebanese in the World: A Century of Emigration*. Edited by A. Hourani and N. Shehadi. London, 1992, pp. 243–84.

Kocabaşıoğlu, Uygur. *Kendi belgeleriyle Anadolu'daki Amerika: 19. yüzyılda Osmanlı İmparatorluğu'ndaki Amerikan misyoner okulları* [America in Anatolia: American Missionary Schools in the Nineteenth-Century Ottoman Empire from Their Own Documents]. Istanbul, 1989.

Konortas, Paraskevas. "From Ta'ife to Millet: Ottoman Terms for the Greek Orthodox Community" in *Ottoman Greeks in the Age of Nationalism: Politics, Economy, and Society in the Nineteenth Century*. Edited by Dimitri Gondicas and Charles Issawi. Princeton, NJ, 1999, pp. 169–79.

Krämer, Gudrun. "Dhimmi or Citizen? Muslim–Christian Relations in Egypt" in *The Christian–Muslim Frontier: Chaos, Clash or Dialogue?* Edited by Jørgen Nielsen. London, 1998, pp. 33–49.

Kunt, Metin. "Ethnic-Regional (*Cins*) Solidarity in the Seventeenth-Century Ottoman Establishment" *International Journal of Middle East Studies* 5 (1974): 233–39.

Kurd ʿAli, Muhammad. *Khitat al-Sham* [Mapping Syria], 6 vols. First edition, Damascus, 1925–28, reprinted, Damascus, 1983.

Kuroki, Hidemitsu. "The Orthodox–Catholic Clash in Aleppo in 1818" *Orient* 29 (Tokyo, 1993): 1–18.

Kushner, David (ed.). *Palestine in the Late Ottoman Period: Political, Social, and Economic Transformation*. Jerusalem, 1986.

Landau, Jacob. "Relations between Jews and Non-Jews in the Late Ottoman Empire" in *Jews of the Ottoman Empire*. Edited by A. Levy. Princeton, NJ, 1994, pp. 539–46.

Leerssen, Joep. *Mere Irish and For-Ghael: Studies in the Idea of Irish Nationality, its Development and Literary Expression prior to the Nineteenth Century*. Cork, 1996.

Leeuwen, Richard van. *Notables and Clergy in Mount Lebanon: The Khazin Sheiks and the Maronite Church (1736–1840)*. Leiden, 1994.

Levitzon, Nehemia. "Conversion to Islam in Syria and Palestine and the Survival of Christian Communities" in *Conversion and Continuity: Indigenous Christian Communities in Islamic Lands, Eighth to Eighteenth Centuries*. Edited by M. Gervers and R. Bikhazi (Toronto, 1990), pp. 263–68.

Levy, Avigdor. "*Millet* Politics: The Appointment of a Chief Rabbi in 1835" in *The Jews of the Ottoman Empire*. Edited by A. Levy. Princeton, NJ, 1994, pp. 425–38.

(ed.). *The Jews of the Ottoman Empire*. Princeton, NJ, 1994.

Lewis, Bernard. *The Emergence of Modern Turkey*. London, 1961.

(ed.). *Islam from the Prophet Muhammad to the Capture of Constantinople*, vol. II, *Religion and Society*. New York, 1974.

Lewis, Norman. *Nomads and Settlers in Syria and Jordan, 1800–1980*. Cambridge, 1987.

Lewis, Warren. *Levantine Adventurer: The Travels and Mission of the Chevalier d'Arvieux, 1653–1697*. New York, 1962.

Little, Donald. "Coptic Converts to Islam during the Bahri Mamluk Period" in *Conversion and Continuity: Indigenous Christian Communities in Islamic Lands, Eighth to Eighteenth Centuries*. Edited by Michael Gervers and Ramzi Jibran Bikhazi. Toronto, 1990, pp. 263–88.

Livingstone, J. W. "Ali Bey al-Kabir and the Jews" *Middle Eastern Studies* 7 (1971): 221–28.

Longrigg, Stephen. *Four Centuries of Modern Iraq*. Oxford, 1925.

Lopasić, Alexander. "Islamization of the Balkans with Special Research to Bosnia" *Journal of Islamic Studies* 5 (1994): 163–86.

Lutfy, Huda. "Coptic Festivals of the Nile: Aberrations of the Past?" in *The Mamluks in Egyptian Politics and Society*. Edited by Thomas Philipp and Ulrich Haarman. Cambridge, 1998, pp. 254–82.

Makdisi, Ussama. *Culture of Sectarianism: Community, History, and Violence in 19ᵗʰ Century Lebanon*. Berkeley, CA, 2000.

"Reclaiming the Land of the Bible: Missionaries, Secularism, and Evangelical Modernism" *The American Historical Review* 102 (1997): 680–713.

Ma'oz, Moshe. "Communal Conflict in Ottoman Syria during the Reform Era: The Role of Political and Economic Factors" in *Christian and Jews in the Ottoman Empire*. Edited by B. Braude, B. Lewis. New York, 1982, vol. I, pp. 91–105.

*Ottoman Reform in Syria and Palestine, 1840–1861*. Oxford, 1968.

Marcus, Abraham. *The Middle East on the Eve of Modernity: Aleppo in the Eighteenth Century*. New York, 1989.

Mardin, Şerif. *The Genesis of Young Ottoman Thought: A Study in the Modernization of Turkish Political Ideas*. Princeton, NJ, 1961.

Marsot, Afaf Lutfi al-Sayyid. *Egypt in the Reign of Muhammad Ali*. Cambridge, 1984.

Martinez Montiel, Luz Maria. " The Lebanese Community in Mexico: Its Meaning, Importance and the History of its Communities" in *The Lebanese in the World: A Century of Emigration*. Edited by A. Hourani and N. Shehadi, London, 1992, pp. 379–92.

Masters, Bruce. "The 1850 'Events' in Aleppo: An Aftershock of Syria's Incorporation in the Capitalist World System" *International Journal of Middle Eastern Studies* 22 (1990): 3–20.

*The Origins of Western Economic Dominance in the Middle East: Mercantilism and the Islamic Economy in Aleppo, 1600–1750*. New York, 1988.

"Ottoman Policies toward Syria in the 17th and 18th Centuries" in *The Syrian Land in the 18th and 19th Century*. Edited by T. Philipp. Stuttgart, 1992, pp. 11–26.

"Patterns of Migration to Ottoman Aleppo in the 17th and 18th Centuries" *Journal of Turkish Studies* 4 (1987): 75–89.

"The Sultan's Entrepreneurs: The *Avrupa Tüccarıs* and the *Hayriye Tüccarıs* in Syria" *International Journal of Middle Eastern Studies* 24 (1992): 579–97.

"The View from the Province: Syrian Chroniclers of the Eighteenth Century" *Journal of the American Oriental Society* 114 (1994): 353–62.

Meinardus, Otto. *Christian Egypt: Faith and Life*. Cairo, 1970.

Memmi, Albert. *Jews and Arabs*. Translated by Eleanor Levieux. Chicago, IL, 1975.

Meriwether, Margaret. *The Kin who Count: Family and Society in Ottoman Aleppo 1770–1840*. Austin, TX, 1999.

Moosa, Matti. *The Maronites in History*. Syracuse, NY, 1986.

Murphey, Rhoads. "Conditions of Trade in the Eastern Mediterranean: An Appraisal of Eighteenth-Century Documents from Aleppo" *Journal of the Economic and Social History of the Orient* 33 (1990): 35–50.

Naff, Alixa. *Becoming American: The Early Arab Immigrant Experience*. Carbondale, IL, 1985.

el-Nahal, Galal. *The Judicial Administration of Ottoman Egypt in the Seventeenth Century*. Minneapolis, MN, 1979.

Nasrallah, Joseph. "Historiens et chroniqueurs melkites du XVIIIe siècle" *Bulletin Études Orientales* 13 (1949–51): 145–60.

Neale, J. M. *A History of the Eastern Church: The Patriarchate of Antioch*. London, 1873.

Nieuwenhuis, Tom. *Politics and Society in Early Modern Iraq: Mamlūk Pashas, Tribal Shayks and Local Rule between 1802 and 1831*. The Hague, 1981.

Ochsenwald, William. *Religion, Society, and the State in Arabia: The Hijaz under Ottoman Control, 1840–1908*. Columbus, OH, 1984.

Owen, Roger. *The Middle East and the World Economy 1800–1914*. London, 1981.

Peri, Oded. "The Christian Population of Jerusalem in the Late Seventeenth Century: Aspects of Demographic Development" in *Histoire économique et sociale de l'Empire Ottoman et de la Turquie*. Edited by Daniel Panzac. Paris, 1995, pp. 447–54.

Perlmann, M. "Notes on Anti-Christian Propaganda in the Mamluk Empire" *Bulletin of the School of Oriental and African Studies* 10 (1939–42): 843–61.

Philipp, Thomas. "Class, Community, and Arab Historiography in the Nineteenth Century – The Dawn of a New Era" *The International Journal of Middle Eastern Studies* 16 (1984): 161–75.

"French Merchants and Jews in the Ottoman Empire during the Eighteenth Century" in *The Jews of the Ottoman Empire*. Edited by A. Levy. Princeton, NJ, 1994, pp. 315–25.

"The Farhi Family and the Changing Positions of Jews in Syria, 1750–1860" *Middle Eastern Studies* 20 (1984): 37–52.

"Image and Self-Image of the Syrians in Egypt; From the Early Eighteenth Century to the Reign of Muhammad ᶜAli" in *Christians and Jews in the Ottoman Empire*. Edited by B. Braude and B. Lewis. New York, 1982, vol. II, pp. 167–84.

"Jews and Arab Christians: Their Changing Positions in Politics and Economy in Eighteenth-Century Syria and Egypt" in *Egypt and Palestine: A Millennium of Association (868–1948)*. Edited by Amnon Cohen and Gabriel Baer. New York, 1984, pp. 150–66.

*The Syrians in Egypt, 1725–1975*. Stuttgart, 1985.

(ed.) *The Syrian Land in the 18th and 19th Century: The Common and the Specific in the Historical Experience*. Stuttgart, 1992.

Pierce, Leslie. *The Imperial Harem: Women and Sovereignty in the Ottoman Empire*. New York, 1993.

al-Qattan, Najwa. "The Damescene Jewish Community in the Latter Decades of the Eighteenth Century" in *The Syrian Land in the 18th and 19th Century*. Edited by T. Philipp. Stuttgart, 1992, pp. 197–216.

"*Dhimmis* in the Muslim Court: Legal Autonomy and Religious Discrimination" *International Journal of Middle East Studies* 31 (1999): 429–44.

Quataert, Daniel. *Ottoman Manufacturing in the Age of the Industrial Revolution*. Cambridge, 1993.

Rahman, Fazlur. *Islam and Modernity: Transformation of an Intellectual Tradition*. Chicago, IL, 1982.

Rafeq, Abdul-Karim. "Craft Organizations and Religious Communities in Ottoman Syria (XVI–XIX Centuries)" in *La Shī<sup>c</sup>a nell'Impero ottomano*. Rome, 1993, pp. 25–56.

"The Impact of Europe on a Traditional Economy: The Case of Damascus, 1840–1870" in *Économie et sociétés dans l'Empire Ottoman*. Edited by Jean-Louis Bacqué-Grammont and Paul Dumont. Paris, 1983, pp. 419–32.

"New Light on the 1860 Riots in Ottoman Damascus" *Die Welt des Islam* 28 (1988): 412–30.

"Ottoman Historical Research in Syria since 1946" *Asian Research Trends* 2 (1992): 45–78.

Raymond, André. *Artisans et commerçants au Caire au XVIII<sup>e</sup> siècle*. 2 vols. Damascus, 1973–74.

"The Population of Aleppo in the Sixteenth and Seventeenth Centuries" *International Journal of Middle Eastern Studies* 16 (1984): 447–60.

Reilly, James. "From Workshops to Sweatshops: Damascus Textiles and the World-Economy in the Last Ottoman Century" *Review* 16 (1993): 199–213.

"Inter-Confessional Relations in Nineteenth-Century Syria: Damascus, Homs and Hama Compared" *Islam & Muslim Christian Relations* 7 (1996): 213–24.

"Past and Present in Local Histories of the Ottoman Period from Syria and Lebanon" *Middle Eastern Studies* 35 (1999): 45–65.

"Urban Hegemony in the Hinterland of Ottoman Damascus: Villages, Estates and Farms in the Nineteenth Century" in *Histoire économique et sociale de l'Empire ottomane et de la Turquie (1326–1960)*. Edited by Daniel Panzac, Paris, 1995, pp. 455–70.

Reimer, Michael. *Colonial Bridgehead: Government and Society in Alexandria, 1807–1882*. Boulder, CO, 1997.

Reinkowski, Maurus. "Late Ottoman Rule over Palestine: Its Evaluation in Arab, Turkish and Israeli Histories, 1970–90" *Middle Eastern Studies* 35 (1999): 66–97.

Rejwan, Nissim. *The Jews of Irak: 3000 Years of History and Culture*. Boulder, CO, 1985.

Repp, Richard. "Qanun and Shari<sup>c</sup>a in the Ottoman Context" in *Islamic Law: Social and Historical Contexts*. Edited by Aziz al-Azmeh. London, 1988, pp. 124–45.

Rodrigue, Aron. *French Jews, Turkish Jews: The Alliance Israélite Universelle and the Politics of Jewish Schooling in Turkey, 1860–1925*. Bloomington, IN, 1990.

Rodinson, Maxime. *Mahomet*. Paris, 1968.

Rogan, Eugene. *Frontiers of the State in the Late Ottoman Empire: Transjordan, 1850–1921*. Cambridge, 1999.

Roland, Joan. *Jews in British India: Identity in a Colonial Era.* Hanover, NH, 1989.

Said, Edward. *Covering Islam: How the Media and the Experts Determine How We See the Rest of the World.* New York, 1978.

*Orientalism.* New York, 1978.

Salibi, Kamal. "The 1860 Upheaval in Damascus as Seen by al-Sayyid Muhammad Abu'l-Su'ud al Hasibi, Notable and Naqib al-Ashraf of the city" in *Beginnings of Modernization in the Middle East.* Edited by W. Polk and R. Chambers. Chicago, IL, 1968, pp. 185–202.

"The Two Worlds of Assaad Y. Kayat" in *Jews and Christians in the Ottoman Empire.* Edited by B. Braude and B. Lewis. New York, 1982, vol. II, pp. 135–58.

Salt, Jeremy. *Imperialism, Evangelism and the Ottoman Armenians 1878–1896.* London, 1993.

Sanjian, Avedis. *The Armenian Communities in Syria under Ottoman Domination.* Cambridge, MA, 1965.

Sasson, David. *A History of the Jews in Baghdad.* Letchworth, UK, 1949.

Schilcher, Linda Schatkowski *Families in Politics: Damascene Factions and Estates of the 18th and 19th Centuries.* Stuttgart, 1985.

Schimmel, Annemarie. "Dreams of Jesus in the Islamic Tradition" *Bulletin of the Royal Institute for Inter-faith Studies* 1/1 (1999): 207–12.

Schlicht, Alfred. *Frankreich und die syrischen Christen 1799–1861: Minoritäten und europäischer Imperialismus im Vorderen Orient.* Berlin, 1981.

Serjeant, R. B. "The 'Constitution of Medina'" *Islamic Quarterly* 8 (1964): 3–16.

Shaw, Stanford. *The Jews of the Ottoman Empire and the Turkish Republic.* New York, 1991.

Shaw, Stanford and Ezel Kural Shaw. *History of the Ottoman Empire and Modern Turkey Volume II: Reform, Revolution, and Republic, the Rise of Modern Turkey 1808–1975.* Cambridge, 1977.

Shelemay, Kay Kaufman. *Let Jasmine Rain Down: Song and Remembrance among Syrian Jews.* Chicago, IL, 1998.

Shields, Sarah. *Mosul before Iraq: Like Bees Making Five-Sided Cells.* Albany, NY, 2000.

Shorrock, William. *French Imperialism in the Middle East: The Failure of Policy in Syria and Lebanon 1900–1914.* Madison, WI, 1976.

Somekh, Sasson. "Participation of Egyptian Jews in Modern Arabic Culture, and the Case of Murad Faraj" in *The Jews of Egypt: a Mediterranean Society in Modern Times.* Edited by Shimon Shamir, Boulder, CO, 1987, pp. 130–40.

Sonyel, Salâhi. *Minorities and the Destruction of the Ottoman Empire.* Ankara, 1993.

Steensgaard, Niels. "Consuls and Nations in the Levant from 1570 to 1650" *Scandinavian Economic Review* 15 (1967): 13–55.

Stillman, Norman. *The Jews of Arab Lands in Modern Times.* Philadelphia, PA, 1991.

"Middle Eastern and North African Jewries Confront Modernity: Orientation, Disorientation, Reorientation" in *Sephardi and Middle Eastern Jewries: History and Culture in the Modern Era.* Edited by Harvey Goldberg. Bloomington, IN, 1996, pp. 59–72.

Stone, Frank Andrews, "The Educational 'Awakening' among the Armenian Evangelicals of Aintab Turkey, 1845–1915" *Armenian Review* 35 (1982): 30–52.

Sutton, Joseph. *Magic Carpet: Aleppo-in-Flatbush*. New York, 1979.

Tabbakh, Muhammad Raghib. *I'lam al-nubala bi-ta'rikh Halab al-shahba'* [Notices on the Nobles in the History of Aleppo, the Milky-White]. 7 vols. Aleppo, 1923–26.

Thieck, Jean-Pierre. "Décentralisation ottomane et affirmation urbaine à Alep à la fin du XVIII<sup>e</sup> siècle" in *Passion d'Orient*. Edited by Gilles Kepel. Paris, 1992, pp. 113–76.

Tibawi, A. L. *American Interests in Syria, 1800–1901*. Oxford, 1966.

*British Interests in Palestine, 1880–1901*. Oxford, 1961.

Tucker, Judith. *In the House of the Law: Gender and Islamic Law in Ottoman Syria and Palestine*. Berkeley, CA, 1998.

Türkmen, A. Faik. *Mufassal Hatay* [Hatay in Detail]. Istanbul, 1937.

Walker, Christopher. *Armenia: The Survival of a Nation*. London, 1980.

Wallerstein, Immanuel. *The Modern World System*. 3 vols. New York, San Diego, 1974–89.

Wallerstein, Immanuel, Hale Decdeli, and Reşat Kasaba. "The Incorporation of the Ottoman Empire into the World Economy" in *The Ottoman Empire and the World Economy*. Edited by H. İslamoğlu-İnan. Cambridge, 1987, pp. 88–97.

J. A. Watt. "The Anglo-Irish Colony under Strain, 1327–99" in *A New History of Ireland*, vol. II *Medieval Ireland, 1169–1534*. Edited by Art Cosgrove. Oxford, 1993, pp. 352–96.

Watt, Montgomery. *Muhammad at Mecca*. Oxford, 1953.

*Muhammad at Medina*. Oxford, 1956.

Winter, Michael. *Egyptian Society under Ottoman Rule 1517–1798*. London, 1992.

"A Polemical Treatise by ʿAbd al-Ghani al-Nabulusi against a Turkish Scholar on the Religious Status of the dhimmis" *Arabica* 35 (1988): 92–103.

Yehuda, Zvi. "Iraqi Jewry and Cultural Change in the Educational Activity of the Alliance Israélite Universelle" in *Sephardi and Middle Eastern Jewries: History and Culture in the Modern Era*. Edited by H. Goldberg. Bloomington, IN, 1996, pp. 134–45.

Dror Ze'evi. "The Use of Ottoman Shariʿa Court Records as a Source for Middle Eastern Social History: A Reappraisal" *Islamic Law and Society* 5 (1998) 35–56.

Zenner, Walter. *A Global Community: The Jews from Aleppo, Syria*. Detroit, MI, 2000.

"'Middlemen Minorities in the Syrian Mosaic: Trade Conflict, and Image Management" *Sociological Perspectives* 30 (1987): 400–21.

"Jewish Retainers as Power Brokers" *The Jewish Quarterly Review* LXXXI (1990): 127–49.

#### *Unpublished*

Abdullah, Thabet. "The political economy of merchants and trade in Basra, 1722–1795." Ph.D. dissertation, Georgetown University, 1992.

Hidemitsu Kuroki, "Dhimmis in Mid-Nineteenth Century Aleppo, an Analysis of Jizya Defters." Unpublished paper.

# Index

Wallerstein, Immanuel, 7, 131–32, 190
women: conversion to Islam, 27, 34–35;
    conversion to Catholicism, 87;
    education of, 87, 114, 149, 151, 155; in a
    Muslim society, 5–6, 28, 87, 128;
    religious orders, 87, 113–14; *see also*,
    divorce, marriage

Yazidis, 45, 70, 152

Zahle, 116, 157, 163
al-Zaᶜim, Kyrillos V, Patriarch
al-Zaᶜim, Makarios III, Patriarch, 83–84, 86,
    89, 101, 113
Zionism, 174, 193

*Titles in the series*

STEFAN SPERL, *Mannerism in Arabic poetry: A Structural Analysis of Selected Texts, 3rd Century AH/9th Century AD–5th Century AH/11th Century AD*  0 521 35485 4
PAUL E. WALKER, *Early Philosophical Shiism: The Ismaili Neoplatonism of Abū Ya'qūb al-Sijistānī*  0 521 44129 3
BOAZ SHOSHAN, *Popular Culture in Medieval Cairo*  0 521 43209 X
STEPHEN FREDERIC DALE, *Indian Merchants and Eurasian Trade, 1600–1750*  0 521 45460 3
AMY SINGER, *Palestinian Peasants and Ottoman Officials: Rural Administration around Sixteenth-century Jerusalem*  0 521 45238 4 hardback 0 521 47679 8 paperback
TARIF KHALIDI, *Arabic Historical Thought in the Classical Period*  0 521 46554 0 hardback  0 521 58938 X paperback
REUVEN AMITAI-PREISS, *Mongols and Mamluks: The Mamluk–Īlkhānid War, 1260–1281*  0 521 46226 6
LOUISE MARLOW, *Hierarchy and Egalitarianism in Islamic Thought*  0 521 56430 1
JANE HATHAWAY, *The Politics of Households in Ottoman Egypt: The Rise of the Qazdağlis*  0 521 57110 3
THOMAS T. ALLSEN, *Commodity and Exchange in the Mongol Empire: A Cultural History of Islamic Textiles*  0 521 58301 2
DINA RIZK KHOURY, *State and Provincial Society in the Early Modern Ottoman Empire: Mosul, 1540–1834*  0 521 59060 4
THOMAS PHILIPP AND ULRICH HAARMANN (eds.), *The Mamluks in Egyptian Politics and Society*  0 521 59115 5
PETER JACKSON, *The Delhi Sultanate: A Political and Military History*  0 521 40477 0
KATE FLEET, *European and Islamic Trade in the Early Ottoman State: The Merchants of Genoa and Turkey*  0 521 64122 3
TAYEB EL-HIBRI, *Reinterpreting Islamic Historiography: Hārūn al-Rashīd and the Narrative of the 'Abbāsid Caliphate*  0 521 65023 2
EDHEM ELDEM, DANIEL GOFFMAN AND BRUCE MASTERS, *The Ottoman City between East and West: Aleppo, Izmir, and Istanbul*  0 521 64304 X
ŞEVKET PAMUK, *A Monetary History of the Ottoman Empire*  0 521 44197 8
RUDOLPH P. MATTHEE, *The Politics of Trade in Safavid Iran: Silk for Silver, 1600–1730*  0 521 64131 4
G. R. HAWTING, *The Idea of Idolatry and the Emergence of Islam: From Polemic to History*  0 521 65165 4
MICHAEL COOPERSON, *Classical Arabic Biography: The Heirs of the Prophets in the Age of al-Ma'mun*  0 521 66199 4
CHASE F. ROBINSON, *Empire and Elites after the Muslim Conquest: The Transformation of Northern Mesopotamia*  0 521 78115 9
ADAM SABRA, *Poverty and Charity in Medieval Islam: Mamluk Egypt, 1250–1517*  0 521 77291 5